DEEP DATA ANALYTICS FOR NEW PRODUCT DEVELOPMENT

T0311911

This book presents and develops the deep data analytics for providing the information needed for successful new product development.

Deep Data Analytics for New Product Development has a simple theme: information about what customers need and want must be extracted from data to effectively guide new product decisions regarding concept development, design, pricing, and marketing. The benefits of reading this book are twofold. The first is an understanding of the stages of a new product development process from ideation through launching and tracking, each supported by information about customers. The second benefit is an understanding of the deep data analytics for extracting that information from data. These analytics, drawn from the statistics, econometrics, market research, and machine learning spaces, are developed in detail and illustrated at each stage of the process with simulated data. The stages of new product development and the supporting deep data analytics at each stage are not presented in isolation of each other, but are presented as a synergistic whole.

This book is recommended reading for analysts involved in new product development. Readers with an analytical bent or who want to develop analytical expertise would also greatly benefit from reading this book, as well as students in business programs.

Walter R. Paczkowski worked at AT&T, AT&T Bell Labs, and AT&T Labs. He founded Data Analytics Corp., a statistical consulting company, in 2001. Dr. Paczkowski is also a part-time lecturer of economics at Rutgers University.

DEEP DATA ANALYTICS FOR NEW PRODUCT DEVELOPMENT

Walter R. Paczkowski

Routledge
Taylor & Francis Group
LONDON AND NEW YORK

First published 2020
by Routledge
2 Park Square, Milton Park, Abingdon, Oxon OX14 4RN

and by Routledge
52 Vanderbilt Avenue, New York, NY 10017

Routledge is an imprint of the Taylor & Francis Group, an informa business

British Library Cataloguing-in-Publication Data
A catalogue record for this book is available from the British Library

Library of Congress Cataloging-in-Publication Data
Names: Paczkowski, Walter R., author.
Title: Deep data analytics for new product development / Walter R. Paczkowski.
Description: First Edition. | New York : Routledge, 2020. |
Includes bibliographical references and index.
Identifiers: LCCN 2019046905 (print) | LCCN 2019046906 (ebook) |
ISBN 9780367077754 (hardback) | ISBN 9780367077761 (paperback) |
ISBN 9780429022777 (ebook)
Subjects: LCSH: New products–Management. | Big data. | Quantitative research.
Classification: LCC HF5415.153 .P33 2020 (print) |
LCC HF5415.153 (ebook) | DDC 658.5/75028557–dc23
LC record available at https://lccn.loc.gov/2019046905
LC ebook record available at https://lccn.loc.gov/2019046906

ISBN: 978-0-367-07775-4 (hbk)
ISBN: 978-0-367-07776-1 (pbk)
ISBN: 978-0-429-02277-7 (ebk)

Typeset in Bembo
by Newgen Publishing UK

CONTENTS

FIGURES

TABLES

PREFACE

When I worked at AT&T Bell Labs (the "Labs") in the 1990s, I was fortunate to be in a division called the Consumer Lab. This was an eclectic group of people: market researchers, computer scientists, mathematicians, statisticians, psychologists, human factors experts, and economists – even an anthropologist at one time. Our charge was simple: to identify and test new products and service concepts ("products" for short) with consumers and business decision makers to determine market potential. In some instances, the concern was how people interacted with the products so bugs could be worked out or eliminated at the beginning of the design stage. We performed both functions by inviting customers into a lab setting where they could test the products, or mock-ups of them, under controlled conditions, but conditions that mimicked the intended environment where they would be used. We then used advanced statistical and econometric methods to estimate demand, sales, and revenue. The results had direct input into the new product business case process and the whole new product development process from ideation to launch and tracking. Members of the Consumer Lab were often involved in new product development right from the very beginning.

My particular group in the Consumer Lab was charged with terminating a new product concept to prevent it from going to market if it was going to fail. We did not earn any money for the company, but, instead, we saved it money. We actually stopped many products from ever seeing the light of day in the market simply because they did not really solve any problems faced by customers or because the product was too awkward or confusing for them to use. We stopped the products in the early stages of concept design. This was important because it was very expensive to fully develop a product concept and eventually bring it to market. If it failed, then the financial losses could be devastating. So it benefited AT&T to maintain a lab such as ours for the sole purpose of testing new product concepts. We were AT&T's Test Kitchen.[1]

I learned a lot from this experience. I learned about developing new product concepts; about the role, importance, and composition of a business case; and about testing demand at different stages of the new product development process. In short, I learned about the new product development process itself. I expanded on this learning with my own consulting after I left the Labs. Most importantly, in my time at the Labs and afterward, I learned about the vital role that *deep data analytics* plays in new product development. A business manager cannot just say that customers, whether consumers or business customers, will buy whatever is produced. *Data*, better yet, actionable, insightful, and useful *information* extracted from data must be used to support decision making and this extraction can only be done by deeply analyzing data using advanced tools and methodologies. It is this set of learnings about deep data analytics for new product development that is in this book.

If the "learnings" are about using deep data analytics in the new product development process, then two logical questions are begged to be answered. The first is "*What is the process?*" and the second is "*What is deep data analytics?*" Let me address these two questions in reverse order.

Analytics is the process of revealing or extracting what is hidden inside data. What is hidden? Information. Insight. Knowledge. The mistake people often make is believing that data are the information needed for decision making. That having a lot of data gives them, almost *ipso facto*, great insight and knowledge. This is incorrect. Data *per se* can be viewed as a veil concealing what is really important to decision makers: information. This veil has to be lifted. The information, insight, and knowledge have to be extracted from the data.

Data are the starting point. With small amounts of data, the extractions are easy; with large amounts of data, the extractions are more difficult and challenging. I conjecture, without empirical basis (i.e., no data), that the extraction difficulty rises exponentially with the amount of data. Meeting this challenge requires tools and methodologies more sophisticated than those needed for the simpler challenges from "small" data. These tools and methodologies are more advanced; hence the analytics are more advanced. *Small Data* can be effectively analyzed, the information can be extracted, using simple means and proportions, simple linear regression models, cross-tabulations, and simple visualizations such as pie and bar charts. *Big Data* requires multiple regressions, panel models, text analyses, and complex data visualizations to extract the information. This is deep data analytics – those tools and methodologies used for analyzing Big Data.

What is Small Data and what is Big Data? Well, Small is small and Big is big. In one sense, the difference is clear once you see them. Big Data, however, is usually defined by the three "V" paradigm: Volume, Velocity, and Variety. This same paradigm applies to small data; it is just magnitudes that differ. For Small Data, volume is "small" and for Big Data it is "big." For Small Data, velocity is slow and for Big Data it is fast. For Small Data, variety is narrow and for Big Data it is broad. It is really the challenge, the cost of dealing with Big Data rather than

Small Data, that is the analytical issue. The cost covers analytical time, tools (e.g., software and hardware), and analytical talent.

Since more emphasis is placed on Big Data in our modern, high-tech economy, I will devote some time discussing Big Data: what it is, its issues, and its implications for new product development, especially the third "V" of variety. This last "V" covers images, videos, audios, textual material, maps, and much more. It is the textual material in the form of product reviews that is important here so this is the one aspect I will stress. But this leads naturally into a discussion of the first question above, "*What is the process?*", because Big Data is important for and plays a major role in the process in the 21st Century.

There are many books and articles written about processes in general and about processes for new product development specifically. All of them stress a continuous, almost linear, flow from some initial point to an end point. For new products, the initial point is an idea. Everything starts with an idea. This book started with an idea. But where do ideas come from? A lot has been written about the origin of ideas, from a strictly philosophical perspective[2] to a practical one of how to create them. Johnson [2011] and Yona [2011] are two good examples of attempts to identify the origin of our ideas and what we can do to cultivate, to create ideas. A traditional approach in business has been to brainstorm. With modern Big Data, brainstorming has been subordinated, but not eliminated, in favor of mining textual messages as direct input from customers. These textual messages are full of gems from new product possibilities to issues and fixes for old products that eventually lead to new ones. Since Big Data is an important source of ideas, I will discuss some Big Data analytics in the beginning and then throughout the book.

I do not want to overstate the role of Big Data analytics and suggest that non-Big Data analytics (Small Data analytics?) are now completely irrelevant. To the contrary. Other deep data analytic methods are important and vital at different stages of the process. Discrete choice analysis, for example, is important for identifying the structure of the product and willingness-to-pay for product features *vis-à-vis* competitive offerings. Similarly, different pricing analytic methods based on market research surveys can inform the development team about price points at different stages of the process. Finally, competitive environment analysis, also based on market research surveys, can inform the development team about competitive obstacles and opportunities that would impact the success of their new product.

The ending point of any process is the final result, the accomplishment, the attainment of a goal. For a business launching a product, the end result should be financial returns (i.e., contribution) or market share that meets or exceeds the business objectives established by executive management. There is only one way to know if these goals have been achieved and that is by tracking performance in the market. This tracking, however, is important not only because it informs the business about how well it did with the new product, but it also provides hints and clues for the new ideas needed for the next new product launch. That new launch could be an addition to the product line or just a fix to the older products, fixes that are revealed by the market. Once again, Big Data plays a role.

Between the beginning point – the ideation – and the ending point – tracking – are a series of stages that feed on each other in a highly nonlinear fashion but that keep moving the product through to completion. These stages form a pipeline the product must flow though to reach the market and succeed. My view is that a new product development process has five stages in a nonlinear pipeline: *Ideation, Development, Testing, Launch, Tracking*. Big Data and deep data analytics are vital at each stage. In this book, I will focus on the deep data analytics at each of these five stages.

The book is divided into eight chapters. The first, the Introduction, expands and elaborates on my perspectives of the new product development process that I briefly outlined above. The role of Big Data and deep analytics will be highlighted. The five stages of my view of the process make up the next six chapters. You may have noticed that there are six chapters for the five stages. The difference is that I divided one stage into two parts: a marketing mix and a forecasting chapter for product launch. The final chapter, Chapter 8, focuses on the analytical talent and software necessary to follow a deep analytical approach to new product development, especially in a Big Data era. The analytical talent is the background, training, and inclination of the development team starting from the market research team members all the way through to the tracking team members. Each requires a different skill set. At the same time, software must be able to handle the demands and requirements for deep analytics. Spreadsheets do not suffice. Some software products will be reviewed in this last chapter. The talent and the tools contribute to the deep data analytical costs I mentioned above.

Who should read this book? The answer is simple: the analysts involved in new product development. As with my previous books (Paczkowski [2016] and Paczkowski [2018]), my focus is on the analytics needed for solving business problems. The management of teams, organizations, and even the business itself is not my focus in what I do or write about. These topics are best left to those more qualified than I in these areas. So those with an analytical bent or who want to develop that expertise are the targets for this book. The book is also targeted to students in business programs including MBA programs with a quantitative orientation.

Since this book is about the deep data analytics for new product development, a background in statistics, econometrics, and some data mining or machine learning will help. I hope this book is self-contained enough, however, so that it "fills in the gaps" in these areas where needed.

I wrestled with some of the technicalities of deep data analytics since these cannot be avoided. In particular, I wrestled with what technicalities to include, how deep to go with them, and where to put them. I eventually decided to present enough technicalities in the text of the chapters to whet the appetite of those who want to superficially know them but place deeper technicalities in appendices so as to not upset the flow of the book or discourage nontechnical readers. I also decided that the technicalities in these appendices cannot be too deep since I do have a length restriction on what can be written. I hope my compromise satisfies some readers and does not become a drawback to others. I had a choice to make and this was it.

I also wrestled with the use of "consumer" versus "customer." In the early drafts, I tended to use "consumer" to refer to someone who bought the new product. This was natural since I have a consumer research background. But then I started to think that this was too narrow since new products are not just consumer oriented but also business or industrial oriented. So "consumer" was not appropriate for this domain. I therefore opted to refer to "customer" throughout except where "consumer" was a natural fit.

Notes

1 See "AT&T Test Kitchen" in *CIO Magazine* (May 15, 1994) for a description of the Consumer Lab.
2 See, for example, "Descartes' Theory of Ideas" at the Stanford Encyclopedia of Philosophy: https://plato.stanford.edu/entries/descartes-ideas/#Oth.

ACKNOWLEDGEMENTS

In my last book, I noted the support and encouragement I received from my wonderful wife, Gail, and my two daughters, Kristin and Melissa, and my son-in-law David. As before, my wife encouraged me to sit down and just write, especially when I did not want to, while my daughters provided the extra set of eyes I needed to make this book perfect. They provided the same support and encouragement for this book so I owe them a lot, both then and now. I would also like to say something about my two grandsons who, now at 4 and 8, obviously did not contribute to this book but who, I hope, will look at this one in their adult years and say "My grandpa wrote this book, too."

1

INTRODUCTION

All businesses simultaneously pursue multiple activities in order to survive in highly competitive, dynamic, and global markets. Among these are supply chain management; billing and account management; human resource management and development; quality control; and financial analysis, control, and reporting to mention a few. Equally important, and certainly not to be overlooked, is the continuous introduction of new products. It should be acknowledged, without discussion or argument, that your competition will be doing this especially in 21st century global markets. The surest way to fail is to let your competition gain the upper hand.

It is not enough, however, to merely introduce new products. It also is imperative that they be one's customers, whether consumers or businesses, will buy. This should be obvious, but knowing and acknowledging this and finding these new products are two different issues. A business's *pipeline*, the collection of new products at their various stages of development from inception to introduction to the market, must always be full of innovative products that satisfy customers' needs and solve their problems and are also one step ahead of the competition. If your pipeline is not full with the right products, new products, or any products, then your business will be forced out of the market.

In today's world, technology evolves quickly and as a result the competitive landscape constantly changes. Technologies change because they tend to feed on themselves, always evolving from one "species" to a new one. The new species of technology could be a new method of doing something (e.g., communicating through social media) or a new device (e.g., smartphone) or modification of an older device (e.g., snap-on modules for smartphones). At the same time, people's needs constantly and continuously change in part because they themselves are part of the market but also because they adapt to the new technologies. In the process of adapting, however, their needs, both materialistic and psychological, or external

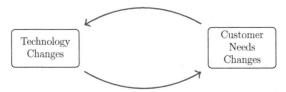

FIGURE 1.1 There is a constant circular pattern from technology changes to customer needs changes and back again.

and internal needs, change and evolve. This evolution itself puts pressure on technology to further evolve to meet changing needs. And so there is a circular pattern from technology changes to people's needs changes and back again. This is depicted in Figure 1.1. How the market changes and how people change are one and the same thing.

This dynamism puts pressure on all businesses to always decide what to produce and introduce as well as what to remove from the market. Old products are therefore an integral part of the cycle in Figure 1.1. So in addition to being full, the content of the pipeline, the nature of the products themselves, must keep pace with the changing technologies and customer wants and needs; basically, their evolving problems. This means technology changes and customer problems must be anticipated and identified. See Arthur [2009] for a good discussion of how technology evolves and the implications of this evolution.

This chapter is divided into four sections. The bases for, not product success, but product failures are described in the first section. The focus is on the failures because this sets the stage for what should be done. It is the failures that motivate people to push ahead and improve, not their successes. The second section draws on these failures and presents a process for generating new products that will have a better chance of success because the process highlights those features that make products fail. In essence, it is a roadmap for what to avoid as much as for what to do. This process is a road map that will be followed and developed throughout the book. The third section describes the main parts of a deep analytical tool set needed for new product development. I refer to this as the heart of the new product development process. The last section is a summary.

1.1 New product failures

All businesses know they must constantly innovate and maintain a full pipeline. The fact that today's markets are highly competitive, dynamic, and global does not change anything. This just intensifies the problem; makes it more imperative; makes it more complex to deal with and manage. Businesses always innovated; to be the first on the block with the newest and most creative products. Unfortunately, not all new products are successful. Some studies of the status of new products soon after their launch have shown that:[1]

- About 80% fail.
- About 66% fail within 2 years of introduction.
- About 80% stay on store shelves less than 12 months.
- About 96% fail to return the cost of capital.

Consider the 80% failure rate. Whether this is too low or too high is immaterial. The fact that it is not 0% or 5% (and not 100%) is the important point. The 80% failure rate implies that the odds of failure are 4:1.[2] Based on this one fact, any new product is 4 times more likely to fail than succeed. The risk of failure is high, so every firm must try hard to "get it right" and get it right the first time; the market very rarely, if ever, gives you a second chance. This risk of failure is important because the cost of developing a new product can be significantly high. These costs include design, retooling of plant and equipment, advertising and promotion, marketing, and personnel hiring and training just to mention a few. If the innovation is just a minor "tweak" to an existing design, the cost may not be substantial, but nonetheless there will be a cost. If the innovation is a major paradigm shift in what the business has traditionally produced or a new-to-the-world innovation, then these cost elements will be substantial. In either case, there is a cost that must be incurred which could lead to financial devastation if the product fails. The higher the risk of a product failure, the greater the risk of financial devastation. So the business has to get it right. But they have only the one chance to get it right! Unfortunately, since there are no guarantees, "getting it right" means reducing the risk of failure, not eliminating it before the product is launched. This reduced risk of failure can only be achieved by having the best information at each stage of a new product's development so that the right decisions are made about it including whether or not it should even be pursued. The information needed for these decisions includes, but is not limited to, what customers want, what is technologically possible, what is the best product design, and what is the best marketing campaign and pricing.

There are many specific reasons for the failure rates listed above, but I will categorize them into three groups displayed in Figure 1.2. These are aggregations

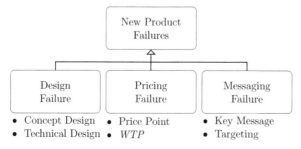

FIGURE 1.2 There are three reasons for new product failures: design, pricing, and messaging. Each one has its own components, some of which are stated here.

of the reasons for the lack of information. A fundamental *Design Failure* involves a concept that does not meet customers' needs or solve their problems. In fact, its use may actually increase the problem rather than ameliorate if there is a fundamental technical fault with the product. The *Pricing Failure* involves a pricing strategy or a price point that is inappropriate for the market, either placing the product out of reach of most customers or giving the impression that the product is "cheap" so customers will not be willing to pay for it. Finally, the product could have a *Messaging Failure* so that the wrong claims are made, especially for the target audience. I will discuss each failure group in the following subsections.

1.1.1 Design failures

Design failures refer to flaws in two design components: concept design and technical design. The concept is an idea, a vision, an intangible statement or description of what should be produced to solve a problem. It consists of a problem statement; a description of the intended target customers who have that problem; an operational statement; and sufficient description so that someone could build it. It is an abstract idea. The technical design, however, is the engineering specification of what can be built given current technology and internal engineering talent. It is a statement of what can be practically done and how. Usually, a prototype or mock-up design reflecting an interpretation of the abstract design concept is constructed from this technical design.

The critical factor for survival is having a new product concept that is brought to market before the competition, but this concept has to be one customers want and need in order to solve a problem, whether real or perceived. It is the customers who count since they buy the product, and this means their wants and needs come first. It is not enough that a business manager "just knows" what should be in the product or what are the customers' needs.

The problem solution, however, is not singularly focused, meaning that one and only one attribute or feature of the product solves a customer's problem. Typically, a product has multiple physical attributes such as form, size, weight, number of buttons, display screen, and so forth. Some of these are important to customers while others are not. Each attribute is a technology unto itself so a product is really a container of subordinate technologies. It is the important ones that customers will key on and that will determine whether or not the product will succeed. The design concept must have these critical and important customer-focused attributes. I will discuss methodologies for assessing physical attribute importances in Chapter 3. See Arthur [2009] on the notion of technology as a series of containers.

The design concept may be a good one if it solves the customer's problem, but it is meaningless if the technical design reflected in a prototype is flawed. Sizes are too small or too large; key buttons (e.g., power button) are difficult to access or operate; the form is awkward; the weight is too high; and so forth. All these interfere with the product's intended use. An area in psychology called *human factors* or *human factors engineering* is concerned with the interaction between humans and the tools they use (e.g., computers, trucks, hammers) to make the tools as effective as possible for their intended use. If a tool is difficult to use or understand, even though the concept is worthwhile, it will fail in the market. If human factors experts are not involved in the technical design of the concept, then the odds of the product failing in the market because of technicalities are higher.

The worst case of a technical design failure occurs when the important physical attributes, those that are important as determined by the customers, are either absent or poorly executed. This can occur because the concept design did not clearly specify the attributes, the technical designers did not implement them well, or the designers' technical knowledge is insufficient to even begin to implement a new technology. Regardless of the reason, the product will not be accepted in the market simply because it will be viewed as insufficient. This will provide an opening for your competition to develop a product that has these attributes.

The two design components (concept and technical) do not always have to agree, primarily because the design concept is abstract. An engineer or other techni-cal designer should have wide latitude and freedom to build a prototype product, within the vision of the concept design, but the goal is certainly to have them agree as closely as possible since they have to solve only one problem, the customer's problem. If the two designs diverge, or solve the wrong problem, or simply fail to solve the problem altogether then the resulting product will fail in the market.

1.1.2 Pricing failures

Even if the concept is a good one and the technical version works as intended, the product can still fail on introduction because the price point is not in line with market assessments or expectations. If the initial price point is too high, then no one will buy the product. If the price point is too low, then the business runs the risk of customers viewing the product as cheap, of poor quality with little or no value for the price. Price acts as an indicator of quality and a price point that is too low relative to expectations could indicate that the product quality is also low. See Monroe [1990] for some discussion about the relationship between price and perceived quality. Also see Paczkowski [2018] for a discussion about assessing the price point below which the product is viewed as "cheap."

A price is needed before the product goes to market to determine if it will be profitable and meet the business's financial goals. All businesses have financial goals both for their current fiscal year and for several years into the future (e.g., five-year plans). One part of the business planning process for new product development is the *business case*. This is a complex assessment of the viability of a product, an assessment usually done at different stages of the development process, i.e., the different times as a product moves through the pipeline. The structure of a business case varies from business to business, but generally it has two major components: a competitive assessment and a financial assessment. For the competitive assessment, a *Competitive Environment Analysis* (*CEA*) shows the space of likely competitive products and *key market players* (*KMPs*) by product attributes and their importance to customers. This shows unmet possibilities in the market but more importantly it also shows the degree of competition in that space. If there are many *KMPs* offering virtually the same product with attributes or features that are almost identical and where those attributes are important to customers, then any new product would face a high barrier to entry. If the product space, however, is sparse and the concept design emphasizes attributes that are important to customers but are not provided by existing products, then the risk of failure is reduced, but certainly not eliminated. A *CEA* will certainly help minimize the risk of a design failure. A *CEA* will be further discussed in Chapter 2.

The financial analysis component of the business case, under the guidance of the Chief Financial Officer (*CFO*) or the *CFO* organization, shows whether or not the product concept will meet the financial goals established by the Chief Executive Officer (*CEO*) and the Board of Directors (*BOD*). The financial requirement may be a return on investment (*ROI*) requirement (e.g., a 10% return on investment) or a market requirement (e.g., garner a 5% share of market in two years). If the target is deemed unattainable with the current design, then it will be terminated and removed from the pipeline as financially nonviable; otherwise, it will continue through the pipeline. So the business case results in a *Go/No-Go* decision.

This is where pricing becomes an issue since the financial assessment involves the calculation of net contribution and contribution margin. Net contribution is what economists typically refer to as profit or the difference between revenue, which is price times units sold, and product-specific costs. Net contribution divided by revenue is the contribution margin and is normally expressed as percent of revenue. Profit *per se* is an enterprise-wide value, not a product or business unit item. A product contributes to the business unit's financial status while the business unit contributes to the enterprise's financial status. There is a rolling-up from the product to the business unit to the enterprise, each piece contributing to the whole.

A new product, and all existing ones for that matter, must contribute to the whole. How much they are required to contribute is determined by the *CEO* and *BOD*. The purpose of the business case is to make sure the contribution goals, the requirements, are met. The price point is needed to calculate the revenue. If the price point is incorrect, then the product will either be viewed as unrealistically profitable or a financial disaster that must not be pursued. A range for key financial measures, rather than definite values, is usually acceptable between the time of concept development and product launch. The range is typically bounded by an optimistic and a pessimistic view of market success. As long as the optimistic to pessimistic range covers the financial target then the product development will continue; otherwise, it will be terminated.

The product-specific costs are also important for the net contribution. These costs are wide and varied, but all internal to the business. These involve, but are not limited to, personnel, marketing, sales, supply chain contracts, and so forth. Obtaining estimates for these is a complex endeavor, but doable. See Chwastyk and Kolosowskia [2014] for a discussion about these costs and how to estimate them for new product development.

The price point for the business case is sometimes compiled by determining how much customers are willing to pay for components of the product. The sum of the amounts they are willing to pay is the overall value or worth of the product to them. This is the price point. Methodologies exist for determining the willingness-to-pay for components. I will describe these in Chapter 4. Unfortunately, they are applicable before launch when the product is almost definitely defined. In the concept stage, the product is still too amorphous for customers to definitely express any willingness-to-pay. Since a price point is hard to determine much in advance of a product launch, another methodology is needed to at least determine a range of feasible prices. It is this range that is used in the business case financial analysis for determining an optimistic and pessimistic financial view of the new product. I will discuss some methodologies for price range assessment in Chapter 3.

1.1.3 Messaging failures

Not only must the product and price be "right" for the market, but how it is sold or positioned must be correct. This involves two intertwined activities: messaging and targeting. The former is part promotional – letting customers know the product exists and where to buy it – but also part customer-specific – having the right messaging to position the product in the customer's product mindset. The messages are claims about what the new product can or will do to satisfy customers' wants and needs and solve their problems; they are about the product's capabilities. Exaggerated or unbelievable, factually baseless or unsupportable, typical, hard to remember, or not very motivating claims will be spotted instantly by potential customers which will make selling it difficult at best or doom the product at worst.

For the targeting activity, customers have to believe the new product fits their lifestyle and requirements, especially their budget. A claim that positions the new product as being very luxurious and targeted to higher income customers will not sell at all to those in the lower income brackets. This is just as important as the claim made about the product's capabilities. This is where the design concept plays a role because the design statement should include a description of the target market. I discuss messaging in Chapter 5.

1.2 An NPD process

All successful businesses have a myriad of business processes they follow, some almost religiously. They range from human resource management (e.g., salary determination, promotion assessment, career moves, hiring) to accounting and invoicing to supply chain management. Three major categories of processes are:[3]

MANAGEMENT PROCESSES: those governing the operation of the business. These include corporate governance and strategic management.

OPERATIONAL PROCESSES: those constituting the core daily operation of the business. Examples include purchasing, manufacturing, marketing, and sales.

SUPPORT PROCESSES: those supporting the core daily operational processes. Examples include accounting, recruitment, clerical, and technical support.

There are a host of subprocesses under each major category such as purchasing under Operation Processes and recruitment under Support Processes. The list of possible subprocesses can, of course, be quite long depending on the size and complexity of the business. One process that should be on this list is new product development. This is needed just as much as any other process any business follows. A new product development process is unique and cannot be subsumed under the three listed above. It may be guided by management, but it is not a management process *per se*. It is not operational process – which is concerned with daily activity, not long-term issues – and new product development is certainly a long-term issue. It is not support which is actually concerned, in part, with existing products through, say, fulfillment houses, call centers, repair centers, and warranty claim centers. So new product development is separate but as equally important as the other three.

Like all processes, a new product development *NPD* process is complex, with many interacting components, each of which is complex in its own right. A large number of books deal with *NPD* processes. See, for example, Cooper [1993], Cooper [2017], and Trott [2017] for some excellent discussions. The classic treatment is Urban and Hauser [1980]. Also see the blog article by Thomas Davenport[4]. This last is particularly important because he outlines five stages for an *NPD* process: ideation, business case, create, test, and launch. This is a good paradigm because it emphasizes the major components of a process. I disagree, however, with a few stages. The business case stage is not a separate one, but is an ongoing check at all stages of the *NPD* process as I mentioned above. It is a gate-keeping function that allows a new product to enter the pipeline and to pass from one stage to the next or be terminated. The launch is not the last stage since once a product is out the door, it must be tracked to see how well it performs and if it is meeting the financial and market targets. If not, then it must be withdrawn from the market. Some may argue that this tracking is not applicable to new products because once the product has been launched, it is no longer "new." It has been "realized" and a new function or team within the business now has ownership of and responsibility for the product. The tracking process, however, is not just for determining how well the product is performing post-launch, but also for determining what is wrong with it or what else may be needed for the next "new" product. In short, a tracking function has two purposes:

1. monitoring performance of the product post-launch; and
2. identifying new opportunities for the next new product.

This second function is, in fact, an input into the beginning of the *NPD* process: ideation or concept formation. In short, the *NPD* process is not linear, progressing from one stage to the next in an almost mechanical fashion allowing, of course, for the business case gate keeping, but rather it is cyclical with the end feeding back to the beginning of the next cycle. In fact, even at a point midway through the process, the product could be "sent back to the drawing board" and redone. Testing, for example, could indicate major design flaws that could terminate the product and force it back into design mode.

My version of the *NPD* process consists of five stages, each one designed to address a logical question:

IDEATION: "*What do we do?*"
DEVELOP: "*How do we do it?*"
TEST: "*Will it work and sell?*"
LAUNCH: "*What is the right marketing mix?*"
TRACK: "*Did we succeed?*"

with the third stage, *Testing*, and the last stage, *Tracking*, cycling back to the beginning Ideation stage. This *NPD* process is illustrated in Figure 1.3.

1.3 The heart of the *NPD* process

The *NPD* process is a decision-making one with key decisions at each stage. These decisions must pass muster by going through various business case gates and overcoming hurdles as established by the executive management. Like all decisions, their quality depends on the input into that decision. That input is information based on data. At the heart of the *NPD* process is *Deep Data Analytics* (*DDA*), a paradigm

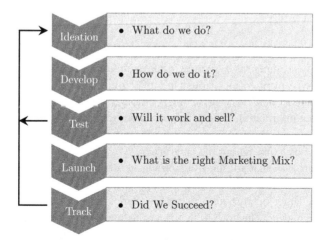

FIGURE 1.3 This illustrates the five stages of the *NPD* process. Although the figure appears to be linear, it is actually a cyclical process with the results of the Tracking and Testing stages feeding back into the Ideation stage as emphasized by the arrows.

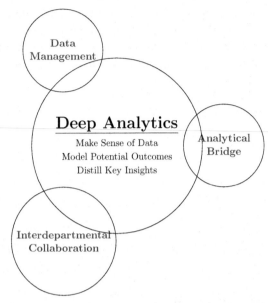

FIGURE 1.4 Deep analytics, a paradigm for converting raw data into actionable, insightful, and useful information consists of three components as illustrated here. This model is based on Wong [2012].

for converting raw data into actionable, insightful, and useful information. Deep Data Analytics consists of three components illustrated in Figure 1.4:

- Data Management;
- Interdepartmental Collaboration; and an
- Analytical Bridge.

Data are often maintained or housed in different settings as simple as personal computer files and as complex as data stores, data warehouses, data lakes, and data marts. Since they are maintained in various types of settings, a method must be devised to manage them so that everyone involved in the *NPD* process can access and use them to extract information. So one important component of Deep Data Analytics is *Data Management*. Data Management involves the organization, cleansing, and distribution of data throughout the enterprise.

More often than not in large organizations, different groups have data that "belong" to them and so are maintained in their personal silos. This is unfortunate since the larger organization, that is the company, suffers from a suboptimal, inefficient use of data. The goals of the larger organization are better served if organizational units share and collaborate. Collaboration across multiple disciplines and functional units, especially when repeated and well orchestrated by a skilled management team, can reduce the costs of analytical work in new product development. As noted by *The Economist* magazine[5]:

The characteristics of information – be it software, text or even biotech research – make it an economically obvious thing to share. It is a "non-rival" good: i.e., your use of it does not interfere with my use. Better still, there are network effects: i.e., the more people who use it, the more useful it is to any individual user. Best of all, the existence of the internet means that the costs of sharing are remarkably low. The cost of distribution is negligible, and co-ordination is easy because people can easily find others with similar goals and can contribute when convenient.

A multicollaborative *NPD* process involves multiple organizations. Figure 1.5 illustrates some possibilities.

Data are not information. They are the raw building blocks for information. They are raw, unfiltered, disorganized pieces of material (i.e., "stuff") that, like clay bricks, you can arrange and assemble in infinite ways reflecting your creativity and questions. Information is contained in the raw data bricks and so must be extracted. This information is not a binary concept meaning that you either have information or you do not. This is how most people view information. Information is better viewed as a continuum as illustrated in Figure 1.6. *Rich Information* is insight built and extracted **from** data by creatively manipulating data bricks while *Poor Information*, in the form of simple means and proportions, can also be extracted, but provides limited insight. You leave a lot of other information in the data when you extract Poor Information. The goal for data analysis should be to minimize the amount of information left in the data. The *Analytical Bridge* is the process of taking raw data bricks and extracting the Rich Information contained in the data by using different data views. Deep Data Analytics consists of the tools and methodologies

FIGURE 1.5 Numerous functional areas contribute to the *NPD* process. Part of this collaboration should be data sharing.

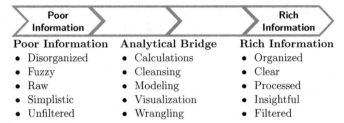

Poor Information	Analytical Bridge	Rich Information
• Disorganized	• Calculations	• Organized
• Fuzzy	• Cleansing	• Clear
• Raw	• Modeling	• Processed
• Simplistic	• Visualization	• Insightful
• Unfiltered	• Wrangling	• Filtered

FIGURE 1.6 Information is not binary, but continuous. At one end is Poor Information while Rich Information is at the other end. It is the Rich Information that provides insight for actionable decision making.

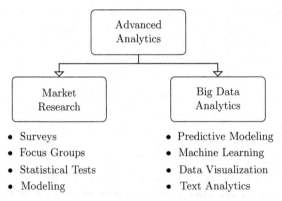

FIGURE 1.7 There are two major components to the Analytical Bridge for extracting information from raw data for new product development: Market Research and Big Data Analytics. These components or functions can certainly be used for other purposes in a business so they are not restricted to just new product development.

of statistics, econometrics, machine learning, and text analysis that are designed to extract the Rich Information. Analytics that are not advanced, that are based on simple means and proportions, extract Poor Information. See Paczkowski [2016] and Paczkowski [2018] for discussions of some methodologies.

The Analytical Bridge component involves two subordinate components:

1. Market Research; and
2. Business Analytics.

These are illustrated in Figure 1.7. They should be considered as frameworks for Deep Analytics since neither is an analytical method *per se*. Subcomponents of each framework, however, are analytical methods, a few of which are listed in Figure 1.7. I briefly discuss these in the following subsections.

1.3.1 Market research

In addition to *Subject Matter Experts* (*SMEs*) and *Key Opinion Leaders* (*KOLs*), market research is the traditional function many businesses turn to and rely on for new product ideas. *SMEs* are people, both internal and external to the business, although they are usually internal employees, who have expertise in a particular area because of advanced training or experience. *KOLs* similarly can be internal or external to the business but are generally external. They are somewhat neutral, unbiased commentators on a wide variety of areas and subjects, such as technology advances, political events, social trends, and so forth. They express their views and opinions in blogs, articles in relevant magazines and professional journals, and at conferences. Both *SMEs* and *KOLs* have valuable insight businesses often draw on for ideas regarding what to put into their product development pipelines.

Although *SMEs* and *KOLs* are important for new product development, they cannot be solely relied on for guidance in what to produce next. They are, after all, not the customers, the ones who actually buy and will buy the business's product and the ones who have problems the products are designed to solve. Ultimately, it is the customers who have the first and last say in what should be produced, but discovering what they have to say is not a trivial task. Market research methodologies are designed, and in fact continually evolve, to hear what they have to say. This is the *Voice of the Customer* (*VOC*). The customers may not know themselves what they want, and they probably do not, so they cannot articulate their requirements in sufficient detail so that product designers (i.e., engineers, technicians, marketers) can design and build a product. Instead, they send messages, sometimes cryptic, that hint at their problems and what they want or need to solve them. The problems are as varied as there are people so there is no one problem and no one solution. The problem could be product specific ("*The power button isn't accessible.*") or universal ("*I spend too much time vacuuming.*").

The purpose of market research is to distill the key or overriding problem (or problem set) from the myriad of hints provided by customers so the new product development team can define and prioritize their efforts. See Inmon [2018] and Barabba and Zaltman [1991] for some discussions about the importance of the *VOC* as market information to be heeded.

Traditional market research uses surveys and focus groups to listen to the *VOC* and to distill the problem set from all the diverse messages sent by the diverse customer base. These tools can yield valuable insights. That is, uncover new market opportunities. At the same time that your business is researching customers, others are doing the same thing for the same purpose. So not only does your business have to assess what is important to its customer base but it also has to assess how other *KMPs* are performing in meeting customer wants and needs.

One approach for assessing what is important and what the competition is doing is the *Competitive Environment Analysis* (*CEA*) mentioned earlier. This is based on survey data to address two problems:

1. The competitive differentiation of the *KMP*s on attributes of a product to identify market opportunities.
2. The strengths and weaknesses of each *KMP* on each attribute.

In essence, *CEA* is a classic Strengths, Weaknesses, Opportunities and Threats *SWOT* analysis. This will aid the concept development team in identifying untapped or unmet opportunities. I will discuss this analysis and others in Chapter 2.

1.3.2 Business analytics

Big Data is all the rage because of the opportunities it offers in many and diverse areas. This is especially true for new product development because of the amount of data available on the *VOC*. Big Data, however, is fraught with problems often overlooked or ignored in many of the commentaries extolling its usefulness and potential for advancing understanding in any area. There are great potentials, but also great problems that have to be noted. See Paczkowski [2018] for a discussion of some problems of Big Data and how to handle them.

The analysis of Big Data falls into two domains: *Business Intelligence* and *Business Analytics*. Business Intelligence is concerned with analyzing data; what did, and what is more important, what is currently happening to the business. It is used to alert management teams of problems, real and potential, so they can take preemptive actions. Business Analytics is more forward looking, telling the same management teams what will happen under different conditions. I further discuss the distinction between the two in Chapter 7 where I emphasize Business Analytics for tracking a new product's post-launch performance. Predictive modeling, Machine Learning, and Text Analysis are the main tool sets.

Both Business Intelligence and Business Analytics rely on Big Data. What is Big Data? The common way to define it is by listing three main features of Big Data, which are its:

1. Volume;
2. Variety; and
3. Velocity.

Volume is the characteristics people immediately think about when they hear or read about Big Data. This should be expected since it is "Big" and not "Small" Data. The volume of data has definitely been exploding because of the different types of data now collected. We used to discuss data in terms of kilobytes, then megabytes, and eventually gigabytes. Now we discuss it in terms of terabytes, petabytes, exabytes, zettabytes, and yottabytes. A kilobyte is 1000 (10^3) bytes which is a basic unit of measure in computer science. A megabyte is 1 million $(= 1000^2 = 10^6)$ bytes. A yottabyte is 1000^8 $(= 10^{24})$ bytes which is 10 followed by 23 zeros. Table 1.1 lists the sizes commonly discussed.

TABLE 1.1 These volumes are in decimal measures. Comparable binary measures are available.

Value	Label	Symbol
1000	Kilobyte	KB
1000^2	Megabyte	MB
1000^3	Gigabyte	GB
1000^4	Terabyte	TB
1000^5	Petabyte	PB
1000^6	Exabyte	EB
1000^7	Zettabyte	ZB
1000^8	Yottabyte	YB

Source: https://en.wikipedia.org/wiki/Yottabyte. Last accessed January 26, 2018.

These volumes definitely present many challenges from storage, to access, to analysis. It also increases pressures placed on analysts and heightens misconceptions of what is possible. Analysts are now expected to analyze all the data to find something of use for all aspects of their business, including new product ideas. Unfortunately, much of the data is useless or so complex that analyzing them with current tools is not trivial and, in fact, daunting. There is also the misconception that statistics and sampling are no longer needed or relevant for Big Data. This view holds that they are needed only to provide measures or estimates of measures of key population aspects (e.g., means) when you do not have complete data on the population under study due to the cost of collecting all that data. With Big Data, however, you have that population data so you can measure aspects directly. Unfortunately, this is not true since the population may not be represented at all. Only those who choose or self-select to be in a database are represented. For example, all the buyers of automobiles are not in any one auto manufacturer's database because people do not buy just one make of automobile. The population is the buyers, not the buyers of one make.

The velocity with which data are arriving into databases is increasing all the time. This is due primarily to new technologies that capture data almost in real-time. Transactions data at grocery centers is an example. In addition to technologies that allow more efficient data capture, new technologies also allow people to almost constantly create data in huge volumes that other technologies capture. Social media in the form of Twitter and Facebook and others of their kind allow people to create text messages at any time and any place they choose. Consider Twitter. One estimate is that there are "350,000 tweets sent per minute" or "500 million tweets per day."[6] This is high velocity. The volume is dependent on this velocity: the higher the velocity, the larger the volume as is evident by these Twitter numbers.

Variety is the main issue for us. Since the advent of the Internet and social media in particular, there has been an explosion in the types of data, from pure text, to photos, to videos and audios, and to maps, captured and stored in data warehouses. Text data in the form of tweets on Twitter and product reviews on company and review websites (e.g., Amazon) have added a new dimension to the data traditionally collected. Prior to the collection of this type of data, the majority of data were well defined and organizationally structured: amounts (dollars and units sold), dates, order numbers, names and addresses in specific formats. They were well defined because those who collected the data knew beforehand the likely values for key concepts such as phone numbers, dollar amounts, dates, ZIP codes, and so forth. This includes predefined key words and phrases. The database designers and managers could plan for these. They were organizationally structured in the sense that the data were in rectangular arrays or data tables with predefined columns for variables and each object (i.e., observation, case, individual, etc.) in each row with one object per row. The type and nature of the data contained in each cell of the data table was pre-specified and filtered before it could be placed in the cell. This is a *structured data paradigm*.

The text data now collected is ill-defined and unstructured. It is ill-defined because it could be any content as determined by the writer of the text: differing lengths, symbols, words, and even languages. Tweets on the social media platform Twitter used to be restricted to 140 characters; now they are restricted to 240, but despite this increase this is still a tight space to express a complex thought. Nothing is well defined or structured the way data used to be. Text data are unstructured so now, in addition to a structured data paradigm, there is an *unstructured data paradigm*. This new type of data is potentially rich in information but, like the traditional well-defined structured data, the information must still be extracted. Since this new form of data, this new variety, arrives so quickly and in such large volumes, the analytical tasks associated with it are now an order of magnitude larger. This is where Big Data Analytics becomes important. This form of analytics not only addresses the volume and velocity issues (the "Big" part), it also addresses the variety issue (the "Data" part).

The sheer volume of data necessitates a new view of analytics but without dropping or ignoring the "old" tools of statistics and econometrics. Those tools, the statistical theory and techniques, still hold and must be relied on. They maintain that there is a population of objects (e.g., people, companies) that exists but that for technical reasons it is too costly to collect data on every object in that population so you cannot directly measure key parameters of that population. One such measure is, of course, the mean. Statistical theory provides tools via sampling that allow you to infer the population measure and to establish ranges (i.e., confidence intervals) around the population measure. Big Data gives the false impression that you now have the population and so therefore the statistical theory and tools, which are based on sampling principles, are no longer necessary. This is incorrect and misleading. Big Data itself, the sheer volume aspect and not to ignore the velocity and variety aspects, present problems that statistical theory directly addresses. See Paczkowski [2018] for a discussion of these problems and how sampling can help.

Although Big Data has issues with the volume aspect that are important to recognize and deal with, it has definite advantages with regard to the variety aspect, especially the text part of variety. Modern technology has enabled everyone to voice their opinions on any topic from politics, to economics, to science. This is especially true for customer opinions about the products they buy. Customer reviews are now the norm rather than the exception on most producer and retailer websites. These review capabilities allow customers to write their opinions, both good and bad, about a product for others to read. Most sites even provide a rating system, usually a five-point "star" system with one star (or less!) indicating a terrible product and five stars a great product. So the reviews have two parts. The star portion can be viewed as a quantitative measure not unlike a five-point Likert Scale measure of customer satisfaction commonly used in many market research surveys. The text portion of the review can be viewed as a qualitative assessment of the product that amplifies or explains the quantitative star rating. It is the qualitative portion that is important for new product development since this is where customers not only voice their opinions but also make their suggestions for improvement. It is the latter that is the key to new product development ideas. These data are not only important for new product ideas but also for follow-up tracking once the product has been launched. You also need to understand how well the product is performing in the market. Sales data can certainly tell you this – this is the "how" of performance – but the customer reviews are invaluable for informing you about the "why" of performance.

The use of text mining and analytics for new product ideas and tracking will be discussed in Chapters 2 and 7. Methods for Business Analytics are discussed in Chapter 7.

1.4 Summary

This introductory chapter laid the groundwork for the rest of this book by highlighting the issues with new product failures and what process could be followed to reduce the risk of failure due to those causes. A risk of failure remains whether the process outlined here is followed or not, but it will be reduced if more reliance is placed on data analytics, the foundational part of the new product development process illustrated in Figure 1.3. The five parts of the process are developed in more detail in the following five chapters, each chapter devoted to one of the parts. A final chapter, Chapter 8, examines resource issues and collaboration needed to make it all work.

Notes

1 See www.forbes.com/sites/onmarketing/2012/04/30/the-need-for-marketing-speed/# 7808acd0768e. Last accessed May 8, 2019.
2 The odds of failure are $^{\text{likelihood of failure}}/_{\text{likelihood of success}} = {0.80}/{0.20} = 4$.
3 Wikipedia: https://en.wikipedia.org/wiki/Business_process_modeling#Business_ process. Last accessed January 24, 2018.

4 http://digitalcommunity.mit.edu/people/tdavenport/blog

5 www.economist.com/node/3623762. Last accessed January 24, 2018.

6 See www.internetlivestats.com/twitter-statistics/. Also see www.americanpressinstitute.org/publications/reports/survey-research/how-people-use-twitter-in-general/. Both sites last accessed January 9, 2019.

2

IDEATION

What do you do?

Generating ideas is not trivial. There is a huge literature in the philosophy of science dealing with where and how ideas originate. These are not only ideas for science, poetry, literature, and art but also, and more importantly for this book, ideas for new technologies and products. In all cases, idea generation, at worst, is considered mysterious, involving a black box (i.e., the brain) from which something just appears; pure creativity. At best, it is considered to be the result of hard work and deep concentration. In neither case is it considered to involve data or deep data analytics.

Since the topic of idea generation is so broad and diverse, I can only hope to describe a few practical approaches relevant for new product development. These are described in the following section. See Johnson [2011] for a discussion about where ideas come from. Also see Couger [1995] for an extensive discussion of different approaches to creative problem solving (*CPS*) which is another way to describe idea generation.

There are nine sections in this chapter. Traditional sources for new ideas, such as brainstorming, are discussed in Section 1 but then the sources are extended in the second and third sections to include Big Data and especially text data as a component of Big Data. In Section 3, I review the key points about text analysis in some detail because I believe this is an untapped area for new product ideas. I then narrow the focus for text analysis in Section 4 to call center logs and warranty claims analysis as special cases of text analysis. *Sentiment analysis* and *opinion mining* as possible sources of ideas are mentioned in Section 5 but these are not developed in detail since I will discuss them in Chapter 7 when I focus on post-launch tracking. Section 6 contains more traditional market research approaches while Section 7 is concerned with some machine learning methodologies that could be used in the ideation stage. Section 8 is a review of software. Section 9 is a summary. An

Appendix presents some higher-level math concepts mentioned in the chapter and that are referred to in later chapters. It is not necessary to be proficient in these concepts, but if you intend to pursue a more data analytics approach to new product development then these concepts are a must to know. Other chapters will have their own technical appendices with more information needed for a data analytics approach.

2.1 Sources for ideas

I categorize idea generation into two broad approaches, *traditional* and *modern*, to make a discussion of idea generation more systematic. The traditional approach consists of time-honored ways of finding ideas: brainstorming, market research surveys, and focus groups. The modern approach is more systematic involving data and statistical, econometric, and machine learning methodologies. I will discuss the traditional approaches in the next subsection followed by the modern approach.

2.1.1 Traditional approaches

There are three (and probably many more) traditional ways to generate ideas: brainstorming, market research surveys, and focus groups. Brainstorming is an old technique that has been in use for 70 years and is applied in many forms depending on the interviewer's training, expertise, and preferences. It was introduced by Osborn [1953] and subsequently used and abused by many in academics, business, and government. There are two central precepts to the approach:

1. idea generation must be separated from idea evaluation[1]; and
2. brainstorming in a group context supplements, not replaces, individual ideation.[2]

Osborn [1953] outlined four guidelines for the effective application of brainstorming:

1. **No criticism** of other participants' ideas. Judgement is reserved for the end of a brainstorming session.
2. **Free thinking** is encouraged. The objective is to generate ideas, so anything and everything is on the table.
3. **Generate quantity**. The more ideas listed, the better the odds of finding a winning one.
4. **Combine ideas**. Part of the creative process is combination and connectivity. Ideas can be formed by combining several already stated ideas as well as by finding a connection between two or more ideas. One idea in a vacuum from others may be insufficient but several in a combination may be a gem.

Brainstorming, despite its wide use, has its detractors and critics who believe it is a waste of time, energy, and money. These are weak criticisms usually proposed by those who do not want to be involved in a brainstorming session; they are basically trite rationalizations because these critics often believe they already "know the answers" or that nothing new will be proposed. Better criticisms have focused on situations with more merit because they get to core psychological reasons participants may not function well in a brainstorming session. Working in groups can be inhibiting and intimidating due to "evaluation apprehension" and "uniformity pressure." The former is a fear of being evaluated and criticized while the latter is a fear of being pressured to conform with the crowd. These are inherent fears many people share but are not reasons for dismissing the process. Other issues are "social loafing" and an associated "free-rider effect." The former occurs when people let others in a group lead the way while the latter occurs when people gain some benefit from a group activity while expending little effort. The free-rider problem is an issue in economics and political science regarding the provisioning of public goods. Basically, a free-rider problem exists when someone benefits from an action or situation without cost. In the case of brainstorming, a team member could simply not participate but yet receive accolades and rewards as a team member if a good idea emerges. If a bad or no idea emerges, that person could simply say "*I had no part in this.*" See Hardin [2013] for a good discussion of the free-rider problem in general. Other reasons include the "sucker effect", the "matching effect" and the "blocking effect." See Couger [1995] for discussions. These criticisms obviously go against two of Osborne's guidelines.

A legitimate issue with brainstorming is a quantity–quality tradeoff. The objective of brainstorming is to generate ideas – lots of them. This is Osborn's third guideline. During a typical session, dozens, if not hundreds, of ideas could conceivably be listed. This is a quantity problem. Someone, or preferably the team, must wade through the list which would definitely be time consuming and thus costly, not to mention fatiguing and discouraging. Buried inside this list could (hopefully) be the gem of an idea that leads to a new product, but finding it may be as daunting as initially compiling the list. This is a quality problem. Further efforts may be needed to cull that single idea or basis for an idea from the list which means other sessions or teams have to be engaged to review and narrow the list.

See Isaksen [1998], Isaksen and Gaulin [2005], and Couger [1995] for reviews of the brainstorming technique and critical appraisals. There are many other techniques that can be used to generate ideas, both individually and in groups. Couger [1995] lists 22 methods, one of which is brainstorming.

Market research methods consist of *quantitative research* and *qualitative research*, or a combination of both in a two-phase approach: qualitative research done first to identify key issues and problems, followed by quantitative research building on and supported by the qualitative research results. Sometimes the quantitative research is followed by another round of qualitative work to verify or further clarify quantitative conclusions.

Included in the qualitative research are in-depth interviews with Subject Matter Experts (*SMEs*), Key Opinion Leaders (*KOLs*), major customers, and company executives. The quantitative research includes extensive questioning of customers using survey research techniques. In either case, the objective is to "hear the voice of the customer" although with *SMEs* and *KOLs* the voice is indirect since you do not speak to the customers *per se*. In-depth interviews with major customers, of course, give you access to that voice, but at the same time the voice might be muddled. In a business-to-business context (i.e., *B2B*), for example, there are two levels of customers. One is the Key Decision Makers (*KDM*) who authorizes buying the product or service for use in his/her company. This person may not be the actual user of the product, the second level of customer. Users may have opinions which, perhaps because of organizational issues or restrictions, were never conveyed or expressed to the *KDMs*. Consequently, the *KDMs* interviewed may not be able to fully express or articulate problems and requirements. The end-users may be buried deep inside the organization and they may be so dispersed throughout the organization or so anonymous that finding a representative sample for interviewing may be more than a challenge. The in-depth interviews are then biased.

2.1.2 A modern approach

A modern approach to idea generation heavily relies on a combination of data and statistical/econometric methods to identify customer – *business-to-business* (*B2B* and *business-to-customer B2C*) – needs, problems, issues, and concerns. These may be known to the customers so they can directly express them, or they may be unaware of them and so they can only express them indirectly. Also, they may not be able to fully and adequately articulate their needs, problems, issues, and concerns because of language issues or a belief that whatever they say or write is "clear enough" even though it is not. This last point introduces what Liu and Lu [2016] refer to as noise and misleading information. In general, methods are still needed to extract the essence of what customers are trying to say that could lead to new product ideas.

Two items are needed for this essence extraction: data and analytical approaches. There are three data sources:

1. Big Data – External
   - Social media and product reviews.
2. Big Data – Internal
   - Service calls
   - Warranty claims
3. Market Research – Voice of the Customer (*VOC*)
   - Surveys
   - Ethnographic research

The analytical methods applied to the data include the trio of statistics, economet-rics, and machine learning, each consisting of a wide array of tools. Within this trio, the actual tools range from the simple to the complex. For example, with the statistical methodologies, means and standard errors are simple while logistic regres-sion is complex. Depending on the data, its magnitude and structural complexity, some methodologies and tools are more appropriate than others.

I will discuss these data sources and the analytical approaches for each in the following sections.

2.2 Big Data – external and internal

As I mentioned in Chapter 1, "Big Data" is a buzz phrase widely bantered around with, in many instances, little definition of what is "big." My discussion put some content behind a definition in terms of Volume, Velocity, and Variety. That discussion was an almost standard one.

Although there is much discussion about the variety component, at the risk of oversimplification, I will categorize it into three classes as illustrated in Figure 2.1: numerical data, imaging data, and textual data. Images are photos, videos, and multimedia. Numerical data are any numbers as well as text that may logically be associated with the numbers. This includes, for instance, a product stock keeping unit (*SKU*), an order number, or a customer ID. The last three are usually alphanu-meric codes. The text class is strictly text, although numbers could certainly be embedded in the text strings. Customer reviews, call center logs, warranty claim notes, and product return notes are a few examples. The numeric and text data are particularly important for new product development, but at different points in the overall process: text in the ideation stage (the focus of this chapter) and numerical data in the pricing and tracking stages. See Mudambi and Schuff [2010] for an anal-ysis of customer reviews on Amazon.com and what aspects of reviews make them useful and informative.

The data in these three classes are a combination of internal and external orig-ination (another artificial distinction). Internal data are generated by the order processing system when a customer places an order. Price point, discount rates,

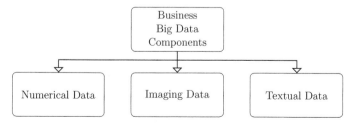

FIGURE 2.1 There are three major components of Big Data: numerical data, imaging data, and textual data. The imaging data could consist of videos and pictures. Textual data are any kind of text ranging from a word or two to whole books.

SKU code, dates, payment options, and so forth are automatically attached to the order by well-established internal protocols of the ordering, tracking, accounting, and financial systems. Most, if not all, of these are hidden from the customers. External data, however, are generated solely by the customers and may not even be maintained by the business. The external data could be product reviews on a product review web site which is divorced from the business or they could be comments on social media. Certainly, they could be on the business's own web site but nonetheless generated external to the company. The particular use of these pieces for ideation is often little discussed although some research is beginning in this area. See Liu and Lu [2016] for an example. They focus on *crowdsourcing* which has several definitions but all fundamentally referring to online reviews by a "crowd" of customers. Liu and Lu [2016], for example, refer to it as "the process of soliciting inputs from a large group of online users via the internet-based platforms." Also see Evans et al. [2016] for a review of the crowdsourcing literature.

For what part of a business's operations are numerical data to be used? Videos? Text? There seems to be little guidance and discussion that I am aware of. The three pieces are illustrated in Figure 2.1.

The use of the text component is discussed in the next section and then again in Chapter 7. The use of the numeric component is discussed in Chapter 7.

2.3 Text data and text analysis

Text data are usually characterized as *unstructured*. To understand why, it is necessary to first understand the structured nature of non-text data; i.e., numerical data. Numerical data are *structured* in that they are stored in well-defined fields with well-defined formats based on well-defined rules and protocols. For example, a transactions database would have the total number of units sold and the total invoice amount. The former would be another field without a decimal format (of course, depending on the product) while the latter is in one field with a two-decimal place format reflecting dollars and cents. The data would be maintained in a data table consisting of rows and columns. For transactions data, the rows would be individual orders while the columns would be the order and invoice amount. Other columns would be included to indicate an order number and transaction date. Another data table would have a column that represents the order number and an additional column for a customer ID. Yet another data table would repeat this customer ID plus have columns for the customer name and address. All the data tables are linked on order number and customer ID. These data are structured in that each datum goes in a specific table, in a specific place in that table, with a specific format, and for a specific purpose. See Lemahieu et al. [2018] for some discussion about structured and unstructured data for database design.

Not all non-text data are numerical. Corporate databases of transactions and customers have always contained text in addition to numerical data. These text data, however, like the numerical data, are structured. Names and addresses are stored in well-defined fields and tables with well-defined formats based on well-defined rules and protocols. Addresses, for example, would be:

- address 1 for street;
- address 2 for apartment or suite number;
- address 3 for possible third part of address such as a post office box number;
- city;
- state or province;
- country; and
- ZIP or postal code.

The same holds for product descriptions and email addresses. This text may best be labeled as character strings or character data to distinguish it from the text data computer scientists, IT managers, and data analysts worry about when they deal with Big Data.

These numeric and character data follow rules for storage and format. There are exceptions to the rules, but most data processing proceeds with few glitches or concerns. True text data are different. They do not follow any rules because the text can contain any type of characters, numeric or strings in any order, and be of any length. In addition, they may make intelligent sense or not. By intelligent sense, I mean that what is stored may be something that a normal person could read and immediately understand; text that basically follows proper grammar and literary rules with complete sentences and correct punctuation. In short, they make sense. They also may not follow grammar rules, be short abbreviated statements with strange letterings (e.g., "*bff*" for "*best friends forever*"; "*lol*" for "*laughing out loud*" or maybe "*lots of luck*"; or "*IMHO*" for "*in my humble opinion*"), contain foreign words or Latin words and expressions such as "*ergo*" for "*therefore*" or "*post hoc ergo propter hoc*" for "*after this, therefore because of this*," and they could be any length from a single word to several pages without punctuation or paragraph indication. In short, they are free-form. These types of data are unstructured. This makes storage and formatting difficult to say the least.

Despite being unstructured in form and format, there is actually a structure in arrangement which helps analysis. The arrangement is *documents* within a *corpus* which may be contained in a collection called a *corpora*. I discuss these arrangements in the next subsection.

2.3.1 Documents, corpus, and corpora

Text data *per se* at one level are unstructured as I just mentioned, yet at another level they are structured. It is from this higher level of structure that even more structure is imposed on text data so that traditional statistical analysis, primarily multivariate analysis, can be used to extract Rich Information useful for product ideas. The higher-level structure involves documents, a corpus of documents, and

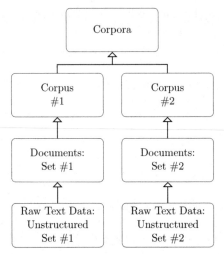

FIGURE 2.2 The raw, unstructured text data are contained in documents, which are contained in a corpus. If there are multiples of these containers, then they form a corpora. Two sets of raw text in two sets of documents are shown here. The documents form each corpus which themselves form a single corpora.

perhaps a corpora (the plural of corpus). This is a hierarchical structure illustrated in Figure 2.2.

In most instances, there is one corpus composed of many documents. As an example, a consumer survey could ask respondents to state why they like a particular product. The responses would be free-form text, the unstructured text in the bottom row in Figure 2.2. Each response is a document. Each document could be just a word (e.g., "Wonderful") or many words depending on what the respondent said about the product. The entire survey is the corpus. If the survey is done multiple times (e.g., once per year), then all the surveys are a corpora. For product reviews on a website, one review by one person is a document while all the reviews on that site is a corpus. Reviews on several sites for that same product is a corpora. These product review documents could also be collected into one data table with, say, two columns: one for the source and the other for the text.

2.3.2 Organizing text data

Since text data, as unstructured data, are fundamentally different from numeric data and other structured data, it would seem that the organization of text data should be different from other types of data. This is, in fact, the case. Consider structured data. By the definition of being structured, these data are maintained in a well-defined *relational database*. The database is relational in the sense that the database consists of tables, each table containing a specific set of information. The tables are linked or "related" based on keys. There are *primary keys* and *foreign keys* that allow you to merge or join two or more tables to answer a query. The primary key is an identifier attached to and is characteristic of the table involved. It identifies a specific element in the table. For example, for a customer table in a transaction database, a customer ID (*CID*) is a primary key for this table because it is directly associated with the data in that table. It identifies a specific customer. An order table in the same transaction database would have an order number (*ONUM*) that identifies a specific order so it is a primary key. But the *CID* is also in the order table because the customer placing the specific order must be identified. The customer ID is a foreign key because it identifies a record in another table. A transaction database, several tables in that database, and primary and foreign keys are displayed in Figure 2.3.

A useful paradigm for a relational database is a building. The building can be expanded in one of two ways: add more floors or add more wings.[3] Adding floors is vertical scaling while adding wings is horizontal scaling. A relational database is vertically scalable to handle more data because it can be expanded by adding more capacity to a server: larger disk storage, more RAM, faster processor. A query language does not care how large the database is. Horizontal scaling is different, however, in that new data structure and organization may have to be added. See Lemahieu et al. [2018] on horizontal and vertical scalability.

Not all databases are relational. By the nature of the data they store, they cannot be relational. Text data, videos, images are examples of data types that do not fit the relational database model because the data do not fit into well-defined

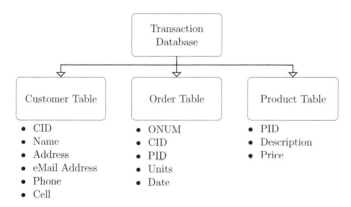

FIGURE 2.3 This shows three tables in a transaction database. Normally, more than three tables would describe an order. The keys are:

Table	Primary Key	Foreign Key
Customer	CID	
Order	ONUM	CID, PID
Product	PID	

structures nor can keys, primary or foreign, be defined for the entries. How do you define a primary key for a customer review for a product? As a result, these databases are unsearchable based on primary keys and can only be scaled horizontally by adding more servers to handle the increased load. These databases are called *document databases* where the documents could be text, videos, images. For our purposes, documents are just text.

Some document databases do have keys in the sense that the data are stored by *key:value pairs*. The key is a unique identifier for the record containing the text, and so is record specific, while the value is the document itself. The keys could be date-time stamps indicating when the text was either created or entered in the database. They allow for faster accessing of the values and are thus a more efficient way to organize the data.

A query language most commonly used to access relational tables, joining them where necessary based on the keys, to address a query is the *Structured Query Language (SQL)*. SQL has a simple, human language-like syntax that allows a user to request data from a table or combination of tables in an intuitive manner. The primary component of a SQL statement is the *Select* clause. As an example, you would select a variable "X" from a data table named "dbname" based on a condition that another variable "Y" has the value "2" using the statement "*Select X from dbname where Y = 2*". More complicated statements are certainly possible.

SQL is the primary language for querying a structured relational database. This is due to the structured nature of the database. A relational database is sometimes referred to as a *SQL* database. A nonstructured database would use *NoSql* and the database is sometimes referred to as a *NoSQL* database.[4] See Lemahieu et al. [2018] for discussion of *SQL* and *NoSQL* databases.

2.3.3 Text processing

Even though a corpus is a collection of documents so there is really some structure to the raw text, this is insufficient for statistical analysis for uncovering patterns or Rich Information in the text. More structure has to be imposed. Basically, the raw text has to be encoded as numeric quantities appropriate for statistical analysis since statistical analysis is based on numbers, not words. In this subsection, I describe the methods for encoding text and the analysis methods applicable to this encoded data.

The "old fashioned" way to encode text data, before modern text processing software, was labor intensive. Consider the market research space where text in the form of verbatim answers to some questions is common (e.g., the ubiquitous "*Other: Please Specify*"). Clerks laboriously examined each verbatim response following a set of guidelines specified by the lead researcher. The guidelines specified key words and phrases expected to appear in responses; assigned a code number to them; specified words and phrases believed to be meaningless or that could be ignored (e.g., articles such as "the", "a", "an" and conjunctive words such as "and" to mention a few). These words and phrases were called, and still are called, *stop-words*. The clerk extracted key words or phrases while ignoring stop-words.[5]. The final result of this text processing is a list of words and phrases the clerk would then sort and tally into simple frequency counts in a manner similar to a Stat 101 initial exercise for a histogram construction. The top few words and/or phrases were then reported. See Leskovec et al. [2014] for some discussion.

This labor-intensive process (actually, the clerk) has been replaced by software but the process is fundamentally the same. A basic list of stop-words is maintained that could, of course, be expanded to include industry, discipline, and geographically local or regional words, phrases, and even symbols that should be ignored. Some words on a stop-word list, however, may be important and should not be ignored. Words such as "The" and "An" (note the capitalization) could be part of a title and may be important. The implication is that not all words are equally unimportant – some should be kept because of their association with other words and thus give those other words more meaning and context. The word "not" is a prime example. There are lists of stop-words but no universal list.[6]

Some words are verbs with different conjugates such as "be", "am", "is", "was", "were", "are", "been", and "being" all of which can be reduced to "be." Other words are written in different forms merely by changing the ending to a base or stem word to create variations on the word. For example, consider a word I just used: "changing." The stem or root word is "change." Variations are "changing", "changed", and "changes." In many applications, only the stem – "chang" in my example – is needed. The process of *stemming*, removing typical endings, is applied to words to extract and return just the stem. For example, stemming might return "chang-" where the "-" indicates that something was dropped, but you do not know what.

Stemming is sometimes described as the crude process of deleting typical endings (i.e., "ed", "es", "ies", "tion") with the goal of returning the stem. Another process, *lemmatization*, is not crude but sophisticated relying on dictionaries and parts-of-speech analysis to reduce words to their core which is called a *lemma*. Stemming, however, is the most commonly used. An algorithm called *Porter's Algorithm* is the most common method for stemming. Stemming may be overdone: it would reduce the words "operator", "operating", "operates", "operation", "operative", "operatives", and "operator" to "oper-". What would happen to "opera?" See Manning et al. [2008, p. 34] for a discussion.

Punctuation and capitalization must also be dealt with. Punctuation marks are of no use for understanding the words themselves, so they need to be removed. Capitalized words, especially the first word of a sentence, are of little value unless they are proper names. These must also be dealt with by changing all words to lower case.

Modern text processing software scans the text in a document and *tokenizes* each word to create *tokens*. *Tokenization* is the process of separating each word and symbol (e.g., the ampersand "&") into a separate entity or *token*. Some tokens are words *per se* and thus meaningful while others are not. It all depends on the text itself. The words "token", "word", and "term" are used interchangeably in the literature and I will use them interchangeably in what follows.

Tokenization is done with a text manipulation software language called *regular expressions*. Regular expressions are powerful, widely used, but yet arcane and difficult to understand and interpret, not to mention difficult to write. It consists of defining a pattern using *metacharacters* (e.g., the asterisk, question mark, and period or dot are three metacharacters) and regular characters (e.g., letters of the alphabet and the digits 0–9) which are meant to match corresponding symbols in a character string. Each metacharacter is a special pattern matching instruction. The question mark metacharacter, for example, instructs the software to match zero or one occurrence of a preceding character in the pattern. The character string could contain letters, symbols, and digits. White spaces are also possible and it is these white spaces that break a string into tokens. For example, the classic string *"The quick brown fox"* has three separating white spaces and would be decomposed into four tokens. Regular expression capabilities are found in many programming languages such as Python, Pearl, and R to mention a few. See Watt [2005] and Frield [2002] for excellent introductions to regular expressions.

There are two forms of tokenization: sentence and word. Sentence tokenization creates a token for each unit of text considered a sentence based on the local rules of grammar and punctuation. In the English language, for example, a period, question mark, and explanation mark denote the end of a sentence. Since much text is now computerized, a newline character is also counted as an ending mark for a sentence. A semicolon might count depending on the text analysis software implementation.

Although sentence tokens are possible, most often only words are tokenized primarily because people are more interested in the frequency of occurrence of individual words rather than sentences. This is changing, however, because collections of words (e.g., phrases and clauses as well as sentences) convey meaning, sentiments, and opinions. I will discuss sentiment analysis and opinion mining in Chapter 7.

Word tokenization is not simple; there are complications. Examples are:

- contractions formed by deleting a vowel, replacing it with an apostrophe, and joining parts (e.g., "won't" rather than "will not"; "can't" rather than "cannot");
- misspellings;
- disallowed repetition of a letter (e.g., in English, a letter cannot be used more than twice in a row in a word);
- shortened versions of words (i.e., *"lol"* for *"laughing out loud"*)

to mention a few. Tokenizing a word such as "won't" could yield "won" and "'t", neither of which makes much sense. Some text softwares recognize this problem and return a single correct token: "won't." See Sarkar [2016] for an in-depth discussion of tokenization problems and how they are handled using Python tools.

Once you have *word-tokenize*d, or just *tokenized* for short, a document you then have a *bag-of-words* (BOW). This is an apt description for exactly what you have: a collection of words that, in and of itself, is useless; you must do something with it. A common operation, the one market researchers traditionally used as described above, is to count the occurrence (i.e., *frequency*) of each term across all documents in a corpus. Let $f_{ij}^C \geq 0$ be the frequency of occurrence of term i, t_i, in document j in corpus C. There is no j subscript on t_i because the document is not important; it is just a term. Term t_i may not occur in document j so $f_{ij}^C = 0$. However, it must occur at least once in all documents so $f_{i.}^C \geq 1$.[7] You could simply array the terms by their frequency counts and focus on those that occur most often in all the documents. The frequencies are usually normalized by the total number of terms in the documents so a relative frequency is displayed. The raw, unnormalized frequencies across all documents are simply referred to as *term frequencies* (*tf*). Note that $tf_i = f_{i.}^C$ is the term frequency for term t_i over all documents in C. A simple display is a barchart with each word listed next to its frequency count and a bar showing the size of the count. An example is shown in Figure 2.4.

A problem with this approach is that documents have different lengths. For example, product reviews could vary in length from one word (e.g. "garbage", "great") to whole paragraphs and pages. Consequently, one word could appear more frequently in one document than in another merely because of the different document lengths. In addition, some words naturally occur more often than others

Example Term-Frequency Display

Number of Terms	Number of Cases	Total Tokens	Tokens per Case	Number of Non-empty Cases	Portion Non-empty per Case
7	1	16	16	1	1.0000

Term List

Term	Count	
high	2	
price	1	
product	1	
rated	1	
service	1	
well	1	
works	1	

FIGURE 2.4 This is an example of a term frequency display for the product review "*the product works well and the service was rated high but the price was too high.*" Stop-words have been filtered out. Seven terms were retained out of 16 in the review. Of the seven terms, "high" occurred twice while the other six occurred once each.

but really do not contribute any meaning in the overall text. Stop-words such as "the", "and", "an" are examples. In a product review, a customer could write "*the product works well and the service was rated high but the price was too high.*" As a *BOW*, there are 16 terms. The term "the" occurs three times so $tf_{the} = 3$ while the term "was" occurs twice so $tf_{was} = 2$. The word "high" also occurs twice so $tf_{high} = 2$. All other words occur once each. Clearly the words "the" and "was" have no importance. They should be filtered out of the *BOW* before any analyses are done. These deleted words are the stop-words. The word "high" is important and should not be filtered out. A frequency count display might look like the one in Figure 2.4. The issue is weighting the terms so those that are important and which occur less frequently across all the documents are given more weight in an analysis while less important ones are given less weight. In Figure 2.4 all the terms have equal weight.

Weighting data is not unusual in empirical work. It is common in survey analysis, for example. In fact, it is probably the rule rather than the exception. See Valliant and Dever [2018] for reasons and methods for weighting survey data. Weights are also used in regression analysis when heteroskedasticity is an issue. In this case, the objective is to weight down those cases with large variances and weight up those with small variances to equalize variances across all the cases. This equalization is tantamount to the classical regression assumption of homoskedasticity which is needed for the *Gauss-Markov Theorem*. In this latter situation, a *variance generating process (VGP)* is assumed and this process is the basis for determining the weights. See Hill et al. [2008] for a discussion.

In sample survey analysis, a *simple random sampling (SRS)* without replacement design is based on every object having the same chance of being selected for the sample as every other object. Problems do occur in real-world applications but this assumption is a good starting point. See Valliant and Dever [2018] for a discussion of problems. In actual applications, an *SRS* design is rarely used. Instead, most sample designs use a probability sampling method in which each element or unit to be sampled (i.e., the *Primary Sampling Unit or PSU*) is assigned a nonzero probability of being selected. So *SRS* is a special case of probability sampling. In an *SRS*, each unit has the same probability of being selected. If N is the population size, then the selection probability is $p_i = 1/N$, $i = 1, \ldots, N$, and sampling is with replacement. If the sample size is n, then the selection probabilities are n/N since each of the n units has the same selection probability. For example, if $n = 3$ and $N = 10$, then $p_i = 3/10$ so each person has a 0.30 chance of being selected for the study (with replacement). These selection probabilities do not have to be all equal for probability sampling. See Heeringa et al. [2010] for a discussion.

A sampling weight is the reciprocal of the selection probability: $w_i = 1/p_i$. Sometimes the weight is interpreted as "the number (or share) of the population elements that is represented by the sample observations. Observation i, sampled with probability $\ldots 1/10$, represents 10 individuals in the population (herself and nine others)." See Heeringa et al. [2010, 35] for a discussion.

Referring to the terms in a corpus C, the probability of any term t_i being randomly selected or found in N^C documents in the corpus is the number of

TABLE 2.1 This illustrates the calculation of term frequencies. The term does not appear in document 3 so $f_{ij}^C = 0$ and the indicator function returns 0. Then $n_i^C = 3$ so $Pr(t_i \in C) = n_i^C/N^C = {}^3/_4$.

Document(j)	f_{ij}^C	$I(f_{ij}^C > 0)$
1	5	1
2	1	1
3	0	0
4	3	1
$N^C = 4$	$f_{i.}^C = 9$	$n_i^C = \sum_{j=1}^{N^C} I(f_{ij}^C > 0) = 3$

documents in which t_i occurs, n_i^C, divided by the number of documents. If $f_{ij}^C \geq 0$ is the frequency of occurrence of term t_i in document j in corpus C and $I(f_{ij}^C > 0)$ is the indicator function that returns 1 if the argument is true, 0 otherwise, then $n_i^C = \sum_{j=1}^{N^C} I(f_{ij}^C > 0)$. Then

$$Pr(t_i \in C) = \frac{n_i^C}{N^C} \tag{2.1}$$

Table 2.1 illustrates a simple example. Note that n_i^C is the number of documents t_i appears in while f_{ij}^C defined earlier is the frequency count of t_i in a single document, document j. Analogous to sampling weights, the weight for term i is ${}^{N^C}/_{n_i^C}$ or the inverse of the probability. This expression is the basis for the *inverse document frequency* (*IDF*). See Robertson [2004]. Applications use log base 2 of this expression, or $IDF^* = log_2({}^{N^C}/_{n_i^C})$. The reason for the log_2 lies in information retrieval theory where a term is either retrieved or not. This is a binary situation, hence the base 2. If term t_i appears in all documents in C so that it is a commonly occurring term, then $n_i^C = N^C$ and $log_2(1) = 0$ so the term has zero weight: it contributes no insight because it occurs all the time.

Variations exist for the *IDF* calculation. For example, JMP software uses

$$IDF(t_i) = log_{10}\left(\frac{N^C}{n_i^C}\right) \tag{2.2}$$

Sometimes the denominator in the log term is increased by 1 to avoid the case of $n_i^C = 0$ (i.e., t_i does not appear in any document in the corpus) which should never occur since t_i would never be under consideration if it did. Sometimes 1 is added to the whole log term to reflect the case where all the terms are contained in all the documents in the corpus. The *IDF* is then written as

$$IDF(t_i) = 1 + log_2\left(\frac{N^C}{1 + n_i^C}\right) \tag{2.3}$$

A final adjustment sometimes done is to divide the *IDF* by the Euclidean distance of the values. This normalizes the *IDF*. See Sarkar [2016] for some discussion.

Since $IDF(t_i)$, however calculated, is a weight, it can be applied to the term frequency, tf_i^C, through multiplication. The result is the *term frequency-inverse document frequency* measure ($tfidf_i$):

$$tfidf_i = tf_i^C \times IDF_i \qquad (2.4)$$

for term t_i. It is merely the weighted term frequency.

Since there is a set of terms for each document in the corpus, a matrix could be created that has as many rows as there are documents and as many columns as there are tokenized terms from all documents. If N^C is the number of documents and $t = \sum_{\forall i} t_i$ is the number of terms across all documents in the corpus, then the matrix has size $N^C \times t$. This is called the *Document Term Matrix* (DTM).[8] This matrix will necessarily be sparse since not all terms will be in each document (i.e., rows of the DTM). A sparse matrix is one with a lot of zeros. Aside from zeros, which indicate that a term does not appear in a document, the cells of the DTM can be populated with any of the following:

- binary values: 0 if the term does not appear in the document and 1 if it does;
- ternary values: 0 if the term does not appear in the document, 1 if it appears once, and 2 if it appears more than once;
- frequency count: number of times the term appears in the document;
- log frequency count: $log_{10}(1 + x)$ where x is the term's frequency count in the document[9];
- *tfidf*, the weighted term frequency.

The *tfidf* is the most common.

Example

Consider a simple example of three product reviews. Each review is a document so $N^C = 3$. This is a corpus of size three. The three reviews are:

1. *The product failed the second time – it failed!*
2. *The product worked the first time.*
3. *It's nice but failed.*

Clearly, one review is favorable (review #2); one is moderate but noted that the product failed (review #3); and one is negative (review #1). There are 18 "terms" or tokens (the "–" is deleted) but only seven unique terms or tokens have meaning. The stop-words and the "–" were removed. A report on the seven terms is shown in Figure 2.5. It is easy to see that "failed" is the most frequently used word. The frequency for each term by each document is shown in Figure 2.6. Looking at the word "failed" you can see that it occurs twice in the first document, not at all in the second, and once in the third.

Example for tfidf Calculations

Number of Terms	Number of Cases	Total Tokens	Tokens per Case	Number of Non-empty Cases	Portion Non-empty per Case
7	3	18	6	3	1.0000

Term and Phrase Lists

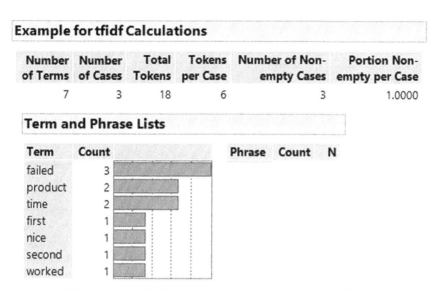

Term	Count
failed	3
product	2
time	2
first	1
nice	1
second	1
worked	1

Phrase	Count	N

FIGURE 2.5 This is an example for three product reviews. Even though there are three reviews (i.e., documents), there are seven terms after stop-words and punctuation are removed.

	text	failed Frequency	product Frequency	time Frequency	first Frequency	nice Frequency	second Frequency	worked Frequency
1	The product failed the second time -- it failed!	2	1	1	0	0	1	0
2	The product worked the first time.	0	1	1	1	0	0	1
3	It's nice but failed	1	0	0	0	1	0	0

FIGURE 2.6 This is the *DTM* corresponding to the example with three cases. Notice that the column sums correspond to the frequency counts in Figure 2.5.

Since "failed" occurs in two documents and there are three documents, the inverse document frequency for "failed" is $N^C/n_{fail} = 3/2 = 1.5$. The $log_{10}(1.5) = 0.17609$. This is shown in Table 2.2. This is a (weighted) *DTM*. This is the structure imposed on unstructured text data. These same calculations would be done for each of the seven terms. The complete set is shown in Figure 2.7.

Multivariate analyses

Once the *DTM* is created, a number of multivariate statistical procedures can be used to extract information from the text data. A common procedure is to extract key words and phrases and groups of words and phrases as topics. Conceptually, phrase extraction is the process of taking groups of words once the document has been tokenized, each group based on a prespecified maximum size. A group of size n is an *n-gram*. If $n = 1$, the group is a *unigram*; for $n = 2$, it is a *bigram*; for $n = 3$, it is a *trigram*; etc. Creating *n-grams* is tantamount to creating a small window of a prespecified size, placing it over a vector of tokens, and treating all the words inside

TABLE 2.2 This illustrates a *tfidf* calculation for the term "*failed*". Column *B* is the term frequency for "*failed*" for each document in column *A*. The frequencies correspond to the values in the "failed" column of the *DTM* in Figure 2.6. Column *C* is the inverse document frequency: the ratio of the number of documents in Column *A* divided by the number of documents that contain the word "*fail*." There are three documents and "*failed*" appears in two of them, so $n_{fail}^C = \sum_{j=1}^{3} I(f_{fail,j}^C > 0) = 2$. The ratio is $3/2 = 1.5$. The log_{10} of the ratio is in Column *D*. The log_{10} is used by JMP which was used for this example. The *tfidf* is in Column *E* and equals the value in Column *A* times the value in Column *D*. Notice that the values in Columns *C* and *D* are constant but the final weight in Column *E* varies because of the frequencies in Column *B*.

Document (A)	Freq. (B)	$\frac{\#Docs}{\#DocsIn}$ (C)	log_{10} (D)	*tfidf* (E)
1	2	$\frac{3}{2} = 1.5$	0.17609	$2 \times 0.17609 = 0.35218$
2	0	$\frac{3}{2} = 1.5$	0.17609	$0 \times 0.17609 = 0.00000$
3	1	$\frac{3}{2} = 1.5$	0.17609	$1 \times 0.17609 = 0.17609$

◁ 8/0 Cols ▼							
▼ text	failed TF IDF	product TF IDF	time TF IDF	first TF IDF	nice TF IDF	second TF IDF	worked TF IDF
1 The product failed the second time -- it failed!	0.35218	0.17609	0.17609	0.00000	0.00000	0.47712	0.00000
2 The product worked the first time.	0.00000	0.17609	0.17609	0.47712	0.00000	0.00000	0.47712
3 It's nice but failed	0.17609	0.00000	0.00000	0.00000	0.47712	0.00000	0.00000

FIGURE 2.7 The weighted *DTM* for the example with three cases.

the window as a phrase. The window can be moved to the right one token and all the words inside the new placement of the window would be a new phrase. This would be continued until the end of the vector of tokens. The phrases are then counted and a report created showing the frequency and (sometimes) length of each phrase. This is largely a counting function. See Sarkar [2016] for a discussion.

Phrases are of limited use in part because many of them would be nonsensical since they are created by selecting groups of words. The groups do not have to make any sense at all. You, as the analyst, must decide what is a useful, meaningful phrase. Many believe that *topics* are more useful, especially because topics are extracted using a statistical modeling method. Topics are viewed as latent, much like factors in factor analysis. In fact, the extraction of topics can be viewed as factor analysis applied to text data. In factor analysis, the resulting extracted factors must be interpreted to give them meaning and usefulness. Interpretation is also needed with latent topics. Nonetheless, a model is still necessary for topic analysis. It is this model that distinguishes topics from phrases.

There are three latent topic methods in common use:

1. *Latent Semantic Analysis (LSA)*, also sometimes referred to as *Latent Semantic Indexing (LSI)*;
2. *Latent Dirichlet Allocation (LDA)*; and
3. *Non-negative Matrix Factorization*.

Some have argued that *LDA* is not a good method because it is inconsistent. A different answer results from the same data set each time it is used. In addition, it uses *hyperparameters* so more "tuning" is required to get the right set of hyperparameters. Hyperparameters are those parameters that are set prior to model estimation in contrast to the parameters that are estimated. Hyperparameters define the model and its complexity. See Alpaydin [2014]. The method, however, is improving at a rapid speed as research continues to add to its foundations.[10]

The *LSA* is the most used method. It is based on the *Singular Value Decomposition* of a matrix; in this case the matrix is the *DTM*.[11] This allows terms that are used in the same context and occur together more often than not to be grouped together, much like numeric data are grouped in factor analysis. The terms are given weights or *loadings*. The *SVD* is preferred because it gives one unique solution regardless how often it is run, it does not have hyperparameters, it is fast, and is unaffected by the sparseness of the *DTM*.

Non-negative factorization is another matrix factorization method, but in this case a matrix is factored into two parts. A property of this factorization is that all three matrices have non-negative elements.[12]

The essence of the *SVD* of the *DTM* is that the matrix is decomposed into three submatrices simply called the left, center, and right matrices. The matrix product of these three submatrices returns the original *DTM*. The left matrix has columns corresponding to the rows of the *DTM*; the right has columns corresponding to the columns of the *DTM*; the center is a connection that has a special interpretation. The center matrix's components are called the *singular values*. The columns in the left and right matrices are called *eigenvectors*. The eigenvectors have the feature that they are independent of each other in their respective submatrix. The squares of the singular values are eigenvalues that correspond to the eigenvectors. See the appendix to this chapter for a discussion of the Singular Value Decomposition.

The weights or *loadings* are the product of the singular values and the right set of eigenvectors. The right set is used because these correspond to the terms in the *DTM*.[13] The products are sometimes called *singular vectors*. Once the *SVD* is applied, other multivariate procedures can be used with the results. This includes cluster analysis and predictive modeling.

Example

There are 22 online reviews of a robotic vacuum cleaner the marketing and product management teams know is not selling well.[14] They want to produce the next generation robotic cleaner and are looking for ideas for a better product. A quick perusal of the reviews reveals the main problems with the current design and a perusal of competitor reviews does the same for their products. Suppose, however, that these reviews were in the hundreds with each review being quite lengthy. Reading them is inefficient. The 22 reviews for this example are just a snapshot to illustrate the technique. Each review is a document and the collection of 22 reviews is a corpus so $N^C = 22$.

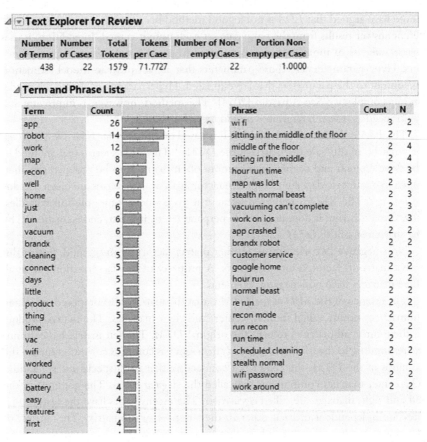

FIGURE 2.8 Word and phrase analysis of 22 robotic vacuum cleaner reviews. The list of terms on the left is truncated for display purposes.

Based on the 22 online reviews, a word and phrase analysis is shown in Figure 2.8. There are 1,579 tokens with 438 terms. This yields an average of 71.8 tokens per case or product review.

Notice that "app", "robot", and "work" are the top three terms. "Robot" should not be surprising since this is robotic technology so this word should be added to a user defined stop-word list but I will leave it in for this example. The word "work" does not convey much insight, but "app" does. This word is at the top of the list, appearing 26 times in the 22 reviews, suggesting that the app is an issue, good or bad. A word cloud, a visual display of the word frequencies, is shown in Figure 2.9. The size of a word is proportional to its frequency.

The phrases column on the right of the report shows the frequency count of each phrase and the number of terms appearing in the phrase. "Wi fi" appears the most and has two terms in the phrase; it is a bigram. A glance at the top phrases, say the top 10, suggests that the vacuum cleaner has a tendency to stop in the middle

Word Cloud

app robot work map recon well home just

run vacuum brandx cleaning connect days little product thing time vac wifi worked around battery easy features first fix hours house lost mode much never seems setup stuck t working works 2 3 access also beast bought classroom d disappointed fi floor hooked job like love network normal now perfectly probably ran re return save started try update use used wi $100 $900 actually alexa amazon better blocked bot charge charged clean cleaned commands complete connected connection cons crashed customer deal even fairly finally finish finished firmware fully getting give go going google great half hallway hour ios issues keeps ll load marketing memory middle new one password perfect performance phone pretty price purchase s say scheduled school secured service set sitting slower something spot stars stayed stealth still stopped technology thought trying vacuuming watch went wireless yes yet

FIGURE 2.9 Word cloud based on the frequency of occurrence of each word. This clearly shows that "app" is important.

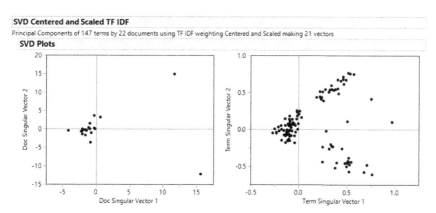

SVD Centered and Scaled TF IDF

Principal Components of 147 terms by 22 documents using TF IDF weighting Centered and Scaled making 21 vectors

SVD Plots

FIGURE 2.10 This is a plot of the first two dimensions of the SVD of the DTM using $TFIDF$ weights. The plot on the left is for the documents while the one on the right is for the terms.

of the room, takes a long time to run, and crashes. Now this is some insight into problems with the product. This is Rich Information.

A Latent Semantic Analysis (LSA) was done on the 22 reviews based on the SVD of the DTM. The *tfidf* was used to weight the DTM. The weighted DTM was scaled to have a zero mean and unit standard deviation. The results for the first two singular vectors for the documents and the terms are shown in Figure 2.10. The graph on the left shows the distribution of the documents and the one on the right the terms. The terms are more important. Notice that there are three clusters of points with two, possibly three, outliers. The large term-cluster on the left, if highlighted, shows that the words "map", "recon", "well", "run", and "vacuum" are the dominant words for this group. This is shown in Figure 2.11. A second group is highlighted in Figure 2.12 while a third cluster is highlighted in Figure 2.13.

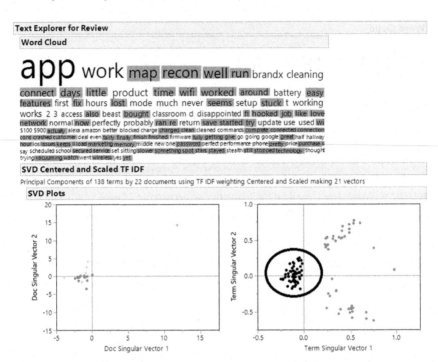

FIGURE 2.11 This set of graphs highlights specific points for the *SVD* of *DTM* using *TFIDF* weights.

The analysis can be extended by basically doing a factor analysis on the *DTM* but utilizing the *SVD* components. This results in "topics" which are like the factors in factor analysis. Each topic has terms comprising that topic with term loadings that show the impact on the topic. These are correlations exactly the way loadings are correlations in factor analysis. Figure 2.14 shows five topics extracted from the *DTM*.

2.3.4 Creating a searchable database

Processing text data and identifying key words, phrases, and topic is only the beginning. What do you do with this processed text data? The objective for the processing methods I outlined above is to enable you to take a large quantity of text data from online customer reviews and distill essential messages useful for developing new product ideas. Unfortunately, someone still must go through the distilled data since ideas will not just "pop out" of them. In addition, the design team may be, and probably will be, large and diverse so that there is not one designer or even one design department. A way is needed to disseminate the distilled text data so that a wide, collaborative group of people can access the text data and use it for their purposes. These purposes could be to identify new ideas and set design parameters.

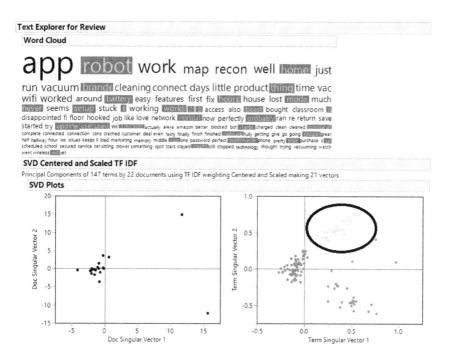

FIGURE 2.12 This set of graphs highlights specific points for the *SVD* of *DTM* using *TFIDF* weights.

A data base structure is needed to link the original text data and the distilled key words, phrases, and topics which would allow users (i.e., designers) to develop queries with returned results linked back to the original text. JMP software, for example, allows you to analyze text data as described above but then pick a key word or phrase and jump to the original document or documents containing that word or phrases. This allows you to scan those documents to better understand the context of what customers said and to interpret their messages for ideas and design parameters. A general system such as this is needed to handle large volumes of text data by the diverse groups. A possible flow chart schema is illustrated in Figure 2.15.

A central feature of the schema in Figure 2.15 is the link from the extracted words and phrases from the corpus back to the corpus itself. The extracted words and phrases provide insight and Rich Information about customer needs, problems, and issues. Their real value, however, can only come from the context they are drawn from which is the documents in the corpus. There must be a link from the corpus to the key words and phrases. Lemahieu et al. [2018] outline an approach for indexing documents that they call an *inverted index*. Basically, once a word (the same holds for phrases) is extracted, based on the methods discussed above, an index is created that consists of a key:value pair: the key is the word and the value is a list of document pointers. The document pointer list contains all the documents that contain the word or term. This can be created from the *DTM* which itself contains

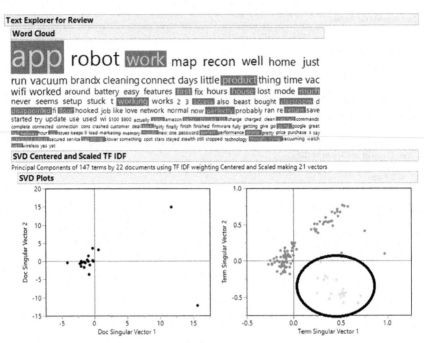

FIGURE 2.13 This set of graphs highlights specific points for the *SVD* of *DTM* using *TFIDF* weights.

Top Loadings by Topic

Topic 1		Topic 2		Topic 3		Topic 4		Topic 5	
Term	Loading	Term	Loading	Term	Loading	Term	Loading	Term	Loading
going	0.98849	new	0.97446	re	0.96385	hour	0.95306	wireless	0.82510
school	0.98849	$100	0.97446	crashed	0.96385	cons	0.95306	watch	0.82510
thought	0.98849	$900	0.97446	vacuuming	0.96385	normal	0.87494	bought	0.82295
hallway	0.98849	google	0.97446	finished	0.96385	2	0.87494	stayed	0.78334
blocked	0.98849	charge	0.97446	stopped	0.96385	seems	0.81390	ran	0.75906
classroom	0.98849	use	0.87560	complete	0.96385	run	0.78743	3	0.66903
disappointed	0.90384	beast	0.87198	recon	0.88202	pretty	0.70092	now	0.65359
access	0.88225	brandx	0.83957	stealth	0.85634	stealth	0.69975	connect	0.65115
set	0.75519	t	0.83563	lost	0.82580	technology	0.68938	marketing	0.60886
alexa	0.75519	setup	0.80636	purchase	0.69423	fairly	0.68385	say	0.59960
perfect	0.75519	cleaning	0.76136	map	0.63458	time	0.67451	fairly	0.58118
went	0.72000	commands	0.71295	clean	0.59998	getting	0.65262	hours	0.57276
trying	0.71774	firmware	0.71295	d	0.58154	also	0.60279	charged	0.55581
phone	0.71774	go	0.70342	save	0.57206	well	0.56122	thing	0.51205
go	0.69416	amazon	0.70342					stars	0.50919
amazon	0.69416	deal	0.70342						

FIGURE 2.14 Five topics with term loadings.

markers for all the documents each word comes from. Lemahieu et al. [2018] also note that the list pointers are of the form (d_{ij}, w_{ij}) for term t_i where d_{ij} is the jth document containing term t_i and w_{ij} is the importance weight associated with that

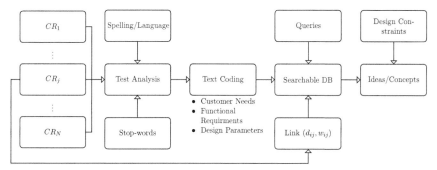

FIGURE 2.15 The results of a text analysis can be made searchable with a system that links words back to their originating documents.

term. This weight would be the *tfidf*. I discussed the *DTM* and *tfidf* weights in 2.3.3.

Product designers could query this full-text search engine for key words (and phrases) and not access the documents *per se* until they feel they have found some problems and suggestions from the reviews based on the key words. Those problems and suggestions, of course, must satisfy design constraints such as what is currently technologically feasible. Once they feel they have some ideas, they could then link back to the corpus to investigate the context for the words they searched for further clarification. This process is not linear so that the search for words and the linking back to the corpus would probably happen at the same time. This issue is whether or not the full-text search engine will allow them to do this.

Lemahieu et al. [2018] note that many existing full-text search engines provide this capability plus other features. Some they cite are:

- a thesaurus;
- a proximity measure so that documents are returned in which the terms are close together;
- fuzzy logic to allow for misspellings and different ways to spell the same word; and
- advanced text mining techniques.

See Lemahieu et al. [2018] for further discussion of these points.

2.4 Call center logs and warranty claims analysis

For most products, especially technologically complex ones and household appliances, calls are placed to service centers by consumers having difficulties. Sometimes these are simple issues and easily handled (e.g., read the manual) but other times they are complex and challenging. In almost all cases, service call centers create a detailed call center log of the call: time of call, the service representative on the call, the issue, the resolution, and any other notes on the call. Many are even recorded, sometimes with the statement "*for training purposes only*." In all cases, these call center logs can provide a wealth of information and insight into issues that could lead to new product ideas. The logs are the same type of information as product reviews, but in a different form. The text analysis described above can be used to glean ideas for new products.

The same holds for warranty claims. Most, if not all, manufacturers issue (limited) warranties and some issue extended warranties, usually for a high price. Third-party providers also offer extended warranties. In essence, warranties are insurance policies against product failures within a reasonable period after the product is purchased, usually one year. The manufacturer clearly incurs a cost if the product fails so it has an incentive to make the product as fail proof as possible and also limit the coverage of the warranty.

Warranty data can be used to predict warranty costs from product failures and take action to fix the issue(s) causing the failure. The latter is important because too many failures would lead to a loss of customer support expressed in poor product reviews. These reviews, however, as discussed above, are a treasure trove of new ideas. Regardless, predicting failures is an important function. For this discussion, however, such predictions are not important. It is the use of warranty claims for new ideas that is important because the warranty claims should explain the nature of the failure.

There are two types of warranty claim analysis: a simple count of the number of claims per product (i.e., *SKU*) perhaps by time since purchase (e.g., 0–1 month, 1–2 months, etc.) and text analysis of problems and reasons for the claim (e.g., "*the dishwasher does not drain*"; "*the oven temperature is not calibrated correctly*"; "*the smoke detector keeps beeping even with a battery*."). Thus, there are two types of warranty data: structured and unstructured. The warranty text data can be analyzed for clues for new products, perhaps as refinements of existing products, the same way product reviews can be used.

2.5 Sentiment analysis and opinion mining

An aspect of text data analysis that is more complex but that is gaining in importance is sentiment analysis and opinion mining. Sentiments are negative, neutral, or positive emotional statements that are made about an object. In our case of text data, the statements would be product reviews, call center logs, warranty claims, and so forth. Opinions are views expressed as pro or con statements about an object. Some analysts believe there is little to no conceptual difference between the two.[15]

Although sentiment analysis and opinion mining are important topics for product ideas, I will relegate discussion of them to Chapter 7 which is concerned with tracking the new product post-launch. Sentiments and opinions would be more important at the stage of the new product development process because they would tell you what is wrong – or right – about the product which may require further action. These actions could, of course, lead to another new product but here, nonetheless, I will restrict any discussion of sentiments and opinions to the tracking function recognizing that they could be used in the ideation phase as well.

2.6 Market research: voice of the customer (*VOC*)

A major theme of this chapter is that new product ideas can come from customers themselves. The market research and marketing literature have emphasized the need to hear "*The Voice of the Customer*" for a long time. See Campos [2012] for an extensive discussion about the voice of the customer and ways to hear that voice. This section focuses on some ways to "hear" that voice using market research surveys.

2.6.1 Competitive assessment: the role of CEA

Ideas for new products and services could come from a two-fold analysis of what is important to customers to satisfy their needs and problems and what competitors, both current and perspective, are doing to satisfy the customers. This is a *Competitive Environment Analysis (CEA)*, a survey-based approach to researching opportunities that could be fueled by an analysis of key words and phrases as described above. In particular, the word and phrase analysis could be used to generate a candidate list of attributes for a new product that might meet customer needs. For example, a text analysis for the robot vacuum could result in a list of attributes that include:[16]

1. Operating Time (hours) on battery power.
2. Charge Time (hours) of batteries.
3. Operating Pattern or area cleaned.
4. Automatic Scheduled Cleaning by time and day.
5. Infrared Sensor allowing the vacuum to navigate around a room.
6. Dirt Sensor for detecting dirt on the floor.
7. Type of Flooring vacuumed: Carpeting, Hardwood, Tile, and Linoleum.
8. Spot Mode for addressing a particularly dirty area.
9. Height Adjustment under furniture.
10. High-efficiency Particulate Air Filter (*HEPA*) for trapping small particles of dust or dirt and certain allergens.
11. Multi-Room Navigation to maneuver through different rooms.
12. Battery Indicator for when the battery is low versus fully charged.
13. Full Bin Indicator indicating when the dust bin needs to be emptied.
14. Cliff Sensor that keeps the vacuum cleaner from falling down stairs.
15. Charging Base to recharge batteries.
16. Return to Charging Base for recharging.
17. Bumper that prevents it from scuffing walls and furniture.
18. Boundary Markers that keep the vacuum cleaner from going where it should not.
19. Virtual Walls or small devices that emit an invisible infrared signal to prevent the robot cleaner from going where it should not go.

20. Remote Control to program or control the cleaner.
21. Price point that is competitive and indicates good value-for-the-money (VFM).

Suppose the competitive assessment group has identified 3 competitor products. How are these competitors meeting each of these attributes? Understanding this competitive environment would help product designers identify which attributes to emphasize and develop, but also identify opportunities, places in the product space where there are unmet needs that are important to customers.

One way to assess the environment is to conduct a survey of customers who have purchased existing products and ask them to assess how well the product they bought performed on the list of attributes. It is also necessary to understand how important each attribute is to them. Some may be very important so they would pay especial attention to the performance of a product regarding that attribute; other attributes may not be that important at all. Therefore, two sets of questions have to be asked:

1. How important is each attribute?
2. How does the brand purchased or used perform on each attribute?

The data set compiled from the responses is a three-way table: attributes by products by different reviewers (i.e., customers). The data could be viewed as a cube with one side the attribute importance measures, another the product performance, and the third the reviewers. One possible form of analysis is to cluster the data and examine the clusters. Another, more simplistic approach, is to collapse one of the dimensions and portray the other two in a two-dimensional map. The obvious dimension to collapse is the customer reviewers since the focus is on the attributes relative to the products; the customers are only the source of the data. The question is how to collapse the customer dimension. First consider the attributes. A question in the survey would ask customers to rate the importance of each attribute to them. Suppose a five-point Likert Scale was used ranging from "*Not at all Important*" to "*Extremely Important*." Although the interpretation of Likert Scales is controversial[17], most analysts interpret the scale as representing an underlying continuous measure and, therefore, they would simply average the quantities. In this case, you would average the ratings over each customer and each product. The mean attribute importance and mean attribute performance can then be compared. The two-dimensional map would be a scatter plot with, say, the importances on the horizontal axis and the performances on the vertical axis. The points would be the attributes. For the robot vacuums, there would be 21 points. Each axis could be (arbitrarily) divided into two equal parts producing four quadrants.

Another map consists of a bar chart of the attribute importances shown in descending order from the most to the least important attribute. The products' mean performance rating on each attribute would be overlaid as a symbol (e.g., ★, +, etc.). This would concisely show how the products are performing on those attributes that are important. A variation is to calculate the overall mean performance and a 95% confidence interval around the overall mean. The overall mean and the two bounds would also be overlaid on the map. All competitive symbols lying within the bounds would indicate products that are statistically performing the same on an attribute.

A better approach regarding performance is to find the standard deviation of the performance ratings over all customers and products. Calculate the mean performance of each attribute for each product. This is a collapsing of the *Customer x Attribute x Product* matrix across the customer dimension leaving an Attribute x Product matrix. The entries in the cells of the table are the mean ratings by all customers who rated the attributes for the products. Sample sizes will necessarily vary because not all customers rate all the products. Further collapse this two-way matrix by finding the standard deviation of the mean performance rating across all products for each attribute. This will yield a one-dimensional table of performance standard deviations by the attributes.

The standard deviation shows the variation among the products for each attribute. This variation can be interpreted as a *degree of similarity* (DOS) of the products. A high DOS shows there is much variation among the competitors on how they provide an attribute while a small DOS shows there is little variation in performance among the competitors; they are similar. A DOS of 0.0 means all competitors are the same on an attribute.

The DOS for each attribute can be plotted against the mean importance rating of each attribute to show the competitive strength among the products relative to what is important to customers. This map can be divided into four quadrants, hence it is also sometimes simply referred to as a *quadrant map*. It shows the market structure for the attributes.

An example report is shown in Figure 2.16 and Figure 2.17. Figure 2.16 shows the mean importance ratings of the 21 robot vacuum attributes and the DOS across the competitors for each of the 21 attributes. Each respondent was asked the brand of robot they have and then were asked to rate that robot's performance or satisfaction on each of the 21 attributes. For each attribute, the mean performance rating was calculated and then the standard deviation of the means for each attribute was calculated. These are shown in a table format in Figure 2.16 and in a map format in Figure 2.17. From the map, it is clear that the competitors all perform about equally on most attributes, all of which are important to customers; see the lower right quadrant of Figure 2.17. However, there is one attribute, *Battery Indicator*, for which performance is an issue, yet this is important to the customers. This suggests an opportunity: build a product with a better battery indicator or some type of low battery warning system. The design team, of course, needs more insight into these two problem areas, but at least they now have a start. More survey research could be done to refine their understanding of issues with both items.

Another level of analysis could be done, data permitting. For each attribute, the difference between the mean performance of your product and the mean of each of

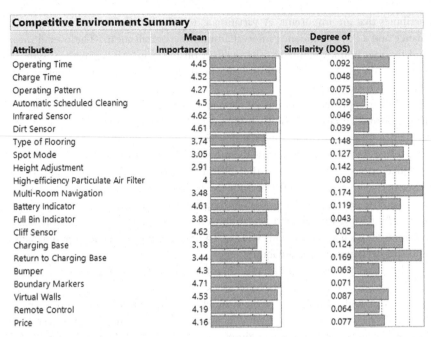

Competitive Environment Summary		
Attributes	**Mean Importances**	**Degree of Similarity (DOS)**
Operating Time	4.45	0.092
Charge Time	4.52	0.048
Operating Pattern	4.27	0.075
Automatic Scheduled Cleaning	4.5	0.029
Infrared Sensor	4.62	0.046
Dirt Sensor	4.61	0.039
Type of Flooring	3.74	0.148
Spot Mode	3.05	0.127
Height Adjustment	2.91	0.142
High-efficiency Particulate Air Filter	4	0.08
Multi-Room Navigation	3.48	0.174
Battery Indicator	4.61	0.119
Full Bin Indicator	3.83	0.043
Cliff Sensor	4.62	0.05
Charging Base	3.18	0.124
Return to Charging Base	3.44	0.169
Bumper	4.3	0.063
Boundary Markers	4.71	0.071
Virtual Walls	4.53	0.087
Remote Control	4.19	0.064
Price	4.16	0.077

FIGURE 2.16 This is a *CEA* summary table showing the 21 robot vacuum cleaner attributes: their mean importance and performance "spread" as measured by the standard deviation of the performance ratings.

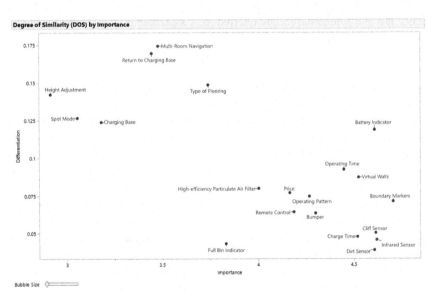

FIGURE 2.17 This is a *CEA* quadrant map showing the 21 robot vacuum cleaner attributes: their mean importance and performance "spread." There were three competitor products and the producer of the new vacuum for a total of four products.

TABLE 2.3 This table shows the effect on the probability of falsely rejecting the Null Hypothesis for different number of tests. Calculations are based on $\alpha = 0.05$.

Number of Tests (k)	Pr(Falsely Rejecting H_0)
1	0.050
2	0.098
3	0.143
4	0.185
5	0.226
10	0.401
100	0.994

the competitors' mean performance can be determined for each attribute. The difference should, of course, be statistically tested. The recommended test is Dunnett's multiple comparison test. In multiple comparison tests in general, there is an issue of performing more than one statistical test on the same data. The standard level of significance, which is the probability of falsely rejecting the Null Hypothesis, used in, say, a t-test is $\alpha = 0.05$.[18] This is sufficient when one test is performed to determine a difference. When more than one test is performed, however, it can be shown that the probability of falsely rejecting the Null Hypothesis, H_0, is greater than 0.05. In fact, $Pr(Falsely\ Rejecting\ H_0) = 1 - (1 - \alpha)^k$ where k is the number of tests. Table 2.3 shows what happens to this probability for different values of k.

Several procedures have been developed to control this inflation of the probability. Tukey's *Honestly Significant Difference (HSD)* test is the most commonly used test. This test does not put a comparison restriction on the items tested: that is, they are not restricted to comparing items to a base item. Dunnett's Test was developed for comparisons against a base. As noted by Paczkowski [2016], this test is "a modification of the t-test, [and] is appropriate when you have a control or standard for comparison." See Paczkowski [2016] for a discussion of multiple comparison tests in general and some comments on Dunnett's Test.

For each competitive comparison for each attribute, there would then be three possibilities: your brand is statistically higher than each competitor, statistically the same, or statistically lower. A heatmap could then be created that shows the attributes on the vertical axis, the competitors on the horizontal axis, and the cells colored coded to indicate the sign of the statistical difference. This would tell you how well you are performing on each attribute relative to your competition. This is, of course, a variation of the bar chart described above.

2.6.2 Contextual design

Contextual design is another approach to designing a new product that involves data collected by directly observing users' interactions with existing systems, tools, materials, and so forth. The belief is that the best way to learn about the problems, needs, and requirements of customers is to observe them in their daily activities and record what they do and how they interact with their environment. Directly observing customers is a qualitative approach in the domain of *ethnographic research*.[19] This approach has been used in a number of industries such as web design and applications, consumer products, manufacturing, automotives, and medical devices.

This approach is not about hearing the voice of the customer but about watching the customer in action. It is based on five principles:

1. Designs must support and extend users' work practices.
2. People are experts at what they do, but are unable to articulate their own practices and habits.
3. Good product design requires the partnership and participation of the end-users.
4. Good design considers the users as a whole entity.

It should be clear that these design principles apply throughout this chapter. See Holtzblatt and Beyer [2013] for more information and discussion of these design principles.

2.7 Machine learning methods

Text mining can be combined with machine learning methodologies to identify ideas in text such as online product reviews. Christensen et al. [2017] discuss an approach using a machine learning classifier known as a *support vector machine* (*SVM*). An *SVM* is one of several machine learning methods that classify objects into groups, usually two groups for a binary classification. Other approaches are *naïve Bayes, decision trees, nearest neighbors, neural networks,* and *radial-basis support vector machines* (as opposed to *linear support vector machines*). See Christensen et al. [2017, p. 27]. These are all in a general class of classification methodologies known as *supervised learning* methods; another class consists of *unsupervised learning* methods. Supervised learning requires a *target variable*, also called a *dependent variable*, that directs the independent variables in the estimation of unknown parameters. In regression analysis, the unknown parameters are the coefficients (and the variance) that are estimated based on the independent variables to give the best estimate of the dependent, target variable. In this case, "best" is defined as the minimum sum of the squared distances between the dependent variable and the predicted dependent variable. Unsupervised learning does not have a target variable or set of unknown parameters. Here, the goal is to find patterns in the data, so the unsupervised learning methods are pattern identifiers unlike the supervised learning methods which are parameter identifying methods. See Paczkowski [2018], Hastie et al. [2001], and James et al. [2013] for discussions of different learning methodologies.

In the approach outlined by Christensen et al. [2017], a set of product reviews is preprocessed using the tools described above: stop-words are eliminated, spelling is corrected, cases are fixed, and words are tokenized. A *DTM* is created which is used in an *SVM*. The target variable is an issue. In the Christensen et al. [2017] approach, a prior set of product reviews is combed through for those that contain ideas and those that do not contain ideas. Those that do contain ideas are coded as 1 while those that do not are coded as 0. This is a binary classification that defines the target variable for the *SVM*. The target variable and the *DTM* are submitted to an *SVM* that produces classification rules. These rules can then be used against a larger untrained set of reviews. This larger set would, of course, have to be preprocessed to produce a new *DTM*. Those reviews classified as containing new product ideas would have to be examined to see which actually did contain new ideas and those ideas would have to be rated for their usefulness. So there is still a human element involved that requires time and energy and thus a cost. Nonetheless, this cost would be smaller than the cost of having personnel read numerous product reviews looking for ideas. In short, this machine learning approach would minimize the cost of new idea identification, but not eliminate it. As machine learning and artificial intelligence (*AI*) develop further, newer more enhanced approaches will be developed that will further aid idea identification for online product reviews.

2.8 Managing ideas and predictive analytics

Few businesses have only one new product in a pipeline at any one time and certainly few have developed only one new product during the course of their existence. They typically have more than one product in the pipeline at any one point in time and they also have a history of pushing new products into the market, some of which succeeded and others not. This history could be used to determine which new product ideas should enter the current pipeline and even remain in the pipeline.

One way to accomplish this is to construct a data table of all past products with an indicator recording their market success or failure. The fields of the table contain the deign parameters of the products: features, characteristics, technical specifications. Basically, everything that describes the products. The launch marketing parameters (e.g., price point) should also be included because the product may have failed in the market simply because the marketing was incorrect. Aside from the marketing parameters, the technical parameters can be used to model the success or failure of each product in the data table and that model could then be used to predict how a new product idea will fare in the market. This is a *predictive analytics* approach to new product management. See Davenport and Spanyi [2016] for comments on this way of approaching new product development.

Predictive analytics is a broad area that is more an umbrella concept than an actual method or approach. It uses a variety of methods from several empirical disciplines such as statistics, data mining, and machine learning to say something about an unknown. Prediction and forecasting are often confused because both aim to accomplish this same objective. Forecasting is specifically concerned with future events. You forecast the sales of a new product "next year and the year after" which are certainly unknown at the present time but you predict whether or not a product will sell. Prediction is more general with forecasting as a subset of prediction. All forecasts are predictions but not all predictions are forecasts. Predictive analytics is concerned with applying different tools to allow us to say something about an unknown but not necessarily about a future time period unknown. Forecasting *per se* for new products, in particular at launch time, is covered in Chapter 6 and forecast errors are covered in Chapter 7.

A major application of predictive analytics is to predict a behavior of customers to buy, sell, attend, make payments, default, and so on. Typically, a *predictive model* is specified and estimated using a subset of historical customer data and then the entire customer database is scored, meaning that each customer in the database is assigned a score which is usually interpreted as a probability. This score as a probability would be, say, the probability of buying a product given past purchase history. Customers can be sorted (in descending order) by their assigned score and those with the highest score are marketed to first. The customers are marketed to in descending order of their scores until the marginal cost of marketing to one more customer exceeds the expected returns from that customer.

Let the success/failure of past products be dummy or indicator coded such as

$$
success = \begin{cases} 1 & \text{if} \quad \textit{Successful} \\ 0 & \text{if} \quad \textit{Otherwise} \end{cases}
$$

Let **X** be a vector of attributes for the products in a product data table. Then a scoring model is the *logit model*

$$
Pr(success) = \frac{e^{\mathbf{Z}}}{1 + e^{\mathbf{Z}}}
$$

where $\mathbf{Z} = \mathbf{X}\beta$ and β is a vector of unknown parameters to be estimated.

Prior to estimating this model, the data table should be divided into two parts: a training data table and a testing data table. The former is used for estimation while the latter is used for testing the predictive ability of the estimated model. Typical proportions are $3/4$ and $2/3$ training data. Whichever proportion is used, it is important that the training data table have more cases than the testing data table. It is also important that the testing data never be used for estimation. See Paczkowski [2016] for some discussion about training and testing data sets. Also see James et al. [2013] and Hastie et al. [2001] for advanced discussions. Also see Chapter 6 for a discussion of splitting time series and Chapter 7 for other comments.

This model is reviewed in some detail in Chapter 5.

There are two issues with this approach: the construction of the product data table and the classification of a product as successful and unsuccessful. First, a business must not only have a sufficient number of past products that it could use in modeling, but it must also have the history on each one. A list of features, characteristics, technical specifications must be available. Such a historical list might be difficult to compile let alone maintain. Second, someone must decide on the criteria for success and failure of a product. Clearly, if nothing was sold, then the product failed. Zero sales are most unlikely for any product. A low number of units sold might constitute a product failure, but what is "low." The most likely candidate for a criterion is the marketing objective originally established for the product. Was that objective met?

Davenport and Spanyi [2016] note that NetFlix is an example of a company that uses this approach. See the various articles at https://research.netflix.com/research-area/analytics regarding the use of predictive analytics at Netflix.

2.9 Software

There are many software products available for text analysis. I will classify them into free and commercial. The free software includes Python and R while the commercial includes SAS and JMP.

Both Python and R are powerful, well established, and definitely known for their text processing capabilities. R is known for its steep learning curve which tends to make it less appealing to those without heavy training in statistics and who do their data analysis in spreadsheets. Not only is the learning curve steep, but everything that has to be done requires some degree of programming. This is a drawback because programming is a specialty skill that requires time to master. Typical new product development managers, regardless of their level, would proba-bly not venture near R if they do not have any intentions of doing other and more sophisticated forms of data analysis. The time cost in coming up to speed with R would not be worth the effort.

Python in many regards is not much better than R. The strong point in favor of Python is its almost cult-like focus on its easily written and interpretable syn-tax. There is a Pythonic way of writing programming code that almost all who write in Python adhere to. Nonetheless, some programming is still required and this factor may be a hindrance to those who only want to get an answer with minimal hassles. The Python package Pandas has a simpler syntax making it eas-ier to do data analysis, including data visualization, but without any loss of power or capabilities. The book by McKinney [2018] provides a great introduction to Python and Pandas.[20] An excellent book on using Python for text analysis is Sarkar [2016].

SAS is the granddaddy of all statistical software products. It is probably safe to say that if some capability is not in SAS, then it is not worth using. SAS, in keeping with being at the forefront of statistical software, has the SAS Text Miner. This strives to make text analysis easier for all users. The problem is that SAS Text Miner, like the SAS software itself, is expensive.

JMP is a product of the JMP division of the SAS corporation. It too has a high price tag, but it also has a more intuitive interface targeted to allowing technical and nontechnical users to more easily interact with their data, whether text and numeric. This interface is graphical meaning that it is dynamic and simple to use and manipulate. The text analysis component of JMP was used in this chapter. See Paczkowski [2016] for using JMP for analyzing market data.

2.10 Summary

In this chapter, I focused on a critical part of new product development – the development of the idea for the product. Any discussion of new product development processes is meaningless unless there is a new product. This should be obvious. Several approaches to product ideation were presented including text analysis using the vast amount of text data now collected through various means. The next chapter will assume that a product idea has been identified and now a design for it must be developed.

2.11 Appendix

This Appendix outlines some mathematical concepts that are useful to know for text analysis methods such as Latent Semantic Analysis. It is not critical that you know or master this Appendix. It is completely optional. If you do want to peruse more, useful references are Lay [2012], Strang [2006], and Jobson [1992].

2.11.1 Matrix decomposition

An important result in matrix algebra is the decomposition of a matrix into three parts. In particular, if $\mathbf{A}$ is a $n \times n$ symmetric matrix, then it can be written or decomposed into

$$\mathbf{A} = \mathbf{V} \mathbf{\Lambda} \mathbf{V}^\mathsf{T}$$

where $\mathbf{V}$ is an orthogonal matrix and $\mathbf{\Lambda}$ is a diagonal matrix with diagonal elements $\lambda_1, \lambda_2, \ldots, \lambda_n$. These diagonal elements are the eigenvalues of $\mathbf{A}$ and the columns of $\mathbf{V}$ are the corresponding eigenvectors. Since $\mathbf{V}$ is orthogonal, then $\mathbf{V}\mathbf{V}^\mathsf{T} = \mathbf{V}^\mathsf{T}\mathbf{V} = \mathbf{I}$. This is the spectral decomposition of $\mathbf{A}$ where the "spectrum" is the set of eigenvalues. See Jobson [1992].

If $\mathbf{X}$ is $n \times p$, then $\mathbf{X}^\mathsf{T}\mathbf{X}$ is $(p \times n)(n \times p) = p \times p$ and is symmetric. Similar, $\mathbf{X}\mathbf{X}^\mathsf{T}$ is $n \times n$ and is also symmetric. Both are symmetric so they can be decomposed as $\mathbf{X}^\mathsf{T}\mathbf{X} = \mathbf{V}\mathbf{\Lambda}\mathbf{V}^\mathsf{T}$ and $\mathbf{X}\mathbf{X}^\mathsf{T} = \mathbf{V}^\mathsf{T}\mathbf{\Lambda}\mathbf{V}$ so $\mathbf{V}$ has the eigenvectors of $\mathbf{X}^\mathsf{T}\mathbf{X}$ and $\mathbf{\Lambda}$ is the diagonal matrix of eigenvalues.

2.11.2 Singular value decomposition (SVD)

An important mathematical operation that plays a pivotal role in a number of statistical methodologies is the *Singular Value Decomposition (SVD)*. It is important for:

1. correspondence analysis;
2. principal components analysis;
3. regression analysis; and
4. text analysis

to mention a few. *SVD* relies on three concepts:

1. eigenvalues;
2. eigenvectors; and
3. similarity of two matrices,

although the last three are inseparably related. I assume that basic matrix operations and concepts are known. If a background is needed or has to be refreshed, see Lay [2012] and Strang [2006] for good introductions and developments. Some of the material in this section draws heavily from Lay [2012]. The eigenvalues and eigenvectors, however, may be somewhat unknown so the following discussion on these two related concepts will help lead into the *SVD* discussion.

If $\mathbf{Ax} = \lambda\mathbf{x}$, λ a scalar, then $\mathbf{A}$, an $n \times n$ square matrix, transforms the vector $\mathbf{x}$ into a multiple of itself, the multiplier being λ. Basically, $\mathbf{x}$ is stretched, shrunk, or reversed by $\mathbf{A}$ but its direction is not changed. As a typical example[21], let

$$\mathbf{A} = \begin{bmatrix} 1 & 6 \\ 5 & 2 \end{bmatrix} \text{ and } \mathbf{x} = \begin{bmatrix} 6 \\ -5 \end{bmatrix}$$

then

$$\mathbf{Ax} = \begin{bmatrix} 1 & 6 \\ 5 & 2 \end{bmatrix} \begin{bmatrix} 6 \\ -5 \end{bmatrix} = \begin{bmatrix} -24 \\ 20 \end{bmatrix} = -4 \begin{bmatrix} 6 \\ -5 \end{bmatrix} = -4\mathbf{x}$$

so the vector $\mathbf{x}$ is expanded by a factor of 4, but in the negative direction. The stretching/shrinking factor, λ, is called an *eigenvalue*.[22] Other names are *characteristic value* and *characteristic root*. There may be multiple eigenvalues, duplicated (sometimes referred to as multiplicities), or none at all. The vector $\mathbf{x}$ that is stretched or shrunk is called an *eigenvector*. There may be multiple eigenvectors, but each eigenvector corresponds to one eigenvalue. The eigenvector **must** be nonzero, but the corresponding eigenvalue may be zero.

There are many ways to decompose or translate a matrix into constituent parts. The most popular from an analytical perspective is the *Singular Value Decomposition* (*SVD*). This decomposition method can be used with large matrices and it is not restricted to square matrices.

The *SVD* method decomposes a matrix $\mathbf{A}$ of size $n \times p$ into three parts which, when multiplied together return the original matrix $\mathbf{A}$:

$$\mathbf{A} = \mathbf{U\Sigma V}^{\mathsf{T}} \tag{2.A.1}$$

where

- $\mathbf{U}$ is an $n \times n$ orthogonal matrix such that $\mathbf{U}^{\mathsf{T}}\mathbf{U} = \mathbf{U}\mathbf{U}^{\mathsf{T}} = \mathbf{I}$ where $\mathbf{I}$ is the identity matrix and is $n \times n$;
- $\mathbf{\Sigma}$ is an $n \times r$ diagonal matrix such that $\mathbf{\Sigma} = diagonal(\sigma_1, \sigma_2, \ldots, \sigma_n)$; and
- $\mathbf{V}^{\mathsf{T}}$ is an $r \times p$ orthogonal matrix such that $\mathbf{V}^{\mathsf{T}}\mathbf{V} = \mathbf{V}\mathbf{V}^{\mathsf{T}} = \mathbf{I}$ where $\mathbf{I}$ is $p \times p$.

Two vectors are orthogonal if their inner or dot product is zero. The inner product of two vectors, $\mathbf{a}$ and $\mathbf{b}$, is $\mathbf{a} \cdot \mathbf{b} = \sum_{i=1}^{n} a_i \times b_i$ and the two vectors are orthogonal if $\mathbf{a} \cdot \mathbf{b} = 0$. This is the same as saying they are perpendicular to each other, or the cosine of the angle between the two vectors is zero.

The main points to know about *SVD* are:

1. The diagonal elements of $\mathbf{\Sigma}$ are non-negative. They can be arranged in any order (as long as the corresponding columns of $\mathbf{U}$ and $\mathbf{V}$ are in the appropriate order) so by convention they are arranged in descending order.
2. The diagonal values of $\mathbf{\Sigma}$ are called the *singular values* and are the square roots of the eigenvalues of $\mathbf{AA}^\mathsf{T}$.
3. The columns of $\mathbf{U}$ are the eigenvectors associated with the eigenvalues of $\mathbf{AA}^\mathsf{T}$. Similarly for the columns of $\mathbf{V}$.
4. The columns of $\mathbf{U}$ are called the *right singular vectors* and the columns of $\mathbf{V}$ are the *left singular vectors*.

As an example of the method, let

$$\mathbf{A} = \begin{bmatrix} 11 & 22 \\ 33 & 44 \\ 55 & 66 \end{bmatrix}$$

which is 3×2. Then the *SVD* of $\mathbf{A}$ is

$$\mathbf{A} = \begin{bmatrix} 0.230 & 0.884 \\ 0.525 & 0.241 \\ 0.820 & -0.402 \end{bmatrix} \begin{bmatrix} 104.781 & 0 \\ 0 & 5.657 \end{bmatrix} \begin{bmatrix} 0.620 & -0.785 \\ 0.785 & 0.620 \end{bmatrix}^\mathsf{T}.$$

Notice that the left and right singular matrices are each orthogonal and that the product of the three matrices is the original matrix, $\mathbf{A}$ (within rounding).

Not all the singular values in the diagonal matrix $\mathbf{\Sigma}$ are positive or even large. Those that are small or negative are often set to 0 and/or dropped. If dropped, then the corresponding eigenvectors in $\mathbf{U}$ and $\mathbf{V}$ must be dropped. A truncated *SVD* results in an approximation.

If $k < r$ is the number of positive, nonzero singular values retained, then the truncated *SVD* is

$$\mathbf{A} = \mathbf{U}_k \mathbf{\Sigma}_k \mathbf{V}_k^\mathsf{T}$$

where

- $\mathbf{U}_k$ is $n \times k$;
- $\mathbf{\Sigma}_k$ is $k \times k$; and
- $\mathbf{V}_k^\mathsf{T}$ is $k \times p$.

Most statistical analyses use a truncated or restricted *SVD*.

There is one final observation about the *SVD*. Let $\mathbf{X}$ by an $n \times p$ matrix. Since $\mathbf{X} = \mathbf{U\Sigma P}^\mathsf{T}$, you can write

$$\mathbf{X}^\mathsf{T}\mathbf{X} = \mathbf{P\Sigma U}^\mathsf{T}\mathbf{U\Sigma P}^\mathsf{T}$$
$$= \mathbf{P\Sigma}^2\mathbf{P}^\mathsf{T}$$

TABLE 2.4 Comparison of Spectral Decomposition and *SVD*.

Spectral	SVD
$\mathbf{A} = \mathbf{V}\boldsymbol{\Lambda}\mathbf{V}^{\top}$	$\mathbf{A} = \mathbf{U}\boldsymbol{\Sigma}\mathbf{P}^{\top}$
$\mathbf{V}$ has the eigenvectors of $\mathbf{A}$ and is orthogonal	$\mathbf{U}$ and $\mathbf{P}$ have the singular vectors of $\mathbf{A}$ and are each orthogonal

so that the right singular vectors of $\mathbf{X}$ are the eigenvectors of $\mathbf{X}^{\top}\mathbf{X}$ from the spectral decomposition. Similarly,

$$\mathbf{X}\mathbf{X}^{\top} = \mathbf{U}\boldsymbol{\Sigma}\mathbf{P}^{\top}\mathbf{P}\boldsymbol{\Sigma}\mathbf{U}^{\top}$$
$$= \mathbf{U}\boldsymbol{\Sigma}^2\mathbf{U}^{\top}$$

so that the left singular vectors of $\mathbf{X}$ are the eigenvectors of $\mathbf{X}\mathbf{X}^{\top}$ from the spectral decomposition. Also, the eigenvalues of $\mathbf{X}^{\top}\mathbf{X}$ are the squares of the singular values of $\mathbf{X}$ based on the spectral decomposition. This is the basis for the correspondence analysis report I will describe in Chapter 3 that shows the singular values and the eigenvalues as their squares.

2.11.3 Spectral and singular value decompositions

The spectral decomposition has a diagonal matrix as middle component that has eigenvalues on the diagonal. The *SVD* has a middle diagonal matrix that has singular values on the diagonal. For a symmetric matrix $\mathbf{A}$, the spectral decomposition and the *SVD* are equivalent so that

$$\mathbf{A} = \mathbf{U}\mathbf{D}\mathbf{V}^{\top} = \mathbf{V}\boldsymbol{\Lambda}\mathbf{V}^{\top}$$

so the singular vectors are the eigenvectors and the singular values are the eigenvalues. See Jobson [1992]. Table 2.4 compares both methods of matrix decomposition.

Notes

1 See Couger [1995, p. 419].
2 See Isaksen [1998].
3 Obviously, both floors and wings can be added at the same time. This complication is an unnecessary one for this example. See www.geeksforgeeks.org/difference-between-sql-and-nosql/ for a comment about buildings.
4 "NoSQL" is interpreted as "No SQL" or "Not SQL" to distinguish it from *SQL*.
5 The Wikipedia entry for stop-words (https://en.wikipedia.org/wiki/Stop_words, last accessed April 27, 2018) notes that the idea for stop-words was introduced in 1959.
6 See https://en.wikipedia.org/wiki/Stop_words for a list of stop-words. Last accessed April 27, 2018.
7 The dot notation indicates summation over all values of j, or all documents in C in this case. That is, $f_{i.}^{C} = \sum_{j \in C} f_{ij}^{C}$.
8 Another reference is *Term Document Matrix* which is the transpose of the *DTM*. I prefer the *DTM*.

9 A "1" is added to the argument of the log function to avoid situations of taking the $log_{10}(0)$ which is undefined.

10 See the blog article by Jim Cox at SAS for a discussion: https://blogs.sas.com/content/sascom/2015/10/22/topical-advice-about-topics-comparing-two-topic-generation-methods/.

11 See the Appendix to this chapter for a discussion of the *SVD*. Sometimes the transpose of the *DTM* is used so the *SVD* is applied to a term document matrix or *TDM*.

12 See https://en.wikipedia.org/wiki/Non-negative_matrix_factorization#Clustering_property. Last accessed July 2, 2019.

13 If a *TDM* is used, then the left set is used.

14 In an actual problem, there would be far more than 22 reviews.

15 See www.quora.com/What-is-the-Difference-between-opinion-mining-and-sentiment-analysis for some discussion. Last accessed June 5, 2019.

16 This list was complied from www.roboticall.com/robotic-vacuum-attributes/. Last accessed on October 9, 2018.

17 See Paczkowski [2018] for some comments.

18 There is nothing special about 0.05. It is more a convention than anything else.

19 See the Wikipedia article on ethnography at https://en.wikipedia.org/wiki/Ethnography. Last accessed July 31, 2019.

20 Wes McKinney is the creator of Pandas.

21 Source: Lay [2012].

22 The prefix "*eigen*" is from the German word "*eigen*" meaning "*proper*" or "*characteristic.*"

3
DEVELOP

How do you do it?

The design of a new product requires a merging of a designer's perception of what works physically and technologically with what customers want, need, and perceive is the right design. The former is an engineering perspective and the latter a user perspective. They do not have to agree, and most often will not since they reflect two different groups of people with different agendas. A new product failure results when a designer's perspective dominates to the exclusion of what matters to customers. Since customer input is absent in the extreme case, the probability is high that the new product would not meet customer requirements and expectations or even solve any problem they have. There is a *Design Failure*. The probability of a design failure varies inversely with the amount of customer input as illustrated in Figure 3.1. This chapter focuses on ways to gather customer input into the design process to minimize the probability of a design failure.

This chapter is divided into five sections. The first provides an overview of product optimization to set the stage for the remaining sections. Conjoint analysis, a traditional methodology for measuring attribute importances, is described in the second section. Conjoint analysis is only useful in the early stage of product development, and should be viewed as a methodology that will be superseded by another in the next stage of product development. This second section is followed by a discussion of the Kansei approach to product design in the third section. This approach expands on conjoint analysis by incorporating customer emotions into the design process. Included in this section is a discussion about merging conjoint and Kansei analysis. Early-stage pricing is discussed in the fourth section. I point out that pricing is needed for business case analysis but it is too early to develop final pricing at this point in the product development. I expand on pricing in later chapters. The fifth section is a summary. Finally, there is a technical appendix that provides background on technical issues mentioned in the chapter.

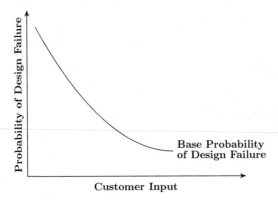

FIGURE 3.1 The design failure rate declines the more customer input there is in the design process.

3.1 Product design optimization

A product is not an entity unto itself. It is actually a collection of parts that, when combined in the "correct" combination or proportions, results in a salable product. A product is a container. A smartphone is a container for a screen, a case, a camera, software, and so forth. The parts in the container are *features* or *attributes* defining the product. These attributes are themselves defined by features or characteristics which are usually called *levels*. The levels are the design parameters I mentioned in Chapter 2. So, the camera in a smartphone is an attribute of the smartphone with two levels: it is either built into the smartphone or not. If the camera is built in, then it has levels of pixel resolution, such as 20 megapixels, 40 megapixels, and 48 megapixels. This means a product, as a container, is actually a combination of attribute levels. See Arthur [2009] for a discussion of how items that are called technologies, such as the smartphone, are really containers of other technologies. The design issue is then two-fold:

1. Which attributes to include in the product container?
2. What level of each attribute to include in the product container?

A design failure occurs when the attributes and/or their levels are incorrect from the customer's perspective so that the product is not optimized to sell in the market. Designers, working independently of customers who would eventually buy the product, may not get the right attributes or the most important ones that would motivate potential customers to buy. The product is not optimized. Designers really have to have input from customers at the product design stage, the point at which the attributes and their levels are specified and assembled to create the product.

Certainly, not all the attributes and/or the levels customers say they want are technologically doable; they may be too costly to implement; the segment of the market requesting or demanding those features may be too small to be financially profitable for the business; or their incorporation into the product would require an increase in the price point to a level that would make it unsalable. In short, marketing concerns must be balanced against technology possibilities when determining what to include in the product design.

A traditional way to optimize a product configuration using explicit physical, engineering attributes is *conjoint analysis*. I describe and illustrate conjoint analysis in the following subsection. Another method, less common in Western product research and design, is *Kansei analysis* which has been successfully applied in Japanese and Chinese new product development efforts for some time. Kansei analysis is described after conjoint analysis. A methodology for combining the two is also described.

Not to be overlooked and just as important as the attributes and their levels is the price point. Customers will, after all, make a purchase decision not only on the product itself, but also on whether or not they can afford it or if the price conveys a sense of quality. This latter quality-based decision is based on the price point. A price that is too high will restrict the market to only those either with a high income level or those who will overlook price because they must have that new product; that is, the early adopters. Demand for this group would be highly inelastic. For the market as a whole, however, a high price would most likely be more than can be tolerated so a large segment of the potential market would be unable or unwilling to buy. This segment would have an elastic demand. At the same time, a low price may be interpreted as a signal that the product is cheap and so not worth the money. Determining the price point is a difficult process but one that is made more difficult by the fact that customers rarely know how to value a new product before it has actually been introduced; that is, when it is still at the design stage. In my opinion, the best they can do is give a range of values they might and might not find acceptable. I discuss how to find a range in Section 3.4.

3.2 Conjoint analysis for product optimization

Conjoint analysis is a member of a family of choice methodologies designed to determine or estimate customer preference for one product versus another. This amounts to determining the optimal combination of attributes and their levels. This family is described in Paczkowski [2016] and Paczkowski [2018]. Another member of the family is *discrete choice analysis* which seeks to handle the same problem but the context of discrete choice differs from that of conjoint analysis. As members of the same family, they share similar features but differ in important ways. The common features are:

1. reliance on attributes with discrete, mutually exclusive, and completely exhaustive levels;
2. an experimental design to arrange or combine the levels into choice alternatives that are interpreted as products;

3. a simple evaluative question used in a survey; and
4. an estimation procedure applied to the data collected in the survey.

They differ in that, for a discrete choice customer survey, respondents are presented with several alternative products at once in *sets*, called *choice sets*, and are asked to select the product from each set they would most likely buy[1]. The minimum size of a choice set is, of course, two. The reason for this choice approach is that it mimics the shopping behavior of customers: they are viewed as facing two or more products on a store shelf and they have to choose one of them. It is this interpretation of shopping behavior that makes discrete choice more applicable for final optimization and market testing than for product optimization at the design stage. Product optimization still occurs at the market testing stage of new product development but it is more product refinement than initial design. In the market testing stage, the focus becomes more on how the product will perform against competitor products. It is for this reason that I discuss discrete choice in Chapter 4 and not here.

In a conjoint customer survey, respondents are also presented with alternative products, but in sets consisting of a single item; they are presented one at a time.[2] They are then asked to rate their preference or likelihood to purchase but they do not "select" or "choose" *per se*. You can only select or choose when you have several items to select or choose from. I describe the general conjoint study framework in the next section and the choice framework in Chapter 4.

3.2.1 Conjoint framework

Conjoint analysis involves presenting survey respondents only one alternative at a time so the choice sets are singletons. Rather than being asked to make a choice, which is not possible since there is only one product placed in front of them, customers instead are asked to rate their preference for the product, usually on a purchase intent scale ranging from 1–10, although other scales are certainly possible.

The singleton sets are created using experimental design principles. Typically, a *fractional factorial design* is created where a *full factorial design* consists of all possible arrangements of the levels of all the attributes. Sometimes a full factorial is too large for any one survey respondent to handle which is why a fraction is used. The fraction is selected to give an optimal design that allows the best estimation of *part-worth utilities*. Part-worth utilities are weights placed on each level of each attribute of a product. See Paczkowski [2018] for design principles for conjoint studies.

An *OLS* regression model is estimated using the preference data with the attributes and their levels, appropriately coded, as the independent variables. A more complicated model is estimated for a discrete choice problem and this estimation will be discussed in Chapter 4. A conjoint model for a product with four attributes for illustrative purposes might be:

$$Y_\tau^r = \beta_0^r + \beta_{aj}^r + \beta_{bk}^r + \beta_{cl}^r + \beta_{dm}^r + \epsilon_\tau^r \tag{3.1}$$

where

$$\beta_0^r = \text{grand mean preference}$$

$$\beta_{aj}^r = \text{part-worth utility for level } j, \text{ attribute } a$$

$$\beta_{bk}^r = \text{part-worth utility for level } k, \text{ attribute } b$$

$$\beta_{cl}^r = \text{part-worth utility for level } l, \text{ attribute } c$$

$$\beta_{dm}^r = \text{part-worth utility for level } m, \text{ attribute } d$$

and Y_τ^r is the *total utility* or *total worth* to customer r of a product defined by a combination of the attributes in a set τ. In this example, τ consists of an arrangement of the four attributes, an arrangement derived from an experimental design. So τ is the product customers are asked to evaluate. The coefficients in (3.1), called *part-worths*, are the contributions of the attributes to the total worth. See Paczkowski [2018] for a thorough discussion of this model. These part-worths show the importance of each attribute and, as I explain shortly, the importance of each level of each attribute in defining a product. It is knowledge of these part-worths that enables product designers to formulate the right combination of attributes and their levels, the combination being contained in the new product. Basically, the attributes and their levels are *design parameters* and conjoint part-worths tell designers how to set these parameters.

3.2.2 Conjoint design for new products

A conjoint design begins with a list of features or attributes that may define or characterize the new product. These are typically physical attributes such as size, color, weight, and so forth. Price is sometimes included but this is not necessary since the objective is to optimize the construction of the product itself. This construction or specification of the attributes is what customers will first evaluate.

The list of attributes may be developed by the design or engineering team based on their knowledge of what must work together for functionality they believe the product should have. In addition, the attributes could, and frequently do, reflect their internal judgement and opinion, sometimes unfounded, as to what they should be with the customers merely providing evidence that their choices are correct. SMEs and KOLs could also be called on to provide input into the attribute list. Occasionally, the list is quite long so it may have to be narrowed to a subset that consists of the most important attributes from the designers' perspective. This subset, however, may still not have the attributes in the right importance order from the customers' perspective so the designers' effort may be misplaced; in short, there is a design resource misallocation.

The attributes could also be the features identified by the methodology I describe in Section 7.2.1 which relies on text analysis of product reviews. That method does not necessarily identify the levels of each attribute, just the attributes themselves. Nonetheless, compiling an attribute list is the important first step. The design team working in conjunction with *SMEs*, *KOLs*, and the marketing team have to specify the levels for the attributes.

The attribute list consists of a set of distinct items that are mutually exclusive but not completely exhaustive. They are mutually exclusive because they are distinct features by definition. They are not completely exhaustive because no product is so simple that it has only a few attributes. Most are defined with multiple attributes, but it is not practical to test all of them. There are probably many designers who can correctly incorporate them in a design without concern about negative customer feedback or that they even notice the attribute. For example, car buyers are more concerned about legroom, number of cup holders, moon roof, and an on-board navigation system while they are less concerned about an on-board computer.

Creating the attribute list is not the end of this phase of a conjoint study. The levels for each attribute must also be defined. These could simply be *"Yes/No"* or *"Present/Absent"* or *"Small/Medium/Large"*. They are discrete and context often determines which to use. Continuous attributes are possible but usually these are discretized. Weight, for instance, might be 6 oz./8 oz./12 oz. for cans of tomato paste where this is obviously a continuous measure but discretized into three levels. The levels that define each attribute are frequently mutually exclusive and completely exhaustive. There is no third possibility "Maybe" for the binary levels "Present/Absent." In some situations, however, the levels of an attribute may not be mutually exclusive. For instance, a home security system could have an attribute "emergency calls" so that the system will call a public help agency in the event of a home emergency. The levels could be "Fire Department", "Police Department", "EMS". These do not have to be mutually exclusive since all three could be included as security help features. In this case, the levels could be redefined as all combinations of "Fire Department", "Police Department", "EMS." With three levels for this example, there are $2^3 - 1 = 7$ combinations consisting of only one level, two levels, and all three levels; the null combination, of course, does not make sense so it is omitted. These seven are mutually exclusive.

It could also be that the levels across two (or more) attributes are not mutually exclusive. For example, suppose a soup manufacturer defines a new soup with two attributes: content and whether or not a soup is vegetarian. The content may be vegetables and sausage while the vegetarian attribute would be *"Yes/No."* But the content cannot be sausage and the soup be vegetarian at the same time. This combination is a *disallowed combination* or *impossible combination* across attributes.

Once the attributes and levels are defined and any disallowed combinations are identified and excluded, unique combinations of attribute levels that will define potential products have to be created. The identification of attributes and their levels is an art part of product design but this formation of combinations is a science part (although there is also an art element to it). The combination is simply called a *design* and the full list of combinations is reflected in a *design matrix*. The design matrix is the list of potential products and a numeric coding of this matrix is used in the statistical estimation of the part-worth utilities. The easiest method for creating a design matrix is to create a full factorial design that consists of all combinations of the attribute levels, but as I mentioned above, a fraction is typically used to lessen the burden on survey respondents.

3.2.3 A new product design example

Musicians have always been hampered as they play an instrument by the need to turn a physical page of sheet music. Sometimes, a human page turner assists them, but this is a distraction, to say the least, and a potential handicap to the musician if the page turner loses the spot on a page and turns the page at the wrong moment.

A manufacturer of automatic page turners developed a new product to solve this physical page turning problem. The solution is a pedal device that communicates with a tablet, smartphone, or computer where a virtual page appears on a screen. The page is turned by stepping on the pedal located on the floor next to the musician. Some practice is needed to get the pedal pressing correct, but the effort is worthwhile since the page turning response rate is high. The device consists of four attributes:

1. device pairing;
2. power source;
3. weight; and
4. page reversibility.

Discussions with individual musicians, focus groups, and reviews of online blogs, chatrooms, and discussion groups using the methods described in Chapter 2 resulted in these four attributes as the primary ones for prototype development.[3] These are the physical attributes. The levels are listed in Table 3.1. Price is not included at this stage of analysis although it could be included.

3.2.4 Conjoint design

A full factorial design consists of all combinations of the attribute levels. For this example, this is $6 \times 3 \times 4 \times 2 = 144$ combinations or *runs* or possible products.[4] In terms of the notation for (3.1), τ is each of these 144 products. In a conjoint study, each customer is presented with each product one at a time and is asked to rate each

TABLE 3.1 Four attributes for an electronic music page turner device. There are six levels for Device Pairing, three for Power Source, four for Weight, and two for Page Reversibility.

Attribute	Level
Device Pairing	iPad, Kindle, IPhone, Android, Windows Laptop, Mac Laptop
Power Source	Internal Rechargeable Batteries, 2 AA Batteries, Mini-USB
Weight (with Batteries)	6.6 oz., 8.2 oz., 10.1 oz., 12.4 oz.
Page Reversibility	Yes, No

Design				
Run	Device Pairing	Power Source	Weight (with Batteries)	Reversible Page Turning
1	iPad	2 AA Batteries	8.2 Oz.	Yes
2	Kindle	Internal Rechargeable Battery	8.2 Oz.	No
3	iPhone	2 AA Batteries	6.6 Oz.	No
4	Android	Internal Rechargeable Battery	12.4 Oz.	Yes
5	Windows Laptop	2 AA Batteries	10.1 Oz.	Yes
6	Mac Laptop	Internal Rechargeable Battery	8.2 Oz.	Yes
7	iPad	Mini-USB	10.1 Oz.	Yes
8	Kindle	Mini-USB	6.6 Oz.	Yes
9	iPhone	2 AA Batteries	10.1 Oz.	No
10	Android	Internal Rechargeable Battery	10.1 Oz.	No
11	Windows Laptop	Mini-USB	12.4 Oz.	No
12	Mac Laptop	2 AA Batteries	12.4 Oz.	Yes
13	iPad	Internal Rechargeable Battery	6.6 Oz.	No
14	Kindle	2 AA Batteries	12.4 Oz.	No
15	iPhone	Internal Rechargeable Battery	12.4 Oz.	Yes
16	Android	2 AA Batteries	6.6 Oz.	Yes
17	Windows Laptop	Internal Rechargeable Battery	6.6 Oz.	Yes
18	Mac Laptop	Internal Rechargeable Battery	10.1 Oz.	No
19	iPad	Mini-USB	12.4 Oz.	No
20	Kindle	Mini-USB	10.1 Oz.	Yes
21	iPhone	Mini-USB	8.2 Oz.	Yes
22	Android	Mini-USB	8.2 Oz.	No
23	Windows Laptop	2 AA Batteries	8.2 Oz.	No
24	Mac Laptop	Mini-USB	6.6 Oz.	No

FIGURE 3.2 This is the design matrix in 24 runs for the music conjoint example. The full factorial is 144 runs. The 24 runs is a one-sixth fraction of the total number of runs.

one separately on a 10-point preference or liking scale, but 144 products is clearly far too much for any one respondent to handle, so a smaller number is needed. This smaller number is a fraction of the full set of combinations and the smaller design is, hence, called a *fractional factorial design*. The minimum size for this problem is 12 combinations, a one-twelfth fraction[5] but a better size is 24, or a one-sixth fraction, since 12 does not allow for any error estimation whereas 24 would. So a fractional factorial design consisting of 24 runs or products was created. This is shown in Figure 3.2.

Each row in the design matrix is a potential product. Referring to the first row of the design matrix in Figure 3.2, one possible music sheet turner is compatible with an iPad, uses 2 AA Batteries, weighs 8.2 Oz., and allows page reversing.

Conjoint model estimation

The statistical objective for conjoint analysis is the estimation of the part-worth utilities, one part-worth for each level of each attribute. These show the value to customers of each level so that by appropriately aggregating the part-worths to form products you can determine which attributes and which levels are most important or critical for the product. The part-worths are, therefore, the basis for the optimal product design parameters.

The part-worths are typically estimated using ordinary least squares regression (*OLS*), although this may not be the best estimation method. As noted in Paczkowski [2018], other estimation methods are available but *OLS* is commonly used because of its ubiquity (it is implemented in most simple software and spreadsheet packages); many analysts are trained in *OLS* estimation to the exclusion of other methods; and calculations are simple to do and understand.

The design matrix is the explanatory data input while the preference ratings are the dependent data. The preference ratings can be used as-is but the explanatory data must be coded since they are qualitative factors. Only numerics can be used in statistical estimations. There are two ways to code the qualitative factors, although they give the same results after interpretation adjustments. The two ways are *dummy coding* and *effects coding*.[6] The former is popular in econometric studies while the latter is popular in market research studies. Dummy coding involves assigning 0 and 1 values (representing "absent" or "turned off" and "present" or "turned on", respectively) for the levels of a qualitative factor. Effects coding uses -1 and +1 values for the comparable settings. In either case, new variables are created for each level of a qualitative factor except one level which is chosen as a base level. For example, if a factor has three levels, then two variables are created; if it has four levels, then three are created. The reason one variable is omitted is to avoid what is commonly called the *dummy variable trap* which leads to a situation of perfect *multicollinearity*. See Gujarati [2003] for a discussion. Dummy variables measure shifts from a base level, which is the one that is dropped, while effects variables measure differences from the mean of the dependent variable. The effects codes can be easily derived from the dummy codes so intuitively you should expect the estimation results with either coding to be the same; just interpretations differ. Regardless of the coding method, the created variables are often simply called "dummies."

An advantage of effects coding is that the coefficient for the base level can be retrieved. As shown by Paczkowski [2018], the coefficient for the omitted base equals $-1 \times \sum (\text{coefficients})$ so the sum of all the levels for an attribute must sum to 0.0. Figure 3.3 shows the estimated coefficients or part-worths for each attribute for the page turner problem in the report labeled *Parameter Estimates*. The *Expanded Estimates* section shows the retrieved part-worths. The sum of all the coefficients for an attribute in this section is 0.0.

Most statistical softwares provide methods for doing the coding. In some instances, the coding is automatic. The selection of the base to be omitted is also sometimes automatic. A common rule for the base is the last level in alphanumeric order. See Paczkowski [2018] for a thorough discussion and comparison of these two coding schemes and the bases.

This coding explains the minimum size of 12 combinations for the page turner problem mentioned above. For each attribute, a series of variables, either dummy or

Response Rating

Parameter Estimates

Term	Estimate	Std Error	t Ratio	Prob>|t|
Intercept	5.125	0.001776	2886.5	<.0001*
Device Pairing[Android]	3.3416667	0.004023	830.69	<.0001*
Device Pairing[iPad]	-1.35	0.004023	-335.6	<.0001*
Device Pairing[iPhone]	-1.366667	0.004023	-339.7	<.0001*
Device Pairing[Kindle]	-1.85	0.004023	-459.9	<.0001*
Device Pairing[Mac Laptop]	1.5916667	0.004023	395.66	<.0001*
Power Source[2 AA Batteries]	-0.033333	0.002593	-12.85	<.0001*
Power Source[Internal Rechargeable Battery]	0.1333333	0.002593	51.41	<.0001*
Weight (with Batteries)[10.1 Oz.]	-0.291667	0.003075	-94.84	<.0001*
Weight (with Batteries)[12.4 Oz.]	-1.125	0.003075	-365.8	<.0001*
Weight (with Batteries)[6.6 Oz.]	1.5416667	0.003075	501.31	<.0001*
Reversible Page Turning[No]	-0.375	0.001776	-211.2	<.0001*

Expanded Estimates

Nominal factors expanded to all levels

Term	Estimate	Std Error	t Ratio	Prob>|t|
Intercept	5.125	0.001776	2886.48	<.0001*
Device Pairing[Android]	3.3416667	0.004023	830.69	<.0001*
Device Pairing[iPad]	-1.35	0.004023	-335.59	<.0001*
Device Pairing[iPhone]	-1.366667	0.004023	-339.73	<.0001*
Device Pairing[Kindle]	-1.85	0.004023	-459.88	<.0001*
Device Pairing[Mac Laptop]	1.5916667	0.004023	395.66	<.0001*
Device Pairing[Windows Laptop]	-0.366667	0.004023	-91.15	<.0001*
Power Source[2 AA Batteries]	-0.033333	0.002593	-12.85	<.0001*
Power Source[Internal Rechargeable Battery]	0.1333333	0.002593	51.41	<.0001*
Power Source[Mini-USB]	-0.1	0.002593	-38.56	<.0001*
Weight (with Batteries)[10.1 Oz.]	-0.291667	0.003075	-94.84	<.0001*
Weight (with Batteries)[12.4 Oz.]	-1.125	0.003075	-365.82	<.0001*
Weight (with Batteries)[6.6 Oz.]	1.5416667	0.003075	501.31	<.0001*
Weight (with Batteries)[8.2 Oz.]	-0.125	0.003075	-40.65	<.0001*
Reversible Page Turning[No]	-0.375	0.001776	-211.21	<.0001*
Reversible Page Turning[Yes]	0.375	0.001776	211.21	<.0001*

FIGURE 3.3 Part-worth utilities. The top panel shows the *OLS* estimates based on effects coding of the qualitative factors. One level, the last in alphanumeric order, is dropped to avoid perfect multicollinearity. The second panel shows the estimates expanded to include the omitted level from each attribute. Notice that the utilities in the Expanded Estimates section sum to 0.0 for each attribute.

effects coded, is defined for estimation. But there is always one less dummy variable than there are levels. The numbers of required dummy variables for each attribute are shown in Table 3.2.

An effects coding was used for estimating the part-worth utilities for the page turner problem. The estimates are shown in Figure 3.3. Notice that there is a separate estimated coefficient for each level of each attribute in the *Expanded Estimates*

TABLE 3.2 This shows the number of required dummy or effects coded variables for each attribute for conjoint estimation. The first attribute, Device Pairing for example, has six levels as seen in Table 3.1. To avoid the dummy variable trap, five dummies are required. The sum of the dummies is 11 so there are 11 variables, each requiring a coefficient in the model. A constant is also included in the model which has its own coefficient. A total of 12 coefficients have to be estimated. The minimum number of observations, or runs in this case, is therefore 12.

Attribute	#Levels	#Required Variables
Device Pairing	6	5
Power Source	3	2
Weight	4	3
Page Reversibility	2	1
Total		11

report. For Device Pairing, for example, which has six levels, there are six estimated coefficients.

These estimates can be used to predict the total utility or total worth of each possible product. As I noted above, there are 144 possible products. The best product configuration is the one identified by the maximum part-worth for each attribute. From Figure 3.3, these part-worths are 3.34, 0.13, 1.54, and 0.38. The intercept is 5.13. The sum is 10.52.

Although the main output of the *OLS* estimation is the part-worth utility estimates, and these are valuable unto themselves, it is the determination of the *attribute importances* that most analysts look at for determining what should be emphasized in the new product. The attribute importances are the scaled ranges of the part-worth utilities of each attribute with the scale being 0–1 (or 0%–100%). The range for an attribute is the maximum part-worth less the minimum part-worth. The sum of the ranges is divided into each attribute range to get the scaled range for all attributes. A typical chart of these importances shows the attributes, not their levels, rank ordered by the importances. The ranges for the part-worth utilities were calculated and scaled to sum to 100% and are shown in Figure 3.4. It is clear that Device Pairing is the most important feature for a new product. See Paczkowski [2018] for a discussion of the importances calculations and interpretation.

3.2.5 Some problems with conjoint analysis

Although conjoint analysis has been a mainstay of market research analysis for a long time, is simple to implement, and is easy to interpret, it has shortcomings that make its continued use for product optimization questionable. One issue, of course, is the assumed setting for the conjoint exercise. Unlike discrete choice analysis mentioned above which mimics shopping behavior, conjoint fails to mimic this behavior, or any behavior for that matter. Survey respondents are merely asked to

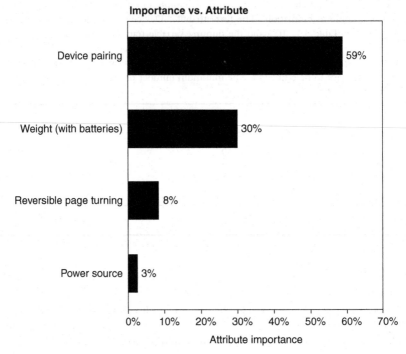

FIGURE 3.4 Attribute importances calculated by scaling the ranges of the part-worth utilities in Figure 3.3 to sum to 100%.

rate a single product in isolation from other products. Occasionally, they are asked to rank products which means they have the full set of products in front of them when they do the ranking. If there are a large number of products, however, then the ranking can become onerous which could make results questionable. Experimental design procedures are available to mitigate this issue but since most analysts are unfamiliar with them they are infrequently used. The fractional factorial is the easiest and this is the one most analysts use. See Paczkowski [2018] for a discussion of other designs.

3.2.6 Optimal attribute levels

The purpose of a conjoint analysis for new product development is to identify the optimal level for each attribute or feature of the product. This is done with the estimated part-worths as I illustrated above. The sum of the part-worths tells you the overall worth to customers of the product configuration. It is important to know this total worth because it can help you decide between two configurations that are reasonably close. Although the conjoint estimates may indicate one clear "winner", marketing and business intuition and intelligence (*a.k.a.*, experience) might indicate that the second-best configuration is better. In addition, since the

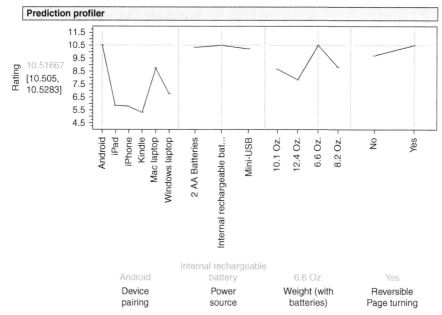

FIGURE 3.5 The effect of the optimal or best level for each attribute is shown along with the worst level. The best configuration has the highest total worth which is the sum of the individual part-worths. This is 10.51. The worst configuration has a total worth that is 8.2 utility units lower at 2.29.

estimated total worth is based on the sum of part-worth estimates, the total really has a confidence band around it. It may be that several configurations have overlapping confidence bands so there is no clear winner.

A tool, such as a *profiler* or *simulator* could easily be constructed to calculate the total worth from different combinations of part-worths. Figure 3.5 shows one such profiler. The optimal total worth has a value of 10.5 while the worst configuration is 2.29. There are three configurations that are close for being the best ones, all of which involve the maximum part-worth estimate for Device Pairing, Weight, and Reversible; only the Power Source differs for each. The Power Source attribute has almost no contribution to the total worth which is consistent with the attribute importances as shown in Figure 3.4. The three top configurations are shown in Figure 3.6.

3.2.7 Software

Software is always an issue. For conjoint analysis, two procedures are required:

- choice set development using an experimental design; and
- part-worth estimation which is usually *OLS*.

Device pairing	Power source	Weight (with batteries)	Reversible page turning	Total worth
Android	Internal rechargeable battery	6.6 Oz.	Yes	10.52
Android	2 AA Batteries	6.6 Oz.	Yes	10.35
Android	Mini-USB	6.6 Oz.	Yes	10.28

FIGURE 3.6 The top three configurations are all close in value. The Page Transport attribute make little to no contribution to the total worth of the product.

All statistical software packages implement *OLS* to varying degrees of sophistication so any package can be used. Some are R and Python which are free, and JMP and SAS which are more comprehensive and commercial which means they are expensive. Stata is excellent but mostly targeted to econometric applications which makes it more specialized than the others.

The experimental design is an issue. My preference is JMP because it has a comprehensive design of experiments (*DOE*) platform which can easily handle conjoint designs although there is no conjoint design component *per se*. See Paczkowski [2016] for an example of using JMP's *DOE* platform for conjoint design. SAS can certainly be used but this requires an advanced understanding of SAS. R has packages that will also create fractional factorial designs. JMP was used for the Case Study.

3.3 Kansei engineering for product optimization

The main problem with conjoint analysis is the lack of an emotional or feelings assessment of the product. Conjoint merely provides an assessment of the materialistic or engineering aspect of a possible design. When you buy a product, you buy more than a material item; you also buy an attachment that transcends the material. A good example is the purchase of a new car. In a simplistic sense, the car is only a physical container composed of many individual physical items: metals, plastics, glass, rubber to mention a few. These are arranged in some fashion to create an object called an "automobile" or "car" that has speed, power, fuel efficiency, maneuverability, and safety. Other design elements, such as the appearance (i.e., the aesthetics), are also embedded in the car as part of the arrangement of the materialistic parts. These are additional important factors customers consider when purchasing a new car along with the materialistic combinations of the metals, plastics, glass and rubber. Because of both the materialistic and aesthetic aspects, people develop an attachment (or not) to a car so that it becomes an extension of themselves. See Sheller [2004] for some discussion about the emotions associated with a car. Also see Edensor [2004] for an interesting discussion about how national identity is also expressed by car and what the author calls "automobility."

Jewelry is another product that has more aesthetic appeal than materialistic. Certainly for a diamond engagement ring, there is concern about the features of the diamond such as its rating on the "4Cs" of diamonds: cut, color, clarity, and carat weight. The shape and perhaps certification may also be important. But by and large, the emotions attached to giving or receiving that ring far outweigh these physical attributes. See Ahde [2010] for a study of the emotions attached to jewelry.

Clothing, foot apparel, and a house are other examples. You have a favorite shirt or blouse, or sneakers you believe make you look sexy, successful, powerful, independent, and so forth. A house shows status, success, lifestyle, and comfort but also embodies memories and emotions, good and bad. These examples illustrate an appeal that transcends purely physical characteristics. Conjoint analysis captures the importance and weight in total value or worth of the physical attributes, but the emotional aspects are absent.

There is research that shows that people form attachments to their material possessions that go beyond the physical attributes of those products, usually durable goods. Schifferstein and Zwartkruis-Pelgrim [2008] argue that some products, such as cars, have a degree of irreplaceability, indispensability, and self-extension that transcend the physical attributes. They claim that there is an emotional bond that ties the product to memories, enjoyment, self-identity, life vision, and market value that new product designers should be aware of and should try to incorporate into their product designs. It may be difficult or next to impossible to incorporate some of these emotional aspects into a physical design (how do you incorporate "memories" or "self-worth"?) so they may be better left to the marketing messaging, a topic I discuss in Chapter 5. But yet for some products that are considered gifts, memories can be invoked or created by the product itself. An example is a silver platter given as an anniversary gift or a picture frame given as a wedding or graduation gift. Nonetheless, they should be considered rather than being either ignored or given scant attention simply because they are difficult to measure. See Schifferstein and Zwartkruis-Pelgrim [2008] for some suggestions on how to incorporate emotions in new product design. Also see Sheller [2004] for more comments on the role, extent, and importance of emotions regarding automobiles.

Since conjoint analysis is materialistically focused with the emotional aspect absent, another approach is needed that captures this emotional aspect. One such approach is called *Kansei Engineering*. "Kansei" is a Japanese word that implies "feelings" or "impressions" or "emotions". The goal of Kansei analysis is to identify, measure, and incorporate emotional aspects of products in the new product design stage. See Matsubara et al. [2011], Lai et al [2006], and Chuang et al. [2001] for discussions and applications. Also see Lokman et al. [2018] for proceedings of an international conference on Kansei methods and emotion research.

3.3.1 Study designs

A Kansei study is multifaceted and, of course, the particulars vary from study to study. In general, the steps are outlined in the following subsections.

Design product prototypes for testing

Similar to conjoint analysis, you need something to show customers so they can evaluate the new product concept. Conjoint analysis relies on card descriptions, although more modern presentations are conducted online utilizing images if the images can clearly illustrate the different attributes and their levels. In many instances, this is difficult to do, but not completely impossible. For a Kansei study, images could be used but the focus is not the attributes *per se* but the product itself as an entity. An effective presentation includes physical prototypes customers could touch, handle, and examine. A diamond engagement ring, for example, does not have the same effect if viewed in a picture as being placed on a finger and held up to light. The problem with a physical prototype is that many versions might be needed which may be too costly to create. In addition, the sample size of customers may be restricted because time has to be allowed for them to examine the prototype which means fewer customers may be allowed per session. Since most studies are time restricted (i.e., the field work has to be completed within a set period and within a set budget) this further means that fewer customers can be recruited. An online presentation in which images could be shown would be more cost effective, faster, and would allow for more customers to participate, but it would be less effective. The image designers could create a number of variations unlike physical designers who would be more restricted in what they can physically produce.

Some Kansei studies use images or physical objects that are readily available for already existing competitive products with only a few of their new versions included in the mix. The competitive images could easily be obtained from media or the competitors' web sites while a physical object could simply be purchased for the study. For example, a car manufacturer could conduct a clinic study in which consumers could look at, sit in, and perhaps drive different cars. Several could be competitor cars and several could be new versions of their car. The competitor cars could be masked so that the consumers would not be able to (easily) identify the make or model. I discuss clinics in Chapter 4.

Create an experimental design

An experimental design is still needed since it may be impractical to present all the prototypes to customers; it could be overwhelming to say the least. Some Kansei studies have used a large number of prototypes. See Matsubara et al. [2011], Lai et al. [2006], and Chuang et al. [2001] for discussions and examples. A possible experimental design is a *Balanced Incomplete Block Design* (*BIBD*) which I discuss in Chapter 5. Fundamentally, a *BIBD* creates sets of products such that each set does not contain all the prototypes but yet all the prototypes are represented in all the sets. A single customer could be shown only one set. There are restrictions on the *BIBD* design which I describe in Chapter 5.

Create a list of emotional descriptors

A list of emotional descriptors is needed. These are usually adjectives such as "beautiful", "strong", "powerful", "artistic" and so forth. The list could be constructed, for example, from a perusal of publications (e.g., popular magazines, newspapers)

TABLE 3.3 A differential semantic scale might use adjectives such as these for a new sheet music page turning product. The adjectives represent (in order): sound level, comfort, responsiveness, aesthetic appeal, obtrusiveness, and innovativeness. A musician would be asked to rate how each adjective pair best describes the product, making one rating per pair.

	1	2	3	4	5	
Noisy						Silent
Uncomfortable						Comfortable
Unresponsive						Responsive
Boring						Stylish
Obtrusive						Unobtrusive
Mundane						Revolutionary

and online reviews. Focus groups could be conducted in which customers would be asked to brainstorm a list of adjectives. Matsubara et al. [2011], Lai et al. [2006], and Chuang et al. [2001] discuss how they compiled a list of adjectives for their studies. Also see the articles in Lokman et al. [2018].

The adjectives *per se* are not used, however. Rather, each adjective is matched with its polar opposite to form a differential pair. So "beautiful" is matched with "not beautiful," "strong" with "weak," "artistic" with "unimaginative." A *semantic differential* scale, designed to measure the "connotative meaning of objects, events, and concepts,"[7] is a listing of the extremes of the adjectives so it is a bipolar scale. One end of the scale is the positive use of the adjective while the other is the negative use. For example, if the adjective is "beautiful", then the two extremes are simply "beautiful" and "not beautiful." Other extremes might be "good–bad", "big–little", "worthwhile–worthless", and "fast–slow." The scale between the two extremes is usually on a 1–5 or 1–7 basis with the former the most common. An example is shown in Table 3.3. The words are called *Kansei words*. The scale is certainly not without controversy. See Beltran et al. [2009] for some discussion of semantic differential scales. Also see Wegman [1990] for some technical discussions.

Present the prototypes and semantic differential questions

Each customer is shown all the prototype images one at a time and for each image is asked to rate or describe it using the semantic differential scale question. If there are four prototypes and 10 semantic differential questions, then each customer is asked to do 40 evaluations.

Basic data arrangement

If there are N respondents who see P prototypes and are asked W Kansei words using a semantic differential scale, then the data form a cube that is $N \times P \times W$. An example is shown in Figure 3.7. Such a cube is actually common in statistical analysis although it is usually not discussed, being more subtle than provoking.[8] Yet

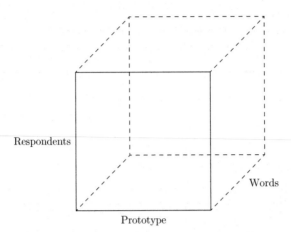

FIGURE 3.7 This is the data cube resulting from a Kansei experiment.

it is important to note that there are several dimensions to any data set, the Kansei data being only one example. See Lemahieu et al. [2018], Basford and McLachlan [1985], and Vermunt [2007] for the use and analysis of three-way data.

The cube is usually collapsed by aggregating across the N respondents. The aggregation is done by averaging the Kansei word ratings for all respondents for each prototype and word. The result is a two-dimensional plane that is $P \times W$ with cells equal to the average across all respondents. That is, if **A** is the resulting $P \times W$ data matrix, then cell $pw, p = 1, \ldots, P$ and $w = 1, \ldots, W$ is

$$A_{.,p,w} = \frac{1}{N} \sum_{n}^{N} A_{n,p,w} \tag{3.2}$$

where the "dot" notation indicates average. In essence, the data cube shown in Figure 3.7 is squashed down or flattened to just the *Prototype* × *Words* plane. The resulting matrix is shown in Figure 3.8

Analyze the data

The objective is to use the prototypes to explain or account for the Kansei word score in each cell of the matrix. The prototypes *per se* are not used, but their attributes and the levels of those attributes are used to account for the Kansei word scores. A regression model is immediately suggested with the attributes and their levels appropriately encoded. Dummy variable coding or effects coding can be used but which encoding is not a major issue. As I noted above, dummy and effects coding are commonly used and are easily handled by most statistical and econometric software packages.

There is an issue with the specification of a model. Since there are W Kansei words whose average scores have to be explained or accounted for by the attributes

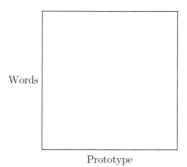

Words

Prototype

FIGURE 3.8 This is the data matrix resulting from collapsing a three-dimensional Kansei data cube.

and their levels, a model would be

$$\mathbf{Y} = \mathbf{X}\beta + \epsilon \tag{3.3}$$

where ϵ is the usual *OLS* disturbance term such that $\epsilon_i \sim \mathcal{N}(0, \sigma_\epsilon^2)$ and independently and identically distributed (*iid*), and $\mathbf{X}$ is the dummy coded matrix of attributes. The $\mathbf{Y}$ is not a column vector as in traditional *OLS* with only one dependent variable, but is now a $P \times W$ matrix. This matrix is often reduced in size using a data reduction method such as *factor analysis* resulting in a $P \times W'$ matrix with $1 < W' < W$. If $W' = 1$ then the usual *OLS* model results.

The $\mathbf{X}$ matrix is of order $P \times L$ where L is the total number of levels for all attributes and their levels. If each attribute has two levels as an example, then $\mathbf{X}$ has size $P \times A$ where A is the number of attributes.[9] The number of attributes can be large enough so it is safe to assume that $P << A$; that is, the number of observations, P, is much less than the number of variables, A. This is a problem for *OLS* because *OLS* requires that $P > A$ for estimation so in this situation estimation is impossible. In addition, the attributes are usually associated with some degree of correlation which, despite the use of an encoding scheme for any one attribute, still introduces multicollinearity. The collinearity jeopardizes estimation by making the estimated parameters unstable and with possibly the wrong signs and magnitudes. Two ways to handle the model in (3.3) are with *partial least squares* (*PLS*) estimation and *neural networks*.

PLS is a variant of *OLS* that allows for

1. a dependent variable matrix rather than a dependent variable vector;
2. $P << W$; and
3. multicollinearity among the independent variables.

I review *PLS* in the next section. Neural networks, which are sometimes considered black boxes, are meant to show the connections among items much as the human brain is considered to have many connecting parts that allow you to understand and reason. I review neural networks below.

Partial least squares review

The *Partial Least Squares* (PLS) methodology has been known for a while but is only now becoming more widely available as data analysts become more aware of it, the problems it deals with become more widespread, and software becomes available. This section provides a high-level overview of this methodology. More technical detail is provided in Appendix C of this chapter. For even more detail, see Tobias [1995], Sawatsky et al. [2015], Ng [2013], and Geladi and Kowalski [1986]. Also see Cox and Gaudard [2013] for a book-length treatment using the JMP software.

To understand partial least squares, it is helpful to briefly state two key assumptions (among many) that enable *OLS* to produce estimates of the model parameters. These are:

1. the independent variables are linearly independent (i.e., there is no multi-collinearity); and
2. the number of observations exceeds the number of independent variables (i.e., $n > p$ where p is the number of independent variables).

If the first is violated, then the matrix formed by the independent variables cannot be inverted. See Appendix C for an explanation. If the second is violated, then there is a chance the model would overfit the data. Overfitting means the *OLS* procedure would attempt to account for each observation rather that some average of the observations. The implication is that the model learned from the data used in the estimation but will most likely be unable to apply those estimates to new data that are unlike those used for estimation. The purpose of a model is to not only indicate the effects on the dependent variable but to also enable predictions for new data. With $n < p$, especially $n \ll p$, then this ability is jeopardized if not impossible.

Partial least squares regression avoids both potential issues by first finding a reduced set of independent variables, the set containing factors that summarize the independent variables. These factors are identified in such a way that they are linearly independent so the first property will be satisfied. Since there is a reduced number of factors, the second property is also satisfied. These factors can then be used in a regression model. If you are familiar with *principal components analysis* (PCA), then this may seem like *principal components regression* (PCR). It differs from PCR in that the information is taken from both the reduced independent factors and the dependent variable at the same time. This is a more complicated procedure. See Appendix C for some high-level details.

Neural networks

Neural networks are sometimes viewed as the quintessential black box for analyzing data. They are difficult to explain and understand primarily because they were originally developed to mimic how the human brain operates. The human brain is a complex organ that has been studied for a very long time. Although we know a

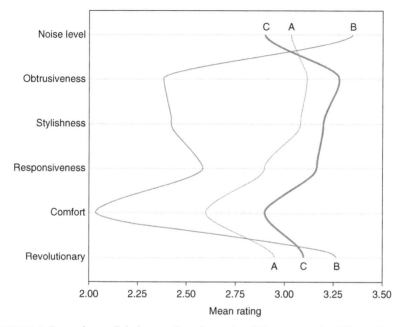

FIGURE 3.9 Example parallel chart or "spaghetti chart" for a semantic differential question. A five-point Likert Scale was used. See Table 3.3 for an example of the question format.

lot about how it works, it is still a mystery. Neural networks are equally challenging. For an intuitive explanation, see Hardesty [2017].

Other analysis methods

The semantic differential scale data are often analyzed with a parallel lines graph, sometimes called a "spaghetti chart." This is illustrated in Figure 3.9. Another possibility is to simply calculate the mean of each item and use these to create a bar chart. See Figure 3.10. These, of course, do not fully utilize the data to provide the richest information. Instead, the final response array can be analyzed using various multivariate methods.

Another possibility is to do a *correspondence analysis* to determine which adjectives are most closely associated with each prototype. The purpose of a correspondence analysis is to reproduce in a two-dimensional plot the relationship in a frequency table (e.g., a crosstab where each cell of the table has the number or *frequency* of observations sharing the features labeling the row and column for that cell) that can be complex to read. A small table, say a 2×2, is easy to read and interpret but is typically uninformative. A large table, say a 10×10, is an order of magnitude more challenging to read and interpret and also typically uninformative merely because of its size. Interpretation is dramatically improved when the complex table of frequencies is plotted in a lower-dimensional space: a two-dimensional plot of

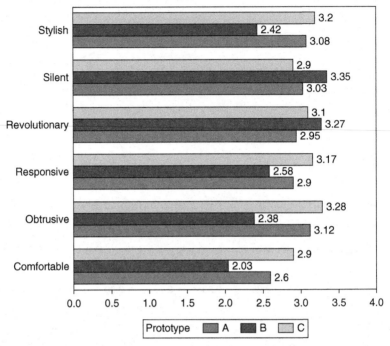

FIGURE 3.10 Example bar chart for a semantic differential question. The mean for each item measured on a five-point Likert Scale was calculated and plotted. See Table 3.3 for an example of the question format.

the rows and columns of the table. The two-dimensional plot is sometimes called a *map*. The map reproduces the differences between the rows and columns of a table in a simple two-dimensional, *X-Y* graph or scatter plot. A two-dimensional plot is typically used because three dimensions are difficult to interpret and more than three cannot be drawn. Two dimensions in most cases completely display the data relationships.

To interpret a map, you have to examine the distances between points on the map for rows, for columns, and, depending on the method used, for both simultaneously. Relative proximities of the points count. If a point on the map for a row category is close to a point on the map for a column category, you cannot say anything about the magnitude of their interaction in an absolute sense, but you can interpret the positions in a relative sense saying that the categories are associated. The word "relative" is important. You cannot say anything about the absolute level of association. You can only say that a pair of points that are close are more strongly associated than a pair that are further apart.

The map is formally called a *biplot* because it simultaneously plots (measures of) the rows and columns of the table on one plot. The "bi" in "biplot" refers to the joint display of rows and columns, not to the dimensionality of the plot, which is two (*X-Y*). In essence, a biplot is one *X-Y* plot overlaid on top of another. The biplot allows you to visualize on one map the relationship both within a structure (e.g., rows) and between structures (e.g., rows and columns) of a table. An example is show in Figure 3.12. See Gower and Hand [1996] for a detailed, technical discussion of biplots.

The correspondence analysis is done using the Singular Value Decomposition (*SVD*) mentioned in Chapter 2 and reviewed in that chapter's appendix. The *SVD* divides the frequency table into three components: a left matrix, a center matrix, and a right matrix. The left matrix contributes to the plotting coordinates for the rows of the table, the right matrix contributes to the plotting coordinates for the columns, and the center matrix contributes to a measure of the variance of the table. See Greenacre [2007] for a classic discussion of correspondence analysis. See the Appendix to Chapter 2 on the *SVD*.

The tables for a Kansei are numbers much like those from paired comparisons, ratings, and distance measures as some examples. These measures are not directly frequencies, but as noted by Greenacre [2007] correspondence analysis can be applied to these tables after being transformed. In the case of ratings, as for the music semantic scale, the data have to be transformed into something that has the interpretation of a frequency, a count so that correspondence analysis can be used. Assume a 1–5 scale as for the music semantic scale. A transformation is to subtract 1 from each value provided by the customer so that a rating of "1", the minimum value possible, becomes "0"; "2" becomes "1", and "5" becomes "4". The new value of "0" is interpreted to mean that the customer is "0" steps from the beginning of the scale (which is "1" on the original scale) and "4" from the end of the scale (which is "5" on the original scale); a new value of "4" means the customer is "4" steps from the beginning and "0" steps from the end. These steps are counts of what the customer must do to get to the beginning and the end from whatever original rating he/she gave. They could also be viewed as offsets from either end of the original scale.[10]. Table 3.4 shows all pairs for a five-point rating scale. Greenacre [2007] and Greenacre [1984] refer to this as *scale doubling*. The steps are counts which is exactly what the correspondence analysis requires. This is illustrated in Figure 3.11.

TABLE 3.4 For a five-point rating scale, the pairs are shown here. Each pair sums to 4 since for any point on the original scale there are only 4 steps in both directions that someone could take.

Rating	Pair
1	(0, 4)
2	(1, 3)
3	(2, 2)
4	(3, 1)
5	(4, 0)

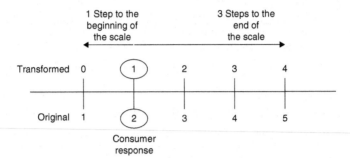

FIGURE 3.11 This rating scale transformation provides a pair of counts for each single rating given by a customer: the number of steps to the beginning of the original scale and the number of steps to the end of the original scale. So the original rating of "2" becomes the pair (1, 3); an original rating of "1" becomes the pair (0, 4); and so forth. Notice that each pair sums to 4, the total number of steps in both directions.

The advantage of the pairs is that a single original rating is transformed into two values: the first of the pair shows the steps to a low or negative part of the scale while the second shows the steps to a high or positive part. A polarity is established. For a semantic differential scale with polar opposites for an adjective, the transformation automatically provides data for the negative pole and the positive pole of the scale. As an example, for a sound level adjective pair "Noisy/Silent", the first of the scale pair is a value for "Noisy" and the second of the pair is a value for "Silent." A "2" rating for the sound level results in a value of "1" for "Noisy" and "3" for "Silent". The music example has six adjective pairs so a single customer provides six ratings on a 1–5 scale as in Table 3.3. After the transformation, there are 12 ratings representing valuations of polar extremes. These 12 ratings are used in a correspondence analysis.

The customer data for the music example were transformed from the original five-point scale to the polar opposite pairs following the scheme in Table 3.4. The labels for the polar opposites were the ones shown in Table 3.3. There is an underlying data table that is a crosstab of the three prototypes and 12 polar opposites labels. The top number in each cell is the sum of steps for that combination of prototype and semantic polar word. This table is shown in Figure 3.5. A correspondence analysis was drawn based on this crosstab data and a correspondence map was created. This is shown in Figure 3.12. This map is quite revealing about the relationships among the products and semantic ratings.

Notice that:

- Prototype *A* is judged as somewhat obtrusive, boring, and revolutionary;
- Prototype *B* is associated with being judged as stylish, unobtrusive, yet noisy; and
- Prototype *C* is closely associated with being judged as unresponsive, uncomfortable, but silent.

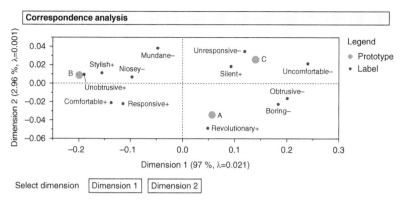

FIGURE 3.12 This is a correspondence map for the means of a semantic differential set of questions in Table 3.3 but for three products. The numbers in parentheses on the axes labels show the amount of variation in the underlying table (i.e., the variance of the data) accounted for by the two dimensions plotted. In this case, the first dimension (the X-axis) accounts for almost 97% while the Y-axis accounts for almost 2.96%. Together, the two axes account for almost 100% of the variation so that the two dimensions almost completely reproduce the data.

The associations for prototypes B and C are somewhat strong since the prototype points are close to the attribute points, but A is somewhat further away from the attribute labels indicating that customers may have had some difficulty judging this product mock-up.

The map in Figure 3.12 has more information about the points in the biplot. The two axes are the first and second dimensions extracted from the SVD of the underlying data table. These are the two that account for the most variation in the table. The most dimensions that could be extracted equals $min(r-1, c-1)$ where r is the number of rows of a table and c is the number of columns. For this problem, $r = 3$ and $c = 12$ so the maximum number of dimensions that could be extracted is $min(2, 11) = 2$. The first dimension is used for the X-axis and the second for the Y-axis, although you can interchange these depending on the software. Certainly, if more dimensions could be extracted, then you could use these for the axes. Typically, only the first two are used. The first dimensions account for the largest proportion of the variation in the data table, in this case this is shown in the label on the x-axis: 97%. The second dimension accounts for the next largest proportion which is 2.96%. Together, the first two dimensions account for almost 100% of the variation. But this should be expected since there are only two dimensions possible for this problem. This is summarized in Figure 3.13. See the Appendix to this chapter for more details on the computations.

3.3.2 Combining conjoint and Kansei analyses

Conjoint and Kansei analyses have been presented as two separate methodologies for optimizing a new product design. Conjoint is associated with the designer's

Details					
Singular Value	**Inertia**	**ChiSquare**	**Percent**	**Cumulative Percent**	**20 40 60 80**
0.14457	0.02090	89.873	97.04	97.04	
0.02524	0.00064	2.740	2.96	100.00	

FIGURE 3.13 The singular values and their transformed values are shown in this table. The first singular value, corresponding to the first dimension extracted, is 0.14457. The square of this is the inertia. The total inertia is the total variation in the table. The total inertia times the sample size, which is 4300 from Figure 3.5, is the total chi-square value for the table: 92.613. The corresponding percents and cumulative percents are also shown. The cumulative percents are in the two dimension labels in the map.

perspective and Kansei with the customer's emotional perspective. Both can, and should, be combined for a total perspective. One procedure for a unified approach involves the following steps:[11]

1. Determine the correlation between the conjoint preference rating and each image evaluation for all prototypes. If there are s image evaluations, then there are s correlations. That is $cor_i = r(Rating, Image_i), i = 1, \ldots s$ where the function $r(\cdot)$ is the correlation function. Note that there is only one conjoint preference rating. These correlations will be used to determine weights as described below.

2. Estimate a key driver model for preference as a function of the image evaluations. The model has preference as the dependent variable and each image rating as an independent variable: $Preference_c = \beta_0 + \sum_{i=1}^{s} \beta_i \times Image_{ci} + \epsilon_c, c = 1, \ldots, n$ customers. The step-wise approach will narrow the list of independent variables to a few key ones.

3. Based on the design elements of the prototypes, estimate a conjoint regression model using the preference rating as the dependent variable and the design elements as the independent variables. Dummy or effects coding can be used but usually effects coding is used as described earlier. The result will show which design elements have the largest weight based on their part-worths. A total utility or worth can be calculated for each configuration. This is standard conjoint analysis.

4. Based on the design elements for the prototypes, estimate additional conjoint models using the key driver image evaluation scores as the dependent variable and the design elements, appropriately encoded, as the independent variables. If there are s' key drivers from Step 2, then there will be s' conjoint models. Each model will show the importance of the design elements on the key image evaluations. A total utility or worth can be calculated for each configuration as in Step 3 but they will now be for the key image words.

TABLE 3.5 This is the crosstab table underlying the correspondence analysis. The first value in each cell is the sum of the steps on the doubled scale for the prototype shown in the column and the polar adjective shown in the row. In the first cell in the upper left, there were 125 steps for Prototype *A* and negative polar word *Boring*.

Contingency Table

	Count Total % Col % Row %	Prototype			Total
		A	B	C	
Label	Boring-	125 2.91 8.75 36.6569	84 1.95 5.87 24.6334	132 3.07 9.17 38.7097	341 7.93
	Comfortable+	144 3.35 10.08 32.3596	175 4.07 12.22 39.3258	126 2.93 8.75 28.3146	445 10.35
	Mundane-	117 2.72 8.19 30.8707	136 3.16 9.50 35.8839	126 2.93 8.75 33.2454	379 8.81
	Noisey-	118 2.74 8.26 31.6354	141 3.28 9.85 37.8016	114 2.65 7.92 30.563	373 8.67
	Obstrusive-	127 2.95 8.89 36.5994	83 1.93 5.80 23.9193	137 3.19 9.51 39.4813	347 8.07
	Responsive+	124 2.88 8.68 32.7177	145 3.37 10.13 38.2586	110 2.56 7.64 29.0237	379 8.81
	Revolutionary+	123 2.86 8.61 36.0704	104 2.42 7.26 30.4985	114 2.65 7.92 33.4311	341 7.93
	Silent+	114 2.65 7.98 33.6283	99 2.30 6.91 29.2035	126 2.93 8.75 37.1681	339 7.88
	Stylish+	115 2.67 8.05 30.6667	152 3.53 10.61 40.5333	108 2.51 7.50 28.8	375 8.72
	Uncomfortable-	96 2.23 6.72 35.4244	61 1.42 4.26 22.5092	114 2.65 7.92 42.0664	271 6.30
	Unobstrusive+	113 2.63 7.91 30.2949	157 3.65 10.96 42.0912	103 2.40 7.15 27.6139	373 8.67
	Unresponsive-	112 2.60 7.84 33.2344	95 2.21 6.63 28.1899	130 3.02 9.03 38.5757	337 7.84
	Total	1428 33.21	1432 33.30	1440 33.49	4300 100.00

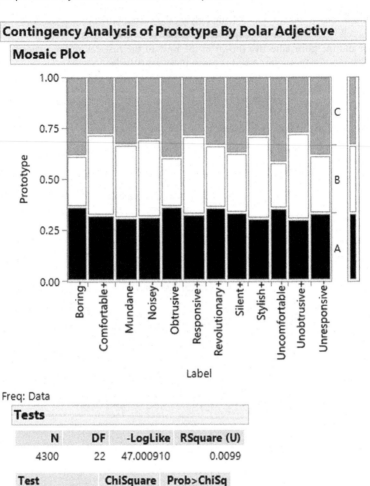

Contingency Analysis of Prototype By Polar Adjective

Freq: Data

	N	DF	-LogLike	RSquare (U)
	4300	22	47.000910	0.0099

Test	ChiSquare	Prob>ChiSq
Likelihood Ratio	94.002	<.0001*
Pearson	92.613	<.0001*

FIGURE 3.14 These are the chi-square tests for the crosstab data in Figure 3.5. The Pearson Chi-square is 92.613 which is the sum of the two chi-square values in Figure 3.13. See Appendix 3.A for an overview of the chi-square statistic and tests.

5. Calculate a weighted average of the image word total utilities from Step 4 using the correlations from Step 1 as the weights. If s_i' is the ith key image word and r_i' is its correlation coefficient, then the weight for the ith key image word is $w_i' = r_i'/\sum_{j \in J'} r_j'$ where $\sum_{j \in J'} w_j' = 1$. These weighted scores are called *simple additive weighted (SAW)* scores.

6. Compare the *SAW* scores and the conjoint total utility scores from Step 3 and select the product configurations with the highest scores for both. One way to do this is to calculate a weighted average or index number of the *SAW* scores

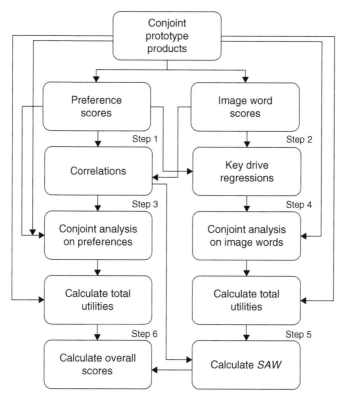

FIGURE 3.15 This flowchart illustrates the steps used in the conjoint analysis of the preference ratings and the image words.

and the conjoint total utility scores perhaps using the first principal component as the weighted index. The corresponding product configuration is the one that should be developed.

These steps are illustrated in Figure 3.15.

3.4 Early-stage pricing

A new product concept must still prove itself at the early stage of the development process even though it has not been introduced to the market. A business case process is typically employed to justify whether or not to continue with development. The contents of the business case, of course, will vary from business to business, each having its own criteria regarding what has to be proven about the new concept. Some components that might be included are a competitive assessment, potential market assessment, legal issues (e.g., patent protection and infringement) to mention a few. Although the requirements will vary, a financial view will almost always be included because the purpose of the new concept is to increase long-run profitability.

A financial case itself involves a cost assessment, a revenue assessment, and a contribution assessment. Costs include the cost of production, marketing, and sales. Revenue includes total quantity sold times price. Contribution is the difference: revenue less costs. Revenue, however, requires a price point but since the product is not available in the market, a market-driven price point is certainly not available. Market research is required to develop a price. The uncertainty surrounding the estimate, however, would be great because of the nature of the problem: the product is, by definition, unknown to the market. One way to handle the issue is to develop a range of acceptable prices. The *van Westendorp Price Sensitivity Meter* can be used for this purpose. I will briefly describe the approach in the next section. A detailed account is provided in Paczkowski [2018]. See Westendorp [1976] for the original presentation and analysis.

3.4.1 van Westendorp price sensitivity meter

The van Westendorp method is used to develop a price range suitable for early business case development. A range estimate is based on a series of four questions, all dealing with customer perception of the quality of the product and how much they are willing to pay conditioned on that quality. Since the method is founded on perceptions, it is ideal for new product development in the early business case stage because customers would not have an actual product to examine and use. A product description would be used so that customers would be able to formulate some judgement or opinion of the product. The description could be supplemented with a prototype or mock-up of the product so that the customer could at least have a visual, or perhaps a textual, experience. The mock-up may not actually work, but it could still help customers form a perception of the new product. [12]

The four questions are:

1. At what price is the product so expensive you would not buy it?
2. At what price is the product so inexpensive you would feel the quality is questionable?
3. At what price is the product becoming expensive so you would have to think about buying it?
4. At what price is the product a bargain – a great value for the money?

The first question is a "too expensive" question; the second is a "too inexpensive" or "cheap" question; the third is an "expensive" question; and the fourth is an "inexpensive" or "bargain" question. The "cheap" question identifies the point where the quality is too suspect so that a customer would not buy the product at all. The "too expensive" question identifies the point where the product is not outside a customer's budget. The "bargain" and "expensive" questions reflect points

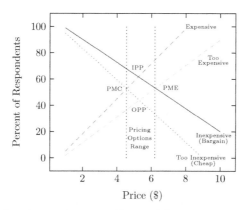

FIGURE 3.16 The four intersections are illustrated here. Source: Paczkowski [2018]. Permission granted by Routledge.

where it is a product that cannot be passed up ("a bargain") or is within a customer's budget and doable.

The cumulative distribution of responses for each question are calculated. By convention, the "bargain" and "cheap" distributions are reversed. The four distributions are then plotted on the same graph space with the two expensive curves sloping upward and the "bargain" and "cheap" curves sloping downward. The two expensive curves should top-out at 1.0 at the upper right of the graph while the other two should bottom-out at 0.0 at the lower right. An example is shown in Figure 3.16.

It is evident from Figure 3.16 that there are four intersections. One possible set is:[13]

Optimal Price Point (OPP) The price at which the number of customers who rated the product too expensive equals the number rating it cheap. It is the equilibrium price between not buying the product and doubting its quality. This is where Too Expensive = Cheap.

Indifferent Price Point (IPP) The price at which the number of customers who rated the product as expensive equals the number rating it a bargain.[14] This is where Expensive = Bargain.

Point of Marginal Cheapness (PMC) The lower bound of a range of acceptable prices where customers are on the edge or "margin" of questioning the product's quality. This is where Expensive = Cheap.

Point of Marginal Expensiveness (PME) The upper bound of a range of acceptable prices where customers are on the edge or "margin" of viewing the product as outside their means. This is where Too Expensive = Bargain.[15]

The difference between the *PMC* and *PME* is usually interpreted as the optimal price range.

TABLE 3.6 These are the price points presented to musicians for the page turner.

$100	$150	$250	$300	$400	$500	$600	$800

Let me return to the music page turning new product. The marketing team of the developer believes the product's price should be in the $100 - $800 range. A more definitive range is needed for the business case to be developed by the business case team. Musicians in several metropolitan areas were surveyed and asked four pricing questions:

1. At what price do you think the cost becomes too expensive to be a good value? (The too expensive question)
2. At what price do you think the cost is starting to get expensive, but not out of the question? (The expensive question)
3. At what price do you think the cost is a bargain? (The inexpensive or bargain question)
4. At what price do you think the cost is too low for the quality to be good? (The too inexpensive or cheap question)

Eight price points were presented as shown in Table 3.6. Each musician respondent selected one of the eight price points for each of the four questions. Some failed to make a selection so their responses were coded as missing and dropped from the analysis. Cumulative distributions were derived for each question across all remaining respondents. The business case development team was advised to develop a business case based on a range of $229 - $265. A follow-up study should be done once the business and marketing plans are approved to determine the exact price.

3.5 Summary

I covered the early stage product design in this chapter. Conjoint analysis is useful at this stage because it helps to identify the product attributes that are important to

TABLE 3.7 This is a summary of the van Westendorp price analysis for the music page turner new product.

Classification	Price	Cum. Respondents (%)
Optimal Price Point (*OPP*)	$239.22	24.3%
Indifference Price Point (*IPP*)	$252.60	34.6%
Point of Marginal Cheapness (*PMC*)	$228.83	26.7%
Point of Marginal Expensiveness (*PME*)	$265.34	30.5%
Pricing Options Range	$228.83 – $265.34 ($36.51)	

the customers who will buy and use the product. The drawback to conjoint is that it is materialistically oriented – only attributes and their levels count for defining a product. The emotions a customer may attach to some features are ignored. The Kansei approach to product design tries to rectify this.

I also discussed developing a price range, not for the purpose of developing a final pricing strategy, but for having reasonable number for a business case. I discuss better pricing approaches in later chapters.

The next chapter takes the development of the new product to the next level – testing with customers to see if it will work and sell. A discrete choice approach, which is akin to conjoint analysis, will be the major focus of that chapter.

3.6 Appendix 3.A

3.6.1 Brief overview of the chi-square statistic

Assume you have a discrete variable measured on L levels. The Null Hypothesis is that the L proportions are equal. If the Null Hypothesis is true, then the expected frequency of cases at each level, E_i, is

$$E_i = \frac{n}{L} = n \times \frac{1}{L} = n \times p \tag{3.A.1}$$

$$i = 1, 2, \dots L \tag{3.A.2}$$

where n is the sample size and p is the proportion in each cell. The factor $p = 1/L$ is the proportion in each level which is a constant if the Null Hypothesis is true. The test compares the observed frequency, N_i, at each level to the expected frequency, E_i. The two frequencies should be equal except for random error, which should be small. The χ^2 test statistic is

$$\chi^2 = \sum_{i=1}^{L} \frac{(N_i - E_i)^2}{E_i}. \tag{3.A.3}$$

This follows an asymptotic chi-square distribution with $L - 1$ degrees-of-freedom. The p-value for this test statistic indicates the significance. As a rule-of-thumb (ROT) for most statistical tests, a p-value $< \alpha$, where $\alpha = 0.05$ is the typical level of significance, indicates significance. This p-value is only for the upper tail of the chi-square distribution since only large values of the chi-square contradict the Null Hypothesis. This test is called the *Pearson Chi-square Test*. The chi-square density is illustrated in Figure 3.17. The hypothesis tests are shown in Figure 3.18.

The χ^2 test can be expanded to test independence of two factors. For example, a sample of customers could be shown four prototypes for a new product and then asked which one they would most likely purchase. The prototype designers want to know if there is any association between the prototype selected and income level. Suppose income is simply divided into three categories: $< \$40K$, $\$41K$ - $\$60K$, and $\$60K+$. The first factor, income, has three levels and the second factor, the prototype selected, has four levels. This results in a two-way table called a *contingency table* which consists of counts or *frequencies* of each combination of the two factors. If the first factor which defines the rows has I levels and the second which defines the columns has J levels, then the contingency table is of size $I \times J$. For this example, the table is 3×4. A contingency table is shown in Table 3.8.

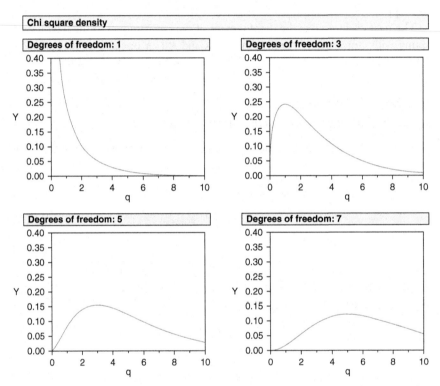

FIGURE 3.17 The density curve for the chi-square distribution varies as the number of degrees-of-freedom. Notice the curve starts as a negative exponential but then quickly morphs into a right-skewed distribution and then begins to look like a normal distribution.

TABLE 3.8 This example contingency table shows the frequency counts of 650 customers who were asked to select one of four prototype products and their income level.

Income	Prototype Selected			
	A	B	C	D
< $40K	30	50	51	20
$41K - $60K	30	40	45	35
$60K+	90	60	104	95

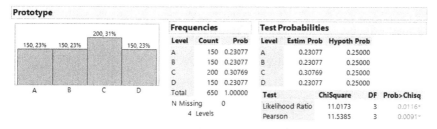

Frequencies			Test Probabilities		
Level	Count	Prob	Level	Estim Prob	Hypoth Prob
A	150	0.23077	A	0.23077	0.25000
B	150	0.23077	B	0.23077	0.25000
C	200	0.30769	C	0.30769	0.25000
D	150	0.23077	D	0.23077	0.25000
Total	650	1.00000			

Test	ChiSquare	DF	Prob>Chisq
Likelihood Ratio	11.0173	3	0.0116*
Pearson	11.5385	3	0.0091*

N Missing 0
4 Levels

Method: Fix hypothesized values, rescale omitted

FIGURE 3.18 Chi-square tests for differences in proportions for the four music prototypes are shown here for the Null Hypothesis that the proportions are all equal. For four levels, the expected proportion per level is 0.25. The Likelihood-ratio Chi-square is 11.0173 and the Pearson Chi-square is 11.5385. The p-values for both are below 0.05 so the Null Hypothesis is rejected by both tests.

Typically, the frequencies are converted to proportions by dividing each value in the table by the sample size, $n_{.}$. If N_{ij} is the frequency in cell ij of a contingency table, then $n = \sum_i \sum_j N_{ij}$ and $p_{ij} = {}^{N_{ij}}/_n$. The Null Hypothesis is that the row (or column) distributions are the same. This amounts to saying that there is only one distribution so you have homogeneity in the distributions. Therefore, any test of this equality is a test for homogeneity. Under independence, based on elementary probability theory, you should have an expected value for each cell of the table equal to the product of the respective row and column proportions. Let $p_{i.}$ be the marginal proportion for row i, then $p_{i.} = \sum_j p_{ij}$. Similarly for $p_{.j}$. Then:

$$E_{ij} = n \times p_{i.} \times p_{.j} \tag{3.A.4}$$

$$i = 1, \ldots, I \text{ rows} \tag{3.A.5}$$

$$j = 1, \ldots, J \text{ columns} \tag{3.A.6}$$

where $p_{i.} = \sum_{j=1}^{J} p_{ij}$ is the marginal proportion for the ith row of Table 3.8 with the dot notation indicating the summation; similarly for $p_{.j}$. The χ^2 test statistic is:

$$\chi^2 = \sum_{i=1}^{I} \sum_{j=1}^{J} \frac{(N_{ij} - E_{ij})^2}{E_{ij}}. \tag{3.A.7}$$

This follows an asymptotic chi-square distribution but with $(I-1) \times (J-1)$ degrees-of-freedom. The p-value again tells you the significance. This is still a Pearson Chi-square Test.

A second test is based on the log of the ratio of the observed to expected frequencies weighted by the observed frequencies:

$$G^2 = 2 \times \sum_{i=1}^{I} N_i \times \ln \frac{N_i}{E_i} \tag{3.A.8}$$

where the N_i and E_i are defined as above. This also follows an asymptotic chi-square distribution with $I-1$ degrees-of-freedom. This is called the *Likelihood-ratio Chi-square Test*.

A contingency table is analyzed using

$$G^2 = 2 \times \sum_{i=1}^{I} \sum_{j=1}^{J} N_{ij} \times \ln \frac{N_{ij}}{E_{ij}}. \qquad (3.A.9)$$

This is also a Likelihood-ratio Chi-square Test.

Figure 3.19 shows the chi-square test results for the data in Table 3.8.

Let me discuss the Pearson Chi-square statistic from a matrix perspective. I change the notation I use because matrix notation is used in Appendix B for correspondence analysis. So this section sets the stage for that discussion.

Consider a $I \times J$ matrix $\mathbf{N}$ of the non-negative frequencies. This could be a crosstab of two measures. If $\mathbf{1}_r$ is a I element column vector of 1s, the size of the vector corresponding to the number of rows of $\mathbf{N}$, and $\mathbf{1}_c$ is a J element column vector of 1s corresponding to the columns of $\mathbf{N}$, then the sample size is

$$n = \mathbf{1}_r^{\mathsf{T}} \mathbf{N} \mathbf{1}_c. \qquad (3.A.10)$$

The frequency matrix is converted to a matrix of proportions, $\mathbf{P}$, by dividing each element of $\mathbf{N}$ by the sample size, n, so that:

$$\mathbf{P} = \frac{1}{n}\mathbf{N}. \qquad (3.A.11)$$

The matrix $\mathbf{P}$ is called the *correspondence matrix*. The data for the example crosstab table are shown in the *Basic Data* portion of Figure 3.20.

Define the *row masses* as the values on the row margin of the matrix, one mass per row. The collection of row masses is the row marginal distribution. These masses are given by

$$\mathbf{r} = \mathbf{P}\mathbf{1}_c \qquad (3.A.12)$$

where $\mathbf{r}$ is $I \times 1$. Similarly, you can define the column masses, or column marginal distribution, as

$$\mathbf{c} = \mathbf{P}^{\mathsf{T}}\mathbf{1}_r \qquad (3.A.13)$$

which is $J \times 1$. The matrix product, $\mathbf{r}\mathbf{c}^{\mathsf{T}}$ is the matrix of expected proportions under independence.

The masses are collected into two diagonal matrices, one for rows, $\mathbf{D}_r$ which is $I \times I$, and the other for columns, $\mathbf{D}_c$ which is $J \times J$. The masses for the example crosstab table are shown in the *Masses* portion of Figure 3.22 and the corresponding diagonal matrices are in the *Diagonal Matrices of Masses* portion of the figure.

These pieces are combined into one $I \times J$ matrix of standardized residuals:

$$\mathbf{S} = \mathbf{D}_r^{-1/2}(\mathbf{P} - \mathbf{r}\mathbf{c}^{\mathsf{T}})\mathbf{D}_c^{-1/2}. \qquad (3.A.14)$$

Residuals are the difference between the matrix of observed proportions and the expected proportions under independence. This matrix is shown in the *Residuals*

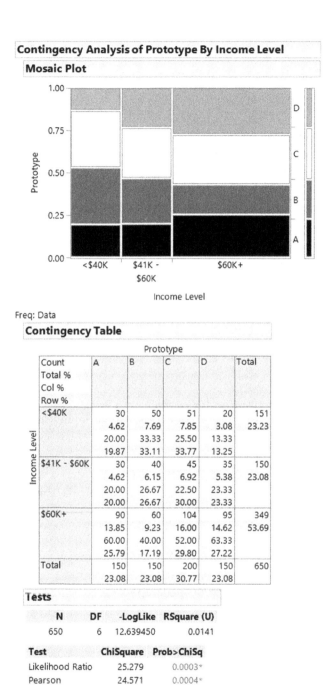

Contingency Analysis of Prototype By Income Level

Mosaic Plot

Freq: Data

Contingency Table

Prototype

Count Total % Col % Row %	A	B	C	D	Total
<$40K	30 4.62 20.00 19.87	50 7.69 33.33 33.11	51 7.85 25.50 33.77	20 3.08 13.33 13.25	151 23.23
$41K - $60K	30 4.62 20.00 20.00	40 6.15 26.67 26.67	45 6.92 22.50 30.00	35 5.38 23.33 23.33	150 23.08
$60K+	90 13.85 60.00 25.79	60 9.23 40.00 17.19	104 16.00 52.00 29.80	95 14.62 63.33 27.22	349 53.69
Total	150 23.08	150 23.08	200 30.77	150 23.08	650

Tests

N	DF	-LogLike	RSquare (U)
650	6	12.639450	0.0141

Test	ChiSquare	Prob>ChiSq
Likelihood Ratio	25.279	0.0003*
Pearson	24.571	0.0004*

FIGURE 3.19 These are the results of the two chi-square tests for the contingency table in Table 3.8. The table is reproduced as part of the output. The table shows the frequency counts and the proportions which are the frequencies divided by the sample size, $n =$ 650. The Likelihood-ratio Chi-square is 25.279 and the Pearson Chi-square is 24.571. The respective p-values are both less than 0.05 so the Null Hypothesis is rejected by both tests.

Basic Data

Frequency Table (N)				Sample Size (n)
30	50	51	20	650
30	40	45	35	
90	60	104	95	

Masses

Rows (r)	Columns (c)	Expected Values (n*r*c')			
0.232	0.231	34.8462	34.8462	46.4615	34.8462
0.231	0.231	34.6154	34.6154	46.1538	34.6154
0.537	0.308	80.5385	80.5385	107.3846	80.5385
	0.231				

Diagonal Matrices of Masses

Rows (Dr)			Columns (Dc)			
0.232	0	0	0.231	0	0	0
0	0.231	0	0	0.231	0	0
0	0	0.537	0	0	0.308	0
			0	0	0	0.231

Residuals

Residuals (P - rc')				Standardized (S)				Cell Deviations (n*Residuals)			
-0.007456	0.0233136	0.0069822	-0.02284	-0.032201	0.1006906	0.0261159	-0.098646	-4.846	15.154	4.538	-14.846
-0.007101	0.008284	-0.001775	0.0005917	-0.030769	0.0358974	-0.006662	0.0025641	-4.615	5.385	-1.154	0.385
0.0145562	-0.031598	-0.005207	0.0222485	0.0413527	-0.089766	-0.012811	0.0632057	9.462	-20.538	-3.385	14.462

Summary Data

Cell Chi-Squares (n*[S^2])				Pearson Chi-Square
0.674	6.59	0.443	6.325	24.571
0.615	0.838	0.029	0.004	
1.112	5.238	0.107	2.597	

FIGURE 3.20 This report illustrates the calculation of a Pearson Chi-square calculation. The Basic Data Frequency Table at the top corresponds to the Contingency Table in Table 3.8. Note that the Pearson Chi-square value (24.571) matches the value in Table 3.8.

portion of Figure 3.22. If **S** is squared and multiplied by the sample size, n, the result is the matrix of Pearson Chi-square values for each cell of the crosstab. That is,

$$Chi-square = n\mathbf{S}^2. \qquad (3.A.15)$$

The observation that these are the chi-square values is based on the discussion above. The sum of these chi-square values is then the Pearson Chi-square for the crosstab table.

3.7 Appendix 3.B

3.7.1 Brief overview of correspondence analysis

The mathematics of correspondence analysis can be a little challenging because it mostly relies on matrix algebra. The main matrix algebra tool is the Singular Value Decomposition (*SVD*) outlined in the Appendix to Chapter 2. Recall from that discussion that the *SVD* method decomposes a matrix **A** of size $n \times p$ into three parts which, when multiplied together return the original matrix $\mathbf{A}$:

$$\mathbf{A} = \mathbf{U}\mathbf{\Sigma}\mathbf{V}^\mathsf{T} \tag{3.B.1}$$

where

- $\mathbf{U}$ is an $n \times n$ orthogonal matrix such that $\mathbf{U}^\mathsf{T}\mathbf{U} = \mathbf{I}$ where $\mathbf{I}$ is $n \times n$;
- $\mathbf{\Sigma}$ is an $n \times r$ diagonal matrix such that $\mathbf{\Sigma} = diagonal(\sigma_1, \sigma_2, \dots, \sigma_n)$; the diagonal values are the singular values; and
- $\mathbf{V}^\mathsf{T}$ is an $r \times p$ orthogonal matrix such that $\mathbf{V}^\mathsf{T}\mathbf{V} = \mathbf{I}$ where $\mathbf{I}$ is $p \times p$.

The following is based on Greenacre [2007] which is the definitive presentation and development of correspondence analysis.

A $I \times J$ matrix $\mathbf{S}$ of standardized residuals is the basis for correspondence analysis. The Singular Value Decomposition (*SVD*) is applied to $\mathbf{S}$ to give

$$\mathbf{S} = \mathbf{U}\mathbf{\Lambda}\mathbf{V}^\mathsf{T}. \tag{3.B.2}$$

The *SVD* is shown in the *SVD Components* portion of Figure 3.22. The matrix $\mathbf{\Lambda}$ is a $I \times J$ diagonal matrix with elements in descending order. The diagonal elements are *singular values*. The left matrix, $\mathbf{U}$, is $I \times I$ and provides information about the rows of the original crosstab. The right matrix, $\mathbf{V}^\mathsf{T}$, is $I \times J$ and provides information about the columns of the crosstab.

The main output of a correspondence analysis is a *map* which means that plotting coordinates are needed. Since the crosstab is rows by columns, a set of plotting coordinates is needed for the rows and another set is needed for the columns. These are given as functions of the *SVD* components. The row coordinates are designated as $\mathbf{\Phi}$ and are based on

$$\mathbf{\Phi} = \mathbf{D}_r^{-1/2}\mathbf{U} \tag{3.B.3}$$

while the column coordinates, designated as $\mathbf{\Gamma}$, are based on

$$\mathbf{\Gamma} = \mathbf{D}_c^{-1/2}\mathbf{V}. \tag{3.B.4}$$

These sets are sometimes called the *Standard Row Coordinates* and the *Standard Column Coordinates*, respectively. For plotting purposes, however, these are usually adjusted as

$$\mathbf{F} = \mathbf{\Phi}\mathbf{\Lambda} \tag{3.B.5}$$

and

$$\mathbf{G} = \mathbf{\Gamma}\mathbf{\Lambda}. \tag{3.B.6}$$

These are the *Principal Row Coordinates* and *Principal Column Coordinates*, respective. These are shown in the *Coordinates* section of Figure 3.22. The full correspondence analysis for the example crosstab is shown in Figure 3.21. Notice that the plotting coordinates agree with the principal coordinates in Figure 3.21.

The *SVD* provides more information than just the plotting coordinates. It also provides measures of the amount of variation in the table explained by the dimensions. These are the *inertias*. The inertia is the variation in the crosstab. See Greenacre and Korneliussen [2017].

It can be shown that the singular values from the *SVD* of the crosstab are related to the Pearson Chi-square value. The singular values are usually arranged in descending order with the corresponding eigenvectors appropriately arranged. The square of a singular value is called the inertia of the table where the concept of inertia comes from the physics of a rigid body. In particular, it is the force or torque necessary to change the angular momentum of the rigid body. The formula for moment of inertia and variance are the same, hence in the correspondence literature the variance of the table is referred to as the inertia.[16] There is a singular value for each dimension extracted from the crosstab table where the total number of dimensions that could be extracted is $d = min(r-1, c-1)$ for r rows and c columns of the table. The singular value for each dimension is SV_i.

If λ_i is the inertia for the ith dimension, then $\lambda = \sum_{i=1}^{d} \lambda_i$. It can be shown that $\lambda_i = SV_i^2$ so $\lambda = \sum_{i=1}^{d} SV_i^2$. It can also be shown that the total chi-square of the table is $\chi^2 = N \times \lambda$ where N is the total sample size. This means that $\chi_i^2 = N \times \lambda_i$. From Figure 3.13, you have the data in Table 3.9.

3.8 Appendix 3.C

3.8.1 Very brief overview of ordinary least squares analysis

Assume there is one dependent variable arranged as a $n \times 1$ vector $\mathbf{Y}$. Also assume there are $p \geq 1$ independent variables arranged in a $n \times (p+1)$ matrix $\mathbf{X}$ where the first column consists of 1s for the constant term. Then a model is

$$\mathbf{Y} = \mathbf{X}\beta + \epsilon \qquad (3.C.1)$$

where β is a $(p+1) \times 1$ vectors of parameters to be estimated with the first element as the constant, and ϵ is a $n \times 1$ vector of random disturbance terms. It is usually

TABLE 3.9 This table illustrates the calculations for the inertia values for the correspondence analysis.

Dimension	SV_i	$\lambda_i = SV_i^2$	$\chi_i^2 = N \times \lambda_i$	$Percent = \dfrac{\chi_i^2}{\chi^2}$	Cumulative Percent
1	0.14457	0.02090	89.873	97.04	97.04
2	0.02524	0.00064	2,740	2.96	100.00
Total		0.02154	92.613	100.00	

$N = 4300$ from Figure 3.5
$\chi^2 = 92.613$ from Figure 3.14.

Correspondence Analysis

Select dimension [Dimension 1] [Dimension 2]

Details

Singular Value	Inertia	ChiSquare	Percent	Cumulative Percent	20 40 60 80
0.19015	0.03616	23.503	95.65	95.65	
0.04053	0.00164	1.068	4.35	100.00	

Row and Column Coordinates

X	Category	Dimension 1	Dimension 2	Y	Category	Dimension 1	Dimension 2
Income Level	<$40K	0.3028	-0.0356	Prototype	A	-0.1156	-0.0513
Income Level	$41K - $60K	0.0681	0.0726	Prototype	B	0.2891	0.0290
Income Level	$60K+	-0.1603	-0.0158	Prototype	C	0.0483	-0.0236
				Prototype	D	-0.2379	0.0538

Contingency Table

Count Total %		Prototype				Total
		A	B	C	D	
Income Level	<$40K	30	50	51	20	151
		4.62	7.69	7.85	3.08	23.23
	$41K -	30	40	45	35	150
		4.62	6.15	6.92	5.38	23.08
	$60K+	90	60	104	95	349
		13.85	9.23	16.00	14.62	53.69
Total		150	150	200	150	650
		23.08	23.08	30.77	23.08	100.00

Tests for Independence

N	DF	-LogLike	RSquare (U)
650	6	12.639450	0.0141

Test	ChiSquare	Prob>ChiSq
Likelihood Ratio	25.279	0.0003*
Pearson	24.571	0.0004*

FIGURE 3.21 this is a comprehensive correspondence analysis report for the example prototype table Figure 3.20.

assumed that $\epsilon_i \sim \mathcal{N}(0,\sigma^2), \forall i$; $cov(\epsilon_i, \epsilon_j) = 0, i \neq j$; and $cov(\epsilon_i, \mathcal{X}_{\geq}) = 0, \forall i$. Then least squares estimation theory shows that an estimator for the parameters is:

$$\hat{\beta} = (\mathbf{X}^\top \mathbf{X})^{-1} \mathbf{X}^\top \mathbf{Y}. \tag{3.C.2}$$

Basic Data

Frequency Table (N)				Sample Size (n)	Correspondence Table (P)			
30	50	51	20	650	0.0462	0.0769	0.0785	0.0308
30	40	45	35		0.0462	0.0615	0.0692	0.0538
90	60	104	95		0.1385	0.0923	0.16	0.1462

Masses

Rows (r)	Columns (c)	Expected Values (n*r*c')			
0.232	0.231	34.8462	34.8462	46.4615	34.8462
0.231	0.231	34.6154	34.6154	46.1538	34.6154
0.537	0.308	80.5385	80.5385	107.3846	80.5385
	0.231				

Diagonal Matrices of Masses

Rows (Dr)			Columns (Dc)			
0.232	0	0	0.231	0	0	0
0	0.231	0	0	0.231	0	0
0	0	0.537	0	0	0.308	0
			0	0	0	0.231

Residuals

Residuals (P - rc')				Standardized (S)				Cell Deviations (n*Residuals)			
-0.007456	0.0233136	0.0069822	-0.02284	-0.032201	0.1006906	0.0261159	-0.098646	-4.846	15.154	4.538	-14.846
-0.007101	0.008284	-0.001775	0.0005917	-0.030769	0.0358974	-0.006662	0.0025641	-4.615	5.385	-1.154	0.385
0.0145562	-0.031598	-0.005207	0.0222485	0.0413527	-0.089766	-0.012811	0.0632057	9.462	-20.538	-3.385	14.462

SVD Components

Left Matrix (U)			Singular Values (LAMBDA)	Right Matrix (V)		
0.767	-0.423	0.482	0.19	-0.292	-0.608	0.269
0.172	0.86	0.48	0.041	0.73	0.344	0.34
-0.618	-0.286	0.733	0	0.141	-0.323	0.772
				-0.601	0.638	0.464

Coordinates

Standard						Principal					
Rows (phi)			Columns (gamma)			Rows (F)			Columns (G)		
1.5922	-0.8772	1	-0.6081	-1.2665	0.5593	0.3028	-0.0356	0	-0.1156	-0.0513	0
0.3385	1.7902	1	1.5205	0.7162	0.7087	0.0681	0.0726	0	0.2891	0.029	0
-0.8429	-0.3899	1	0.2542	-0.5831	1.3922	-0.1603	-0.0158	0	0.0483	-0.0236	0
			-1.2512	1.3278	0.9664				-0.2379	0.0538	0

Summary Data

Singular Values	Inertias (lambda)	Chi-Square (chisq)	Pearson Chi-Square
0.19	0.03616	23.503	24.571
0.041	0.00164	1.068	
0	0	0	

FIGURE 3.22 These are the details for the Singular Value Decomposition calculations for the correspondence analysis in Figure 3.21.

It is easy to show that

$$\hat{\beta} = (\mathbf{X}^T\mathbf{X})^{-1}\mathbf{X}^T\mathbf{Y}$$
$$= (\mathbf{X}^T\mathbf{X})^{-1}\mathbf{X}^T\mathbf{X}\beta + (\mathbf{X}^T\mathbf{X})^{-1}\mathbf{X}^T\epsilon$$
$$= \beta + (\mathbf{X}^T\mathbf{X})^{-1}\mathbf{X}^T\epsilon.$$

Then $E(\hat{\beta}) = \beta$ and $V(\hat{\beta}) = \sigma^2 \times (\mathbf{X}^T\mathbf{X})^{-1}$.

See Greene [2003] for a detailed development of this result. Also see Goldberger [1964] for a classic derivation. If there is perfect multicollinearity, then the $\mathbf{X}^T\mathbf{X}$ matrix cannot be inverted and the parameters cannot be estimated.

3.8.2 Brief overview of principal components analysis

Principal components analysis works by finding a transformation of the $\mathbf{X}$ matrix into a new matrix such that the column vectors of the new matrix are uncorrelated.

An important first step in principal components analysis is to mean-center the data. This involves finding the mean for each variable and then subtracting these means from their respective variable. This has the effect of removing any large values that could negatively impact results. To mean-center, let $\mathbf{X}$ be the $n \times p$ matrix of variables. Let $\mathbf{1}_n$ be a column vector with a 1 for each element so that $\mathbf{1}_n$ is $n \times 1$. Then a $1 \times p$ row vector of means is given by

$$\mathbf{M}_X = \mathbf{1}_n^{\mathsf{T}} \mathbf{X} (\mathbf{1}_n^{\mathsf{T}} \mathbf{1}_n)^{-1}$$

where $(\mathbf{1}_n^{\mathsf{T}} \mathbf{1}_n)^{-1} = {}^1\!/_n$. The mean-centered matrix is then

$$\tilde{\mathbf{X}} = \mathbf{X} - \mathbf{1}_n \mathbf{M}_X.$$

I can now do an *SVD* on $\tilde{\mathbf{X}}$ to get $\tilde{\mathbf{X}} = \mathbf{U}\boldsymbol{\Sigma}\mathbf{P}^{\mathsf{T}}$ where $\mathbf{U}$ and $\mathbf{P}$ are orthogonal matrices. Since $\mathbf{P}$ is orthogonal, then $\mathbf{P}\mathbf{P}^{\mathsf{T}} = \mathbf{I}$ implying that $\mathbf{P}^{\mathsf{T}} = \mathbf{P}^{-1}$. Similarly for $\mathbf{U}$. Let $\mathbf{T} = \mathbf{U}\boldsymbol{\Sigma}$ so that $\tilde{\mathbf{X}} = \mathbf{T}\mathbf{P}^{\mathsf{T}}$. Then $\tilde{\mathbf{X}}\mathbf{P} = \mathbf{T}\mathbf{P}^{\mathsf{T}}\mathbf{P}$ or $\mathbf{T} = \tilde{\mathbf{X}}\mathbf{P}$. The matrix $\mathbf{T}$ is the matrix of principal component scores and $\mathbf{P}$ is the matrix of principal components that transform $\tilde{\mathbf{X}}$. See Ng [2013].

Following Ng [2013], you can now write the covariance matrix for the principal component scores, $cov(\mathbf{T}, \mathbf{T})$, as

$$cov(\mathbf{T}, \mathbf{T}) = \frac{1}{n-1} \times \mathbf{T}^{\mathsf{T}}\mathbf{T}$$
$$= \frac{1}{n-1} \times (\mathbf{P}^{\mathsf{T}}\tilde{\mathbf{X}}^{\mathsf{T}})(\tilde{\mathbf{X}}\mathbf{P})$$
$$= \frac{1}{n-1} \times (\mathbf{P}^{\mathsf{T}}\tilde{\mathbf{X}}^{\mathsf{T}}\tilde{\mathbf{X}}\mathbf{P})$$
$$= \mathbf{P}^{\mathsf{T}}\mathbf{S}\mathbf{P}$$

where $\mathbf{S} = {}^1\!/_{(n-1)}\tilde{\mathbf{X}}^{\mathsf{T}}\tilde{\mathbf{X}}$. The matrix $\mathbf{S}$ is a covariance matrix and is square so a spectral decomposition can be applied to get $\mathbf{S} = \mathbf{U}\mathbf{D}\mathbf{U}^{\mathsf{T}}$. Then,

$$cov(\mathbf{T}, \mathbf{T}) = \mathbf{P}^{\mathsf{T}}\mathbf{S}\mathbf{P}$$
$$= \mathbf{P}^{\mathsf{T}}\mathbf{U}\mathbf{D}\mathbf{U}^{\mathsf{T}}\mathbf{P}.$$

Let $\mathbf{P} = \mathbf{U}$, then

$$cov(\mathbf{T}, \mathbf{T}) = \mathbf{P}^{\mathsf{T}}\mathbf{P}\mathbf{D}\mathbf{P}^{\mathsf{T}}\mathbf{P}$$
$$= \mathbf{D}.$$

Since $\mathbf{D}$ is diagonal, the diagonal elements are the variances and they are in decreasing order. Also, since $\mathbf{D}$ is diagonal, the off-diagonal elements are all zero implying independence. Finally, as noted by Lay [2012], the matrix of principal components, $\mathbf{P}$, makes the covariance matrix for the scores diagonal.

Without loss of generality, the columns of **T** are arranged in descending order of the variance explained so that the first column explains the most variance in **X**, the second column explains the second most variation, and so forth. That is,

$$\mathbf{T} = \mathbf{XP} \tag{3.C.3}$$

where **P** is an $p \times p$ transformation matrix called the *principal components* and **T** is the resulting $n \times p$ matrix of *principal components scores* resulting from the transformation. Usually, only the first $k < p$ columns of **T** are needed since they account for most of the variation in **X**. This reduced matrix can be denoted as $\mathbf{T}_k$. In principal components regression, the reduced matrix $\mathbf{T}_k$ replaces the matrix **X** in the *OLS* formulation.

See Jolliffe [2002] for the definitive treatment of principal components analysis.

3.8.3 Principal components regression analysis

Principal components regression analysis involves using the principal components scores as the independent variables in a regression model. The columns of this score matrix are orthogonal by construction so multicollinearity is not an issue. If **Y** is a column vector for the dependent variable, then the model is $\mathbf{Y} = \mathbf{T}\beta$, ignoring the disturbance term vector for simplicity, and *OLS* can be used.

3.8.4 Brief overview of partial least squares analysis

Partial least squares (*PLS*), initially developed by Wold [1966b], works by finding linear combinations of independent variables, called *manifest variables*, which are directly observable. The linear combinations are latent or hidden in the data and are sometimes called *factors*, *components* (as in *PCA*), *latent vectors*, or *latent variables*. The factors should be independent of each other and account for most of the variance of **Y**. This is akin to principal components analysis. *PLS* uses the result that **X** can be decomposed into $\mathbf{X} = \mathbf{TP}^{\mathsf{T}}$ as shown above. The vector **T** is the score vector for **X**. In particular, a single linear combination or factor can be extracted from the **X** matrix, say **t**, which is one of many such possible factors. This factor represents a reduced combination of the variables in **X** which means it can be used in regression models for predicting **X** and **Y**. Let the predictions be $\hat{\mathbf{X}}_0$ and $\hat{\mathbf{Y}}_0$. The subscript "0" on both predictions indicates that this is the base or initial prediction. The two predictions are based on *OLS* estimations using the *OLS* estimation formula from above. In this case, the extracted factor, **t**, is the independent variable and $\hat{\mathbf{X}}_0$ and $\hat{\mathbf{Y}}_0$ are the dependent variables. The prediction for $\mathbf{X}_0$ is given by $\hat{\mathbf{X}}_0 = \mathbf{t}(\mathbf{t}^{\mathsf{T}}\mathbf{t})^{-1}\mathbf{t}^{\mathsf{T}}\mathbf{X}_0$. Similarly, $\hat{\mathbf{Y}}_0 = \mathbf{t}(\mathbf{t}^{\mathsf{T}}\mathbf{t})^{-1}\mathbf{t}^{\mathsf{T}}\mathbf{Y}_0$.

The factor **t** as a linear combination of the manifest independent variables is important. This is, however, only one factor combination out of many possible combinations. The combination used should meet a criterion and this is that the factor for **X** should have the maximum covariance with a factor extracted for **Y**. The extracted factor for **Y** is $\mathbf{u} = \mathbf{Y}_0\mathbf{q}$. The covariance is $cov(t, u) = \mathbf{t}^{\mathsf{T}}\mathbf{u}$. So the objective is to extract factors (or latent linear combinations of manifest indepen-dent and dependent variables) such that the covariance between them is as large as possible.

Once the first pair of factors are extracted, you have to find another pair that meets the same criterion. You cannot, however, have the first set be used again so they have to be deleted. This is done by subtraction, thus creating two new matrices. That is, you now have $\mathbf{X}_1 = \mathbf{X}_0 - \hat{\mathbf{X}}_0$ and $\mathbf{Y}_1 = \mathbf{Y}_0 - \hat{\mathbf{Y}}_0$. This is sometimes referred to as "partialing out" the effect of a factor. The process outlined above is repeated using these two new matrices. The overall process of doing *OLS* regres-sions and partialing out the predicted values is continued until either you reach a desired number of extracted factors or no more factors can be extracted. The com-bination of *OLS* regressions and partialing out predicted values is the basis of the name *partial least squares*.[17]

Since predicted values are partialed out of both the $\mathbf{X}$ and $\mathbf{Y}$ matrices, an iterative algorithm can be specified. This is usually written as four successive steps from $i = 0, 1, \ldots, n$ where n is the maximum number of iterations of the algorithm:

1. Estimate the $\mathbf{X}$ weights as $\mathbf{w} = \mathbf{X}_i^\top \mathbf{u}(\mathbf{u}^\top \mathbf{u})^{-1}$
2. Estimate the $\mathbf{X}$ factor scores as $\mathbf{t} = \mathbf{X}_i \mathbf{w}$
3. Estimate the $\mathbf{Y}$ weights as $\mathbf{c} = \mathbf{Y}_i^\top \mathbf{t}(\mathbf{t}^\top \mathbf{t})^{-1}$
4. Estimate the $\mathbf{Y}$ factor scores as $\mathbf{c} = \mathbf{Y}_i \mathbf{c}$

Stop the iterations either when the number of desired iterations (i.e., factors) is reached or no more factors can be extracted as determined by a convergence crite-rion.[18] The SAS Proc PLS implementation uses a default of $n = 200$ iterations and a default convergence criterion of 10^{-12}.

The algorithm outlined here is called the *NIPALS Algorithm* which stands for "Nonlinear Iterative Partial Least Squares." It was developed by Wold [1966a]. An alternative algorithm is *SIMPLS*. See de Jong [1993] for a discussion.

There are software packages that implement this *PLS* algorithm. SAS has *Proc PLS* and JMP has a partial least squares platform. The book by Cox and Gaudard [2013] gives an excellent overview of *PLS* using JMP.

An interesting history of *PLS* is provided by Gaston Sanchez: "The Saga of PLS" at sagaofpls.github.io.

Notes

1 A "no selection" option is often included so that the respondents are not forced to select anything from a choice set if nothing appeals to them.
2 In some conjoint studies, all the products are presented at once and respondents are asked to rank them in terms of their preference. I do not like or advocate this approach because it becomes impractical if the number of products become moderately large of if they are similar.
3 See   https://performingarts.uncg.edu/patech/airturn-vs-pageflip-cicada-a-bluetooth-pedal-showdown/   and   www.musicnotes.com/now/tips/the-3-best-hands-free-page-

turners/ for commentary on devices with these, and other, features. Also see *Page turning solutions for musicians: A survey* pdf file in Notes

4   The term "runs" comes from the design of experiments literature.

5   See Paczkowski [2016] and Paczkowski [2018] for an explanation.

6   Dummy coding is also called *indicator coding*. In the machine language literature, it is called *one-hot encoding*.

7   Source: https://en.wikipedia.org/wiki/Semantic_differential#Use_of_adjectives

8   The concept of a data cube is foundational to relational database design and management. See my discussion in Chapter 7 as well as Lemahieu et al. [2018].

9   Recall that for two levels, two dummy variables can be created, but only one is needed to avoid the dummy variable trap. Hence, there is only one dummy variable per attribute for my example.

10   The idea of an offset from one end, say the beginning, is not unique. It also appears in many programming languages. The Python package called Pandas, for example, has data tables, called DataFrames, for which the rows are indexed beginning at zero. The zero indicate that the row is 0 rows from the beginning; the row indexed by 1, which is the second row, means the row is offset from the beginning by 1 row.

11   This is based on Chuang et al. [2001].

12   Based on my experience at Bell Labs, we often created mock-ups of new service concepts that were used in customer testing. The actual services were too far from actual development so using something from the development team was not practical. The mock-up served a good purpose. See "AT&T Test Kitchen" in *CIO Magazine* (May 15, 1994).

13   See www.ipsos-ideas.com/article.cfm?id=2166 for some discussion of these definitions.

14   Some refer to this as the "normal" price in the market.

15   These descriptions are from Paczkowski [2018]. Permission to use granted by Routledge.

16   See https://stats.stackexchange.com/questions/85436/what-could-it-mean-to-rotate-a-distribution. Also see https://en.wikipedia.org/wiki/Variance. Both last accessed on February 9, 2019.

17   There is some controversy regarding what "partial" really means. See the discussion at https://stats.stackexchange.com/questions/135527/what-is-the-partial-in-partial-least-squares-methods, last accessed March 1, 2019.

18   The convergence criterion is based on the difference $\mathbf{X}_i - \mathbf{X}_{i-1}$.

4
TEST

Will it work and sell?

Once there is a design that is believed will meet customer requirements and, therefore, will sell in the market, it may seem the work is done. The new product must now just be produced (a manufacturing, not a new product development, issue) and then sold (a sales issue). But this is not the end. The design must still be tested before being manufactured and launched because it could still fail in the market. As I noted in Chapter 1, 80% of new products fail soon after launch. So product failure is more the norm and not the exception. Pre-launch testing will not guarantee success but it will help reduce or minimize the probability of failure. Pre-launch testing, of course, is costly and these costs will increase in direct proportion to the amount of testing which could kill a product before its launch. The testing costs consist of prototype or description production, test subject recruiting (someone has to use the product in a test), test design, test implementation, test surveillance (for security and confidentiality), and results analytics, interpretation, and reporting. An excessive amount of testing could also delay launch since testing also requires time so the product is then late to market. The competition is then given a window of opportunity that your product may never be able to close. This is another cost of testing.

Despite these costs, pre-launch testing actually serves several purposes. Since the product has not been launched, there is still time to hone and refine the product concept. Have the settings for all the product attributes, those identified as the most critical for customers, been properly set? What should the price point be now that this has to be set for launch? In many instances, what name should be attached to the product? And how will the product fare against competitive products? What market share can be expected? What volume can be expected? These are all pre-launch questions.

There are two forms of pre-launch testing that, in one instance, could be used separately but in another could be used jointly. The first form is discrete choice modeling and the second is market testing. The former is an econometric analysis procedure with a well-established methodology. The second is a more traditional way of testing: put the product in the market and see what happens. The problem with this latter approach is that many intervening market forces will impact customers' purchase decisions about the product, just as in real market settings, as well as for other products; both the new product and competitive products are affected. This may produce unwanted sales impacts. For instance, a new consumer product will have to be sold in a retail store. This new product could adversely impact all sales of the store which means the merchant has to be compensated for any losses.

A better approach is to combine the two in a controlled setting. At the AT&T Consumer Lab[1] mentioned in the Preface, consumers were brought into a lab setting and given a new product or, in most instances, a prototype of the new product to touch, look at, and use (if possible with a prototype). The potentially expensive market test was avoided. Once the consumers had examined the new product, they were surveyed about their opinions and in many instances were asked to complete discrete choice exercises regarding the product. A variation of this approach is sometimes called a *clinic* which I describe below.

This chapter is divided into six sections. In the first, I discuss discrete choice analysis for determining take rates (i.e., expected market share), expected volume sold, and willingness-to-pay. This constitutes an experimental approach to market testing. The second section is focused on actual market testing, primarily in hands-on clinics. I discuss issues associated with clinics and some ways to analyze data. The third section is devoted to market segmentation for more focused testing. The fourth section deals with multiple versions of a product, not just testing them but determining which combination should be marketed. This is *TURF* analysis applied to product testing. The fifth section contains the usual software discussion while the sixth section is a summary.

4.1 Discrete choice analysis

In this section, I will describe the fundamental principles for a *discrete choice study*. A study is called "discrete choice" because a customer is observed to choose one product over one or more other products in some type of setting, hence the choice is discrete. The setting could be part of a market research survey so the choice is a *stated preference choice*: the customer states his or her preference for one product over another. This framework was developed to mimic actual market choices in a consumer market in which a consumer goes to a store, sees several products on a store shelf (e.g., cereals) and selects just one to buy on that shopping occasion.

Another setting could be in an actual market (e.g., a grocery store) so the consumer reveals his/her preference for one product over another. This is a *revealed preference choice*. If the store is, again, a grocery store and the product is cereal, then a consumer is observed to select one cereal over another from the store shelf. This might seem comparable to the market studies I just mentioned. There is a difference, though. In a market test study, sales are tracked in the same manner as a post-launch tracking study which I discuss in Chapter 7. In a revealed preference study, however, only the selection is analyzed; not the unit sales. The end result is the same: product performance. The approach is different.

A stated preference choice study is common in market research. Paczkowski [2018] provides a good, complete discussion of stated preference market research studies. For a theoretical discussion and application to revealed preference choice studies, see Train [2009]. In some instances, revealed and stated preference studies are combined. See Paczkowski [2018] for a brief discussion. Regardless of the setting, the underlying principles are the same and it is these principles that I will discuss in the next subsection.

4.1.1 Product configuration vs. competitive offerings

A central concept in a discrete choice study is the *choice set* containing discrete product options presented to a customer. The product options are typically some composition or configuration of the new product as well as competitor products. Each product, new and competitor, consists of a collection of product attributes or characteristics much like the conjoint attributes I described in Chapter 3. Examples of attributes are size, weight, form, portability, warranty, brand name, and, of course, price. Each attribute has specified levels. If weight is an attribute, its levels could be 1 ounce, 3 ounces, 5 ounces. In a stated preference choice study, the attribute levels are prespecified both for the new product and the competitive products. They are then arranged using statistical design of experiment principles to create choice sets, each set consisting of one variant of each product. It may be difficult to vary attribute levels for a competitive product simply because that product is not under the control of the market researcher. They could, however, artificially change some features they believe the competitor might change in the future based on competitive analysis and assessments. The price point is an easy example. Size is another, especially if there is a history of size changes or competitive market forces are pushing for, say, smaller sizes.

A revealed preference choice study is more difficult to design because product attributes cannot be easily changed. It may be possible to manipulate price points, but other attributes may be impossible. Some creative methods have to be devised to artificially change them after data are collected by calculating new variables that will change. In transportation mode studies, for example, price per commute time can be calculated where the price of a ticket does not change. The commute time from different stations and by time-of-day and day-of-week, however, do change so the price per commute time will change.

Several choice sets are typically created that meet desirable criteria. One criterion is that no product clearly dominates others in the same choice set. Suppose the attributes for all products are weight, size, and price point. If all products in a single set have the same weight and size but one has the lowest price, then that lowest priced product will always be selected by consumers; it would dominate all others and always "win." A second criterion is that the same configuration cannot repeat in a single choice set because a consumer could not distinguish between them (they are, after all, the same product) so no insight into consumer choice is gained. See Paczkowski [2018] for a discussion of choice set construction. Also see Paczkowski [2016] for an example application using the JMP software.

Once the choice sets are developed, they are presented to a customer, one set at a time. Following each presentation, the customer is asked to select his/her preferred product in the set. This is repeated for each choice set. Sometimes a likelihood to purchase question is asked after each customer choice. The idea for this follow-up question is to develop a calibration weight for choice to adjust the choices to reflect the fact that what customers say they would buy is not what they would buy if they really went to a store. In a revealed preference study, they are observed to actually make a choice and pay for it; in a stated preference study they do not pay for anything. The act of paying makes a big difference. The calibration weight is supposed to adjust for this.

4.1.2 Discrete choice background – high-level view

A discrete choice model was outlined in the above paragraphs. In the remainder of this section I will describe the model and some key output. See Paczkowski [2016] and Paczkowski [2018] for more details.

The basic model

A fundamental concept in the microeconomic theory of consumer demand is utility maximization. A consumer buys a combination of products that maximize the utility he/she receives from that combination. These products are continuous so they can be infinitely divided. The products considered in this section are not continuous: you either buy a product or not; it is not infinitely divisible. A box of cereal is purchased or not; you cannot buy half a box or a quarter of a box. The unit of measure is discrete. The utility maximization concept, however, can still be applied to the discrete product case but with modifications.

Suppose there are C consumers in a market consisting of J products. Define a measure of utility, U, for consumer i, $i = 1, \ldots, C$, for product j, $j = 1, \ldots, J$, as

$$U_{ij} = V_j + \epsilon_{ij}. \tag{4.1}$$

The term V_j is a measure of the average utility received by all consumers for product j. This is sometimes called systematic utility. Each consumer's utility for product j will differ from this average by an unobserved and unobservable random factor characteristic of the individual. The term ϵ_{ij} is a measure of this random variation. Total utility is thus composed of two parts: a systematic part, the V_j, and a random part, ϵ_{ij}. It is a random variable because of the random part of utility.

A specific product is purchased if the total utility received from it is greater than that received from any other product. That is, utility is maximized when

$$U_{ij} > U_{ik}. \tag{4.2}$$

Unfortunately, because of the random part of utility, you cannot make definitive statements about what will be purchased by an individual consumer. You can, however, make a probabilistic statement. That is, you can determine the probability a consumer, selected at random in the market, would buy product j, $j = 1, \ldots, J$. This is expressed as

$$Pr_i(j) = Pr(U_{ij} > U_{ik}), \ k \neq j. \tag{4.3}$$

Substituting (4.1) into (4.3) and rearranging terms yields

$$Pr_i(j) = Pr(V_j + \epsilon_{ij} > V_k + \epsilon_{ik}) \tag{4.4}$$

$$= Pr(\epsilon_{ik} - \epsilon_{ij} < V_j - V_k). \tag{4.5}$$

This has the form of a cumulative probability function. To complete the specification, a probability function is needed for the random components. As noted in Paczkowski [2018], three possibilities are

- Linear;
- Normal; and
- Extreme Value Type I (*Gumbel*)

distributions. The Linear distribution results in a linear model; the Normal results in a *Probit* model; the Extreme Value Type I distribution results in a *logit* model. The linear model is just *OLS*. The Probit model is popular in academic research but is a challenge to use in model estimation. The logit model is popular in market research and other practical applications because of its simplicity. Assuming the Extreme Value Type I distribution, the logit model is

$$Pr_i(j) = \frac{e^{V_j}}{\sum_{k=1}^{J} e^{V_k}}. \tag{4.6}$$

This is sometimes called a *multinomial logit choice model* (*MNL*) although this is not a good name since there is another multinomial logit model that is more complicated. A better name is a *logistic model* or *conditional logit model* (*CLOGIT*). The latter name emphasizes that the model is conditioned on the systematic utility. I often refer to the probability as a *take rate*. For a discussion of the derivation of (4.6), see Paczkowski [2018] and Train [2009]. Also see McFadden [1974] for the original discussion and derivation of the conditional logit model.

As I noted above, each product is defined by a set of attributes with each attribute defined by different levels. These attributes and their levels define the systematic utility. In particular, the systematic utility is specified as a linear function of the attributes and their levels:

$$V_j = \beta_1 \times X_{j1} + \beta_2 \times X_{j2} + \ldots + \beta_p \times X_{jp} \tag{4.7}$$

where X_{jm}, $m = 1, \ldots, p$ is the measure for attribute m for product j. The parameters, $\beta_1, \beta_2, \ldots, \beta_p$, are sometimes called part-worth utilities as in conjoint analysis. They are the same for each alternative product in the choice sets so there is just one set of part-worth utilities. This is the sense in which the choice probability is "conditional" – the probability is conditioned on the parameters being the same for all products in a choice set. See Paczkowski [2018] for some comments about this conditionality.

If the attributes are discrete, then the measures are appropriately coded dummy or effects variables. See Paczkowski [2018] for a thorough treatment of both types of coding for discrete choice as well as conjoint studies. Notice that a constant term is omitted from the systematic utility specification in (4.7). This is due to a property of this class of models called the *Equivalent Differences Property* which states that a constant factor will have no effect on the choice probability because the constant factor cancels from the numerator and denominator of the choice probability. The intercept is certainly such a constant. Sometimes you may want to have a constant in the model so this property is a potential drawback. There are ways around it which are discussed in Paczkowski [2018].

There is another property called the *Independence of Irrelevant Alternatives (IIA)*. Consider a case of just two products. The *IIA* property states that only the features of these two products count for the choice probabilities while the features of other products do not. This could be a problem or a benefit. The issues are too complex to develop here, but see Paczkowski [2018] for an extensive discussion.

The discrete choice model (4.6) is estimated using a maximum likelihood procedure. McFadden [1974] presents the details of estimation. Also see Train [2009] for an excellent discussion of estimation.

Main outputs and analyses

The estimated part-worth utilities are of some interest in a discrete choice problem just as they are in a conjoint problem because they show the importance of each level of each attribute. An attribute importance analysis could be done as for conjoint. This helps the product designers finalize their design because they would know the weight placed on each attribute. A better way to finalize the design is to recognize that the estimated part-worth utilities used in conjunction with different settings of the attributes' levels produce an estimate of the choice probability for each possible product defined by the attributes. If there are J products, then there are J probabilities. These can be interpreted as estimates of market share given the settings of the attributes. A simulator could be built that allows the product designers and the product managers to try different levels of the attributes, basically different sets of assumptions about the attributes, to determine which settings give the maximum estimated market share. Since competitive products are usually included in choice sets, a competitive scenario analysis can also be done to gauge competitive reactions and possible counter-moves. The results of these simulations would help finalize the design for launch. See Paczkowski [2018] for some mention of simulators.

Pricing and willingness-to-pay analysis

One attribute included in the choice study must certainly be the price, both for the new product and the competition's product. Marketing and pricing management could then use the simulator to test different price points, along with the settings of the other attributes, to determine the best price point for the product's launch.

There is more, however, that could be gained by including prices in a choice study. The willingness-to-pay (*WTP*) for different settings of the attributes (excluding price, of course) can be estimated. The estimated *WTP*s show the value consumers attach to each level of the product. Product managers could then determine which attributes and their levels should receive the most emphasis in the final design: those attributes and levels the consumers are willing to pay the most to get.

Since the part-worth utilities show the importance of each attribute and the levels, it stands to reason that the *WTP* should be a function of these part-worths. And they are. The actual formulation depends on the coding used for the discrete attributes. Without loss of generality, assume the price is designated as attribute 1 so β_1 is its part-worth. You should expect $\beta_1 < 0$: the higher the price, the lower the utility received. If dummy coding is used, it can be shown that the willingness-to-pay for a level m of attribute k is given by

$$WTP_{km} = -\frac{\beta_{km}}{\beta_1}.$$

The negative sign offsets the negative value of β_1 so $WTP_{km} > 0$. The *WTP* is just the scaled part-worths. If effects coding is used, then

$$WTP_{km} = -\frac{2 \times \beta_{km}}{\beta_1}.$$

A full discussion of these results and their derivations is in Paczkowski [2018].

Volumetric estimation

The estimated choice probabilities could be used to estimate total sales volume and expected revenue. To estimate volume, an estimate of the potential market size is needed. I call this the *addressable market*: the number of customers in the segments targeted for the new product. If N is the size of the addressable market and $Pr(j)$ is the estimated choice probability for product j, that is, the estimated market share for product j, then the expected sales volume is simply $N \times Pr(j)$. Given the price point used to determine the choice probability, the expected revenue is $N \times Pr(j) \times P_j$ where P_j is the price for product j. Paczkowski [2018] outlines this estimation procedure in more detail.

Software

The commercial software products that can handle discrete choice problems include JMP, SAS, Stata, and Limdep. JMP is especially good because it has platforms to handle all aspects of design, estimation, and reporting. The open source software R will also handle these problems but this will require some programming.

Case study

As a case study, consider an example used in Paczkowski [2018] of a drone manufacturer, FlyDrone Inc., that developed a new drone model targeted to hobbyists. FlyDrone's marketing team identified five attributes and their levels plus two competitive brands, Birdie Inc. and SkyFly Inc., for a total of six attributes. The attributes and their levels are:

- Price: $79.99, $99.99, $119.99
- Maximum Flight Time (in minutes): 5, 7, 9
- Integrated GPS: Yes, No
- Integrated Camera: Yes, No
- Video Resolution: 640x480, 720x576, 1280x720
- Brand: FlyDrone Inc, Birdie Inc, SkyFly Inc.

A panel of hobbyists were recruited to complete a survey of their drone use: how many drones they own; when they started using drones as a hobby; how much they paid for their drone; how often they fly it; and any plans to buy another one and at what price range.

As part of the survey, they were asked to complete a choice exercise for the new drone product. Each hobbyist was shown 12 choice sets, each set consisting of two alternative products identified by the six attributes listed above. In addition to the two products, a Neither option was included so there were really three options in each choice set. The Neither option allows the hobbyist the chance to not select one of the two products if neither is satisfactory. For each choice set, the hobbyist had to select one product or the Neither option. An example choice "card" (which actually appeared on a computer monitor) is shown in Figure 4.1.

A choice model was estimated using a maximum likelihood procedure. The dependent variable was the choice (including the Neither) for each choice set, for each hobbyist. The independent variables were the six attributes, each one effects coded. The estimated part-worth utilities are shown in Figure 4.2.

Take rates for different settings of the independent variables can be calculated in a specially written program, a spreadsheet, or with a simple hand-held calculator. The *WTP* calculations for the drone study are shown in Figure 4.3. See Paczkowski [2018] for an interpretation of these results.

Please review the following two drones and indicate the one you would most likely buy. You could select *Neither drone* if neither appeals to you.

Drone 1	
Flight time	7 Minutes
Integrated GPS	No
Integrated camera	Yes
Video resolution	720x576
Brand	SkyFly, Inc.
Price	$99.99

Drone 2	
Flight time	5 Minutes
Integrated GPS	Yes
Integrated camera	No
Video resolution	640x480
Brand	Birdie, Inc.
Price	$79.99

☐ Drone 1   ☐ Drone 2   ☐ Neither drone

FIGURE 4.1 This is an example of what a choice card presented to the drone hobbyist. Each card had two alternative products and a *Neither* option. Each hobbyist had to select one of the products or Neither. See Paczkowski [2018]. Permission to reproduce from Routledge.

Parameter Estimates

Term	Estimate	Std Error
Price[$79.99]	0.77049679	0.1103996375
Price[$99.99]	0.37311430	0.0867925613
Flight Time (Minutes)[5]	-1.21593652	0.1366752407
Flight Time (Minutes)[7]	0.28426310	0.0908197873
Integrated GPS[Yes]	1.13176337	0.1009827445
Integrated Camera[Yes]	1.18701196	0.0881097009
Video Resolution[640x480]	-1.70624332	0.1387596708
Video Resolution[720x576]	0.38107503	0.0738225339
Brand[FlyDrone Inc]	-0.23973118	0.0908926646
Brand[Birdie Inc]	0.33850802	0.0737032993
No Choice Indicator	-1.20800256	0.1125166504

AICc	1504.4171
BIC	1560.1857
-2*LogLikelihood	1482.1948
-2*Firth LogLikelihood	1424.9818

Converged in Gradient

Firth Bias-Adjusted Estimates

FIGURE 4.2 Estimated choice parameters for the drone example. See Paczkowski [2018]. Permission to reproduce from Routledge.

Willingness to Pay

Factor	Baseline Value
Price	79.99
Flight Time (Minutes)	5
Integrated GPS	No
Integrated Camera	No
Video Resolution	640x480
Brand	FlyDrone Inc

Baseline Utility
-9.4386

Factor	Feature Setting	Price Change	Std Error	Lower 95%	Upper 95%	New Price
Flight Time (Minutes)	5	$0.00	.	.	.	$79.99
Flight Time (Minutes)	7	$24.62	3.21487	$18.32	$30.92	$104.61
Flight Time (Minutes)	9	$41.05	3.67542	$33.84	$48.25	$121.04
Integrated GPS	Yes	$41.70	2.88593	$36.05	$47.36	$121.69
Integrated GPS	No	$0.00	2.88593	($5.66)	$5.66	$79.99
Integrated Camera	Yes	$48.03	3.2594	$41.64	$54.42	$128.02
Integrated Camera	No	$0.00	3.2594	($6.39)	$6.39	$79.99
Video Resolution	640x480	$0.00	3.2594	($6.39)	$6.39	$79.99
Video Resolution	720x576	$42.04	3.92523	$34.34	$49.73	$122.03
Video Resolution	1280x720	$59.38	4.43677	$50.69	$68.08	$139.37
Brand	FlyDrone Inc	$0.00	4.43677	($8.70)	$8.70	$79.99
Brand	Birdie Inc	$11.00	3.0672	$4.99	$17.01	$90.99
Brand	SkyFly Inc	$3.60	3.80256	($3.85)	$11.05	$83.59

Standard deviations for Price Change calculated by Delta method.

FIGURE 4.3 The *WTP* was calculated for each attribute for the drone example. See Paczkowski [2018]. Permission to reproduce from Routledge.

4.2 Test market hands-on analysis

Experimental testing using a discrete choice framework is definitely a cost-effective way to test a new product concept. Testing costs are lower, testing is more targeted to specific customer segments, and the new product concept is more secure from competitive discovery. More importantly, the effect of specific parameters, the attributes and their levels, can be isolated because of the use of experimental design principles. This, in fact, is the purpose of experimental designs: to allow you to isolate effects. Despite these advantages, hands-on actual market testing is still preferred by many researchers because they believe that only by observing actual market behavior can one tell if a product will not only sell but also reveal any product issues. In this section, I will discuss some ways to conduct actual market tests.

4.2.1 Live trial tests with customers

The development of a discrete choice model for "market" testing was certainly an advance in market research. Discrete choice studies are sometimes referred to as experimental choice studies simply because they are experimental. Sometimes, however, actual market tests are conducted in which a new product is placed in a market for a period of time and its performance tracked to see how it fares against the competition. It is believed that such market tests are superior to experimental tests because they involve actual market conditions.

In-field studies: advantages and disadvantages

There are some advantages and disadvantages to live market testing. A major advantage is that actual consumer purchases are observed under the same conditions that would exist when the product is finally launched. In addition, if a prototype is in the market for a sufficient period of time, enough data could be collected to allow you to build a model to forecast sales once the product is actually marketed. I comment on new product forecasting in Chapter 6.

There are disadvantages that include:

1. Signaling to the competition what the new product will be, how it will be offered, and the likely price points. Just as you monitor your competition to determine their tactical and strategic plans, so they are doing the same regarding your plans. They will become fully aware of the test offering which will allow them to develop their own new product.
2. Test marketing is expensive. Placing any new product into the market is not cost-free, so why should it be any different for a test product? Actual products have to be developed which means that manufacturing must be able to produce sufficient quantities for sale. This may require a retooling of current manufacturing operations which is typically not a trivial issue.
3. Adverse publicity could be created for the product and company if consumers do not like it or something goes dramatically wrong simply because the product is not yet ready for market introduction. The public relations damage could be devastating.
4. Customer and service representatives must be trained regarding the test product so that they are prepared for customer complaints, questions, and product failures that have to be addressed.
5. Some advertising or promotional material has to be developed for the test markets just to get the "word" out for the test product. This is also costly.

In my opinion, the experimental approach to testing a new product is a more cost-effective way to test than an actual market test.

A consumer lab setting: clinics

Some industries use a compromise between actual market tests and experimental tests. The automobile industry, for example, uses car clinics to test new car designs.[2] The concept of a clinic is not restricted to cars. It could be applied to any durable good for which consumers have to make a major purchase decision.[3] Food and beverage taste testing are also forms of clinics since consumers are brought into a controlled environment and are asked to evaluate a new product (usually several), so clinics are not restricted to durable goods.[4]

There are some issues associated with running a clinic, security being a major one. Since customers would be shown actual prototypes of a new product, they could conceivably divulge properties of the prototype. Customers should be asked to sign a nondisclosure agreement (NDA) prior to taking part in the clinic. The NDA may be difficult to enforce, however, since a specific person divulging clinic information may be difficult to identify.

An important aspect of a clinic is the data collected. Data collection could be in the form of routine survey questions and/or in the form of a stated preference discrete choice experiment. For the former, questions regarding

- likelihood to purchase;
- attribute importance ratings;
- performance ratings if the consumers could use the product;[5]
- attribute liking;
- measures of emotion stimulated by the product (e.g., power, confidence, prestige); and
- Just-About-Right measures

to mention a few.

The analyses conducted for these measures could be just stand-alone analyses (e.g., simply tabulate the number of responses regardless of the characteristics of the respondents) or they could be by major customer characteristics (e.g., income level, education, socioeconomic status, marketing segment membership).

Data from the first five question types can be analyzed via the techniques I described earlier in Chapter 3 on the design of a new product. The sixth question type, Just-About-Right measures, is more complicated. It is typical for managers in the sensory areas (e.g., beverages, foods, and fragrances) to want to understand consumers' reactions to the sensory experience of their product. This also holds for personal items such as jewelry and automobiles. Automobiles are in this category because of the emotions attached to them as discussed above. These products appeal to a subjective state – the senses – so objective measures are hard to determine. Consequently, the measures commonly used are more subjective regarding "getting it right." Basically, managers need to know if customers believe some attribute is

- too little or insufficient;
- just-about-right (JAR); or
- too much or too intense.

Penalty analysis is a methodology for determining if a product attribute is less than optimal (i.e. above or below a JAR level) on an overall liking-the-product scale.

An Overall Liking scale is part of the measurement because how customers "like" a product is a predictor of their potential to purchase it. If they say they do not like the product at all, then it is a safe bet they will not buy it. If they say they really like it, the probability of buying should be high. The probability of purchase should vary directly with the degree of liking.

A *JAR* scale is used because a measure is needed for a sensory evaluation of an aspect of the attribute. Sensory evaluations are, by their nature, highly subjective. It is believed that customers (primarily consumers) cannot exactly express their sensory evaluation but can only say that the attribute is "about right." This is a less definitive response to a question regarding whether or not the attribute is correct.

The amount by which an attribute is not correct (i.e., not *JAR*) indicates the amount of improvement that has to be made. The improvement could be an increase (reflecting "Too Little") or a decrease (reflecting "Too Much") in the attribute. Making the indicated improvement would increase the product's Overall Liking. In general, the Overall Liking will rise as the customers' sensory subjective evaluation rises to an optimal *JAR* level, but then fall as the sensory subjective evaluation rises past the optimal *JAR* level: Too **Little** of the attribute has a negative impact on Overall Liking while Too **Much** also has a negative impact on Overall Liking. This is illustrated in Figure 4.4.

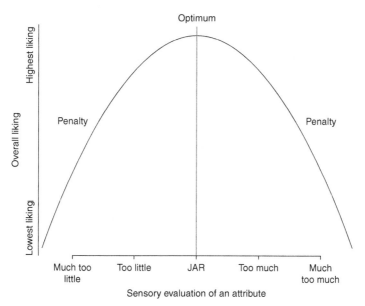

FIGURE 4.4 This illustrates the impact on Overall Liking of not having the setting of an attribute "just about right." A setting that is too much or too intense or too overpowering will make the product unappealing to customers so their Overall Liking will fall. The same holds if the attribute is too little or insufficient or not enough. The goal is to get the attribute setting "just about right."

Data collection for a penalty analysis is quite simple. Consumers are first asked to rate their Overall Liking for a product. Typically, a 7-point hedonic scale is used. An example set of points might be:

- 1 = Do Not Like the Product at All
- 4 = Neither Like nor Dislike
- 7 = Like the Product Very Much.

After providing an overall product rating, they are then asked to rate specific sensory attributes of the product. This rating is typically on a 5-point scale. The scale must have an odd number of points so as to have an unambiguous middle – the JAR value. An example might be:

- 1 = Too Weak/Little/Small/etc. depending on the product
- 3 = Just About Right (JAR)
- 5 = Too Strong/Big/Much/etc. depending on the product.

The sensory attributes evaluated depend on the product. Some typical sensory attributes are shown in Table 4.1.

There are several steps in the penalty calculations. For illustrative purposes, consider a food company that developed a new set of flavors for a popular young-adult product they sell. The product managers wanted to assess consumer reactions to the flavors to see if they "got it right." Since getting it right is personal to the consumer and sensory, a penalty analysis was conducted. First assume that the sensory attribute is flavor. A 5-point *JAR* scale is used with the left, middle, and right points being "Too Mild", "Just About Right", and "Too Spicy." The five points are recoded so that

TABLE 4.1 These are some sensory attributes that might be used in three diverse consumer studies. The Food/Beverage attributes are common. The automotive attributes vary but are representative. The personal care products could be item such as deodorants, perfumes, aftershave lotions, sun screen lotions, general skin lotions, and hair care such as shampoos, conditioners, and colorings.

Food/Beverage	Automotive	Personal Care
Aftertaste	Metal	Uniqueness
Amount	Glass	Better than others
Appearance	Length of hood	Strength of fragrance
Bitterness	Angle of front windshield	Fragrance intensity
Flavor	Length of trunk	Application amount
Size	Angle of rear windshield	Strength of applicator
Sourness	Overall shape	Dryness
Strength	Overall length	Stickiness

- Bottom-two boxes is *Too Little*
- Middle box is *JAR*
- Top-two boxes is *Too Much*.

In addition to the sensory attribute question, an Overall Liking question is asked on a 7-point scale. The average Overall Liking for the product is calculated for each level of the recoded assessment. The drops in the average Overall Liking rating for *Too Little* and *Too Much* from the *JAR* level are determined. These are sometimes called (appropriately) *Mean Drops*. The weighted average of the *Mean Drops* is the *Penalty* for not "getting it right." Getting it right is the *JAR* level.

There is disagreement as to exactly what is the "penalty." Some view it as the *Mean Drops* and others view it as the weighted average of the *Mean Drops*. I view the penalty as the weighted average, but a best practice is to report both *Mean Drops* and the weighted average labeled as "Penalty." Penalties are usually analyzed by plotting the mean drops against the percent of respondents for that mean drop.

Extending the example just mentioned, 107 young-adult consumers were asked to taste the flavors. They were asked to rate them on overall liking using a 7-point hedonic scale and then to indicate their opinion on flavor as mentioned above plus sweetness, sensation, and sourness. A penalty analysis is shown in Table 4.2. For each attribute, the responses on the 5-point *JAR* scale were recoded as described

TABLE 4.2 This is an example penalty analysis table summarizing the calculations for four sensory attributes for the new flavors for a popular young-adult product. The *Percent* column is the percent of the respondents in each *JAR* category for each attribute. These percents sum to 100% for each attribute (within rounding). The *Liking* scores sum to 585 for each attribute because the liking rating was for the product regardless of the individual attributes. The table shows the sum of the *Liking* scores by attribute by *JAR* category.

Attribute	JAR Level	Percent	Liking	Mean Liking	Mean Drop	Penalty
Flavor	Too Weak	9.3%	52	5.2	−0.6	
Flavor	JAR	68.2%	427	5.8	0.0	−1.2
Flavor	Too Strong	22.4%	106	4 4	−1.4	
Sensation	Too Weak	9.3%	55	5.5	−0.4	
Sensation	JAR	57.0%	362	5.9	0.0	−1.1
Sensation	Too Strong	33.6%	168	4.7	−1.3	
Sweetness	Too Weak	15.0%	89	5.6	−0.2	
Sweetness	JAR	69.2%	423	5.7	0.0	−0.8
Sweetness	Too Strong	15.9%	73	4.3	−1.4	
Sourness	Too Weak	25.2%	133	4.9	−0.8	
Sourness	JAR	46.7%	288	5.8	0.0	−0.5
Sourness	Too Strong	28.0%	164	5.5	−0.3	

above and the percent of young adults in each *JAR* group was calculated. For *Flavor/Too Weak*, there were 10 respondents which is 9.3% ($= {}^{10}/_{107} \times 100$). The *Liking* score from the 7-point liking scale was calculated by simple summation. The 10 respondents for *Flavor/Too Weak* assigned a total of 52 points to this category. The *Mean Liking* is just the *Liking* points divided by 10 respondents. The *Mean Drop* is the drop in the mean liking for each category from the *JAR* value. For the *Flavor* attribute, the *Too Weak* category is 0.6 points below the *JAR* value ($= 5.2 - 5.8$) while the *Too Strong* category is -1.4 points below ($= 4.4 - 5.8$). Obviously, the *JAR* category has a zero mean drop. The *Penalty* for not getting *Flavor* just right is a drop in the overall liking of the product by 1.2 points. This is calculated as the weighted average of the mean drops, the weights being the proportion of respondents in the *Too Weak* and *Too Strong* categories. For the *Flavor* attribute, the weights are $0.093/(0.093 + 0.224) = 0.293$ for *Too Weak* and $0.224/(0.093 + 0.224) = 0.707$ for *Too Strong*. The proportion for the *JAR* category is not included since the respondents in this group do not contribute to either mean drop. The *Penalty* is then $0.293 \times (-0.6) + 0.707 \times (-1.4) = -1.2$.

If a stated preference discrete choice experiment is included, take rates could be estimated as described in the previous section and then used for volumetric forecasting.[6] The advantage of this approach is that the consumers would have first-hand experience with the new product as opposed to just reading a description of it. Personal experience always dominates.

4.3 Market segmentation

Market segmentation has been an important component of marketing operations for a long time. Fundamentally, segmentation involves dividing the market into homogeneous subgroups and developing a different marketing campaign for each segment. Segmentation also includes developing a different pricing strategy and price point for each segment. This is called *price segmentation* in the marketing literature and *price discrimination* in the economic literature. See Paczkowski [2018] for a discussion of price segmentation.

Many different approaches have been proposed for segmenting a market all of which could be summarized in three categories:

1. *a priori* segmentation;
2. unsupervised learning segmentation; and
3. supervised learning (or model based) segmentation.

A priori segmentation refers to those situations in which the marketing team, the corporate culture, or the executive management have decided on the segments without regard to any data. Basically, they just intuitively know the segments because they just seem to fit the business. An example is electricity customers. Utilities sometimes divide their market into residential, commercial, and industrial customers merely because this is intuitive.[7] Marketing campaigns and pricing would be developed for these segments.

Unsupervised and supervised learning refer to how understanding is gained from data. The analogy is learning in an educational situation, say a college class. The traditional education model consists of a professor who guides a student (called a "learner") in processing, interpreting, and learning from books, articles, and lecture notes (i.e., input), and then tests the learner's performance in learning via a test with an assigned grade. There is a teacher, a learner, an input, and a performance measure; this is supervised educational learning. In statistical analysis, a model (e.g., a linear, logistic, or Poisson model) guides how a learner (the estimation techniques such as least squares or maximum likelihood) processes inputs (i.e., data) with the processing performance measured by a goodness-of-fit measure such as R^2 or badness-of-fit measure such as Akaike or Bayesian Information Criteria (*AIC* or *BIC*, respectively). This is called supervised learning in the statistical and Machine Learning spaces. The estimation technique learns from the data under the guidance of the model. The entire regression family of statistical methodologies are supervised learning methods.

If there is no college professor so the students are left on their own to learn, then they are clearly unsupervised. In the statistical analysis and Machine Learning spaces, if there is no model but there is data, an algorithm for operating on that data, and (maybe) a performance criteria, then this situation is called *unsupervised learning*. The algorithm is not guided by a model but follows some procedure which is the algorithm itself. Cluster analysis, both hierarchical and k-means as the two most popular examples, is in the family of unsupervised learning techniques. A performance measure may not exist for these methods. For hierarchical clustering, a *Cubic Clustering Criteria* (*CCC*) is sometimes used, but this is not without controversy. See Paczkowski [2016] for some discussion of the *CCC* and references.

The two learning approaches and their college counterparts for reference are summarized in Table 4.3.

Regarding segmentation, a latent class regression analysis is an example of a supervised learning segmentation method. Unsupervised learning segmentation would be some form of clustering. Of the two, the more popular is the unsupervised clustering with the supervised latent class segmentation becoming more popular as software develops in this area and more market researchers are trained in supervised learning methods.

TABLE 4.3 Learning comparisons.

College Setting	Supervised Learning	Unsupervised Learning
Professor	Model	*NA*
Student Learner	Estimation Method	Algorithm
Lectures/Notes	Data	Data
Performance	R^2, *AIC, BIC*	*CCC*, etc.

The advantage of supervised learning is that a model guides the learning process. The model reflects assumptions about how the world works and what the important drivers are for determining a key variable as reflected in the model specification, the key variable being the dependent variable. Given the data (the independent variables) for the model, there could be only one solution for the unknown parameters, the weights on the independent variables, that produce the best predictions for the dependent variable. Consider *OLS* as an example. The best predictions are those that minimize the sum of the squared differences between the actual values of the dependent variable and their predictions. Estimates of the unknown parameters are chosen that yield this minimum. In this sense, the dependent variable and the model for it guide the selection of those parameters. There is only one set of estimated parameters; there is only one solution that weights the independent variables to predict the dependent variable.

For unsupervised learning, there is no model since there is no dependent variable or model. There cannot be. There are no assumptions about how the world works. In fact, the search is for something that yields relationships among a set of variables without any prior view of a relationship. The supervised learning has a prior view of a relationship, the model, while unsupervised learning does not. The unsupervised learning takes place using an algorithm with a specific set of parameter settings that search for relationships. These parameters are hyperparameters. You specify the hyperparameters; you do not search for them. Consequently, by a simple change in the hyperparameters, a different relationship can be found. Consider hierarchical cluster analysis which is an unsupervised learning method. The parameter set before clustering can be done is the type of clustering algorithm to be used. Most software allows you to select one of five algorithms: *Average Linkage, Centroid Linkage, Ward's Method, Single Linkage*, and *Complete Linkage*. Each method can generate a different cluster solution. Most practicing statisticians, marketing researchers, and Machine Learning experts use Ward's minimum variance method and select the most appealing solution from this method. See Everitt et al. [2001] and Jobson [1992] for discussions of clustering methods.

A supervised learning segmentation method is superior because it uses a model. In this category, there is latent regression analysis which is a combination of regression analysis and latent class analysis. This will work well if the dependent variable is continuous. See Paczkowski [2018] for an example using latent regression analysis for price segmentation. The latent class regression approach has been extended to a discrete choice case. Referring to (4.6), the modification involves conditioning the model on a grouping of the dependent variable. This leads to $Pr_i(j \mid s)$. The seemingly small change in notation, the conditioning on a segment or group s, complicates estimation since the groupings are unknown. They have to be estimated simultaneously with the unknown systematic utility parameters. See Greene and Hensher [2003] for a discussion and application. Also see Wen et al. [2012] for an application to transportation carrier choice.

Another supervised learning option is *decision trees*, sometimes called *recursive partitioning*. Unlike latent regression analysis, decision tree analysis can handle a dependent variable that is continuous or discrete or categorical. If the dependent variable is continuous, then the decision trees are referred to as *regression trees*; if discrete, then they are referred to as *categorical trees*. The method, regardless of the nature of the dependent variable, is a recursive partitioning model because it proceeds in a recursive fashion to partition or divide the dependent variable space into smaller spaces using constants determined by the independent variables. These constants that partition the dependent variable space are selected based on the best independent variable, the one that does the best at accounting for the dependent variable based on a criterion measure, and the best division of that variable. If a "best" independent variable is discrete with, say, two levels, then the constants are the two levels. If the "best" independent variable is continuous, then the constants are based on the point or value that optimally divides that variable into two parts. In either case, a constant is determined. Once a partition, based on a constant, is determined, then the algorithm proceeds to find the next best variable and a constant that divides the space, but all given the first variable and its partition. The identification of succeeding variables that contribute to explaining the dependent variable and the associated partitions continues until some stopping rule is met. The resulting set of variables and partitions are displayed as a tree with the dependent variable as the root and the successive "best" variables and partitions as branches emanating from the root. The final set of partitions are interpreted as segments. See Paczkowski [2016] for some discussion of decision trees in JMP.

4.4 TURF analysis

In the previous sections, I focused on newer methods for testing new products in the marketplace. This was predicated on there being just one version of a product. But suppose there are several. An older methodology for determining which of several versions of a product will sell is based on finding the best combination of those products with the notion that the combination will sell the best. It may be that each product alone does not garner enough market share to meet business objectives, but in combination with one or two others they could produce total sales to meet the objectives. A good example is ice cream. Offering one flavor (e.g., chocolate) may not attract enough customers to be profitable. Several flavors, however, could attract customers because of the wider selection even though they would still buy only one; they would buy at least one of the offered flavors. Offering a huge selection of flavors may not be practical because of the cost of producing, maintaining, and marketing them all. An optimal subset, a small combination, may be more profitable. Also, too many options may stifle purchases because customers could be overwhelmed and therefore just not make a purchase. There is a paradox of choice that involves creating purchase anxiety which customers may not be able to resolve and overcome, so they just do not purchase. See Schwartz [2004] for the classic discussion of this interesting paradox.

A market research methodology named TURF, an acronym for "Total Undupli-cated Reach and Frequency," was developed to handle situations such as this. It has its origins in advertisement research and is quite old and simplistic, but still used, especially beyond its original intent. I will briefly discuss TURF in this section for product research. MaxDiff is a modern approach to testing claims and messages, as well as different versions of a product. I will discuss this approach in Chapter 5 and then show how it can be combined with TURF.

TURF was developed to determine the best or optimal set of magazines (or newspapers or TV shows) to use to promote a product. If there are five magazines, it may not be cost effective to promote in all five, not just because of the costs of placing an ad, but because customers may only buy, say, two of the five so placing an ad in two will have the best exposure; it is not necessary to have all five. The percent exposure in the set of magazines is the set's *reach*. The set is the combination of magazines. If there are $n = 5$ magazines, then the number of combinations of size two is

$$\binom{5}{2} = \frac{5!}{(5-2)! \times 2!}$$
$$= 10.$$

There are 10 combinations or sets of magazines, each consisting of 2 magazines. The question is: "*Which combination of size two of the 10 possible combinations has the largest reach*"? The number of times a customer is reached is the *frequency*. The proportion of times at least one item in the set is responded to is the *reach*. A complete discussion of reach and TURF is in Paczkowski [2016].

To implement a TURF study for new products with different versions, customers are surveyed and asked their preference for the versions. They could simply be asked a *Yes/No* question such as "*Would you buy this product*"? Or they could be asked their preference on a nine-point Likert Scale. Regardless of the underlying scale, TURF requires that responses be dummy coded as 0 for *No* and 1 for *Yes*. For the first way to ask a question, the *Yes/No* responses just have to be encoded. For the second way, the preference rating could be dummy coded as 1 if the rating is a 7 or higher, 0 otherwise. This would create a top three box scale (*T3B*).

Suppose there are n products. The number of combinations of size $r, r = 1, 2, \ldots, n$, is given by

$$\binom{n}{r} = \frac{n!|}{(n-r)! \times r!}.$$

Suppose r is restricted to some number less than n. All combinations of size $i = 1, i = 2, \ldots, i = r < n$ can be determined. Let $\tilde{c}$ be the total number of these combinations. That is,

$$\tilde{c} = \sum_{i=1}^{r<n} \binom{n}{i}.$$

For example, if $r = 1$ and $n = 5$, then $\tilde{c} = 5$; if $r = 1$, 2, then $\tilde{c} = 15$.

Out of the class of n candidate designs, only a few would be marketed, say $r < n$. This may be the case because of manufacturing constraints or marketing budget constraints that allow only a few products be brought to market. Which r has the largest reach?

The TURF reach calculation proceeds by creating an indicator matrix that is $\tilde{c} \times n$. The rows are the combinations and the columns are the products. For our example of $r = 2$, there are 10 rows for the 10 combinations and five columns for the five products. The cell values are either 0 or 1: 1 if the product is in a combination and 0 otherwise. A second $m \times n$ indicator matrix identifies the preference for each of the n products for each of the m customers surveyed.

The two indicator matrices are matrix multiplied. The result is an $m \times \tilde{c}$ matrix with cell values representing the number of products purchased in a combination. In our example of $r = 2$, the number of products in a combination could only be 0, 1, or 2.

Reach is formally defined as the proportion of customers purchasing at least one item in a combination. This is implemented by dummifying the $m \times \tilde{c}$ matrix of frequencies. If a frequency is greater than or equal to 1, the cell is recoded as 1; otherwise it is recoded as 0. Since the mean of 0/1 values is a proportion, the mean for each column in the recoded indicator matrix is the proportion of customers reached by the respective combination. This is the reach part of the TURF acronym. The sum of each column of the original frequency matrix is the frequency part in the TURF acronym. The Appendix to this chapter shows these calculations in matrix notation.

As an example, consider a shampoo manufacturer with five new forms of shampoo for deeper and richer cleaning. All five cannot be marketed; just two. But which two? A sample of 275 consumers were recruited and asked to try the shampoos in home tests for five weeks, one shampoo per week. At the end of each week, they were asked to rate their likelihood to buy the tested shampoo on a 1–9 Likert Scale: 1 = *Not at all Likely* and 9 = *Very Likely*. The resulting scores were converted into the top three box using the encoding definition

$$encoding = \begin{cases} 1 & \text{if} \quad rating \geq 7 \\ 0 & \text{if} \quad Otherwise \end{cases}$$

All combinations of the five shampoos taken one-at-a-time and two-at-a-time were determined. The one-at-a-time combinations are just simple proportions. There are a total of 15 combinations. The results of the TURF calculations are shown in Figure 4.5.

Some analysts extend the TURF framework to include the marginal contribution of each item to each set the item belongs to. That is, which item contributes the most to the set's reach, followed by the second most contributory item, and so on. The objective is to identify which item in the set should be marketed first. An example report is shown in Figure 4.6.

TURF Analysis Report

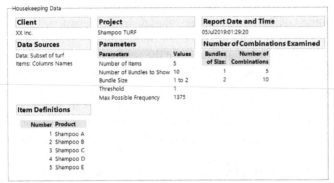

Housekeeping Data

Client	Project	Report Date and Time
XX Inc.	Shampoo TURF	05Jul2019:01:29:20

Data Sources

Data: Subset of turf
Items: Columns Names

Parameters

Parameters	Values
Number of Items	5
Number of Bundles to Show	10
Bundle Size	1 to 2
Threshold	1
Max Possible Frequency	1375

Number of Combinations Examined

Bundles of Size:	Number of Combinations
1	5
2	10

Item Definitions

Number	Product
1	Shampoo A
2	Shampoo B
3	Shampoo C
4	Shampoo D
5	Shampoo E

TURF Details

Top 10 Bundles

Run	Bundle Composition	Reach Count	Reach Percent	Frequency	Frequency Percent of Max
1_1	Shampoo A	119	0.43273	119	0.08655
1_2	Shampoo C	91	0.33091	91	0.06618
1_3	Shampoo E	59	0.21455	59	0.04291
1_4	Shampoo B	23	0.08364	23	0.01673
1_5	Shampoo D	2	0.00727	2	0.00145
2_1	Shampoo A/Shampoo C	151	0.54909	210	0.15273
2_2	Shampoo A/Shampoo E	145	0.52727	178	0.12945
2_3	Shampoo A/Shampoo B	123	0.44727	142	0.10327
2_4	Shampoo A/Shampoo D	119	0.43273	121	0.088
2_5	Shampoo C/Shampoo E	114	0.41455	150	0.10909
2_6	Shampoo B/Shampoo C	99	0.36	114	0.08291
2_7	Shampoo C/Shampoo D	93	0.33818	93	0.06764
2_8	Shampoo B/Shampoo E	78	0.28364	82	0.05964
2_9	Shampoo D/Shampoo E	60	0.21818	61	0.04436
2_10	Shampoo B/Shampoo D	24	0.08727	25	0.01818

Items Summary

FIGURE 4.5 TURF shampoo example for five shampoo products simply labeled *A–E*. The number of combinations were based on $r = 1$ and $r = 2$ giving 15 combinations. Of the 275 customers in the study, 119 would buy *A*, 92 would buy *C*, and 151 would buy at least of the two shampoos giving a reach of 0.549. So 55.0% of the market would buy at least one of *A* or *C*.

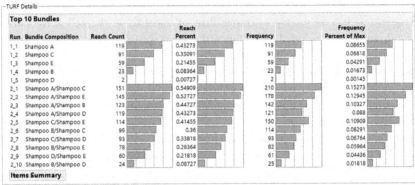

Contribution Report

Incremental Items	Cumulative Reach		Delta Reach	
Shampoo A	0.43273		0.43273	
Shampoo C	0.54909		0.11636	

FIGURE 4.6 This illustrates the marginal contribution of the two products, *A* and *C*, in the top reach bundle of Figure 4.5. Shampoo *A* contributes the most to the combination, having a marginal reach of 0.43273, which happens to be its stand-alone reach proportion. Shampoo *C* contributes 0.11636 to the combination resulting in a total reach of 0.54909 as in Figure 4.5.

4.5 Software

Stated preference discrete choice experiments can be designed using JMP from the SAS Institute Inc. This software has a powerful platform for choice designs as well as a good platform for estimating choice models. Nlogit, an extension of the econometric software Limdep, is the gold standard in choice modeling. This package has all the latest developments in the choice analysis area as it should since its developer is a leading researcher in choice analysis.[8] Stata will also handle choice estimation. R has packages for estimation but they are a challenge to use.

Latent class regression modeling can be done using Latent Class Gold by Statistical Innovations, Inc. Decision trees can be grown using JMP, SAS, Python, and R. I recommend JMP for its simple interface. Cluster analysis, both hierarchical and k-means, can be handled by almost all software packages. JMP has a good interface and is my typical choice.

The TURF calculations in this chapter were done using a JMP script written just for TURF analysis.

4.6 Summary

In this chapter, I described methods for testing a product design just prior to launch. Some of the testing relied on discrete choice analysis, a methodology that has become very popular in the market research space. This is a useful framework for testing products with customers to determine demand and final attribute setting before the product is released to the market. The advantage of this approach is the fact that you do not actually have to market the product to determine its demand. You can set up mock situations and use prototypes and achieve almost the same effects. Another advantage is that competitive products can be included in a study so a competitive effect can be derived. A disadvantage is that an experimental design is needed. Conjoint analysis, which I described in the previous chapter, also requires an experimental design, but the discrete choice design is more complicated. Special skill-sets are required for its implementation.

I also described the use of clinics for assessing demand. A discrete choice study could be included in a clinic, and usually is.

Finally, I gave an overview of price segmentation and TURF analysis to further your understanding of product testing at this stage of development.

4.7 Appendix

This Appendix contains some detail on the TURF calculation.

4.7.1 TURF *calculations*

Let $\mathbf{X}$ be an appropriately dummy-coded matrix of customer preferences for n products. If there are m customers, then $\mathbf{X}$ is $m \times n$. An example of $\mathbf{X}$ is shown in Figure 4.7 for seven customers.

TURF Example

Raw Data

X: Customer Preference Indicators

Customers	Product 1	Product 2	Product 3	Product 4	Product 5
Customer1	1	0	0	1	0
Customer2	0	1	1	1	0
Customer3	0	0	1	0	1
Customer4	1	1	0	0	1
Customer5	0	0	0	0	0
Customer6	0	0	0	0	1
Customer7	1	1	1	0	0

C: Combinations Indicators

Product 1	Product 2	Product 3	Product 4	Product 5
1	0	0	0	0
0	1	0	0	0
0	0	1	0	0
0	0	0	1	0
0	0	0	0	1
1	1	0	0	0
1	0	1	0	0
1	0	0	1	0
1	0	0	0	1
0	1	1	0	0
0	1	0	1	0
0	1	0	0	1
0	0	1	1	0
0	0	1	0	1
0	0	0	1	1

Processed Data

F: Frequency Matrix

1	0	0	1	0	1	1	2	1	0	1	0	1	0	1
0	1	1	1	0	1	1	1	0	2	2	1	2	1	1
0	0	1	0	1	0	1	0	1	1	0	1	1	2	1
1	1	0	0	1	2	1	1	2	1	1	2	0	1	1
0	0	0	0	0	0	0	0	0	0	0	0	0	0	0
0	0	0	0	1	0	0	0	1	0	0	1	0	1	1
1	1	1	0	0	2	2	1	1	2	1	1	1	1	0

R: Reach Indicators Matrix

1	0	0	1	0	1	1	1	1	0	1	0	1	0	1
0	1	1	1	0	1	1	1	0	1	1	1	1	1	1
0	0	1	0	1	0	1	0	1	1	0	1	1	1	1
1	1	0	0	1	1	1	1	1	1	1	1	0	1	1
0	0	0	0	0	0	0	0	0	0	0	0	0	0	0
0	0	0	0	1	0	0	0	1	0	0	1	0	1	1
1	1	1	0	0	1	1	1	1	1	1	1	1	1	0

TURF Results

Reach	Frequency
0.429	3
0.429	3
0.429	3
0.286	2
0.429	3
0.571	6
0.714	6
0.571	5
0.714	6
0.571	6
0.571	5
0.714	6
0.571	5
0.714	6
0.714	5

FIGURE 4.7 This illustrates the TURF calculations for responses by seven customers to five products. The notation corresponds to that in this Appendix.

Let me C be an appropriately dummy-coded matrix of all combinations of $1 < r < n$ products. You could have $r = n$ but this would not be practical if n is large. If $\tilde{c}$ is the number of combinations, then C is $\tilde{c} \times n$. It is not unusual for r to vary from $r = 1, 2, \ldots, < n$. For example, you could have combination sizes of $r = 1$ for each product independent of the others, $r = 2$ for pairs of products, $r = 3$ for 3-tuples of products, and so forth. The matrix C would contain dummies for all the needed possibilities. If $r = 1$ and $r = 2$ and $n = 5$, then C is 15×5. Obviously, for $r = 1$, an $n \times n$ identity matrix, I, is created and C is the $\tilde{c} \times n$ matrix augmented by I. An example of C for $n = 5$ is shown in Figure 4.7.

Frequencies are calculated as

$$F = XC^{\mathsf{T}}.$$

See Figure 4.7 for an example.

To calculate the reach for each combination, **F** must be transformed into a matrix of 0 and 1 values based on a threshold defining the reach. The threshold is usually 1: a customer is reached if he/she buys at least one of the products in the bundle. Larger thresholds are certainly possible. For example, referring to the ice cream example I mentioned earlier, people generally buy several flavors at once when they shop at grocery stores, especially if they have young children with differing tastes and preferences. A threshold might be set at, say, three ice creams in this case. Let $\mathbb{I}$ be the matrix indicator function such that

$$\mathbb{I}(\mathbf{F}) = \left\{ \begin{array}{ll} 1 & \text{if} \quad F_{ij} \geq 1 \\ 0 & \text{if} \quad \textit{Otherwise} \end{array} \right\}$$

where F_{ij} is the value in row i, column j of **F**. The resulting matrix is the reach matrix, **R**. See Figure 4.7.

The reach for each combination is the vector of column means of **R** and the total frequency for each combination is the vector of column sums of **F**. See Figure 4.7.

Notes

1　See "AT&T Test Kitchen" in *CIO Magazine* (May 15, 1994) for a description of the Consumer Lab.

2　See the Decision Analysts white paper "Car Clinics (The Head-to-Head Contest)" at www.decisionanalyst.com/whitepapers/carclinics/. Last accessed April 22, 2019.

3　The Decision Analysts white paper "Car Clinics (The Head-to-Head Contest)" lists bulldozers, construction cranes, lawn mowers, chain saws, vacuum cleaners, refrigerators, and washing machines as examples.

4　Food and beverage taste testing is in the general area of sensory evaluation. See O'Mahony [1986] and Meullenet et al. [2007].

5　For cars, use could involve a test drive. For a household durable product such as a washing machine, it could involve actually doing a small laundry. For a food or beverage, it could involve eating or drinking the product(s).

6　See the Decision Analysts white paper "Car Clinics (The Head-to-Head Contest)" for brief discussion of possibilities.

7　I was once the chief forecaster at a utility company that divided its market into these three groups. There was no reason for it other than this was what made sense.

8　The developer is William H. Greene of Econometric Software, Inc.

5

LAUNCH I

What is the marketing mix?

The Marketing Mix concept is an old one both in the marketing literature and in practice. It originated in the 1960s to systematize thinking about how marketing should operate and therefore succeed in its mission to motivate customers and sell a product.[1] Traditionally, the mix consists of what is known as the *Four Ps*, although the number has increased as academic researchers put their mark on this approach.[2] Whatever the count, I will stick with the traditional four: *Product, Price, Place,* and *Promotion.* This whole book is about the first, Product, so nothing more will be said about it here. This chapter is concerned with the Promotion, Price, and Place components.

This chapter is divided into five sections. I will first discuss Promotion followed by Price and the Place. The promotion of a product, especially a new product, involves an optimal message and claim about it. The message is what you want a customer to hear or read that will motivate a product purchase. This message is not simple or straightforward, but complex because it actually has to appeal to a customer's intelligence, reasoning, and emotion about the product. Claims are what you want a customer to believe, statements that describe the product as being superior to other products. I normally view messages and claims as the same so I use the terms interchangeably.

Message delivery can be by traditional print media, TV ads, radio spots, and, increasingly, through digital channels. The last offers great opportunity for message delivery since messages can be quickly changed (almost instantly, in fact) if a message is not resonating with customers and motivating them to buy the product. Several messages can be tested at once to discover which is the best because of this adjustment speed and the way they are displayed. One group of online shoppers could be shown one message and another group shown another message with the results statistically compared for their effectiveness in converting an online shopper to an online buyer. Testing messages this way is termed *A/B Testing* and is the subject of a subsection below.

The product price is all-important because no matter how right the other components of the Mix, if the price is not right then either a sale will not be made or money will be "left on the table," which means lost revenue opportunities. Pricing was discussed in Chapter 3 from the business case perspective. The business case acts as a gate keeper process in which it is decided whether or not development, and even launch, of a product will continue. As I discussed in Chapter 3, a price point or price range is needed in the early stages of development to calculate potential revenue. Usually, a range is used so that a reasonable revenue range can be developed. At launch, however, the pricing problem narrows and becomes more focused on a specific price point. More specifically, a pricing strategy must be developed. As noted in Paczkowski [2018], a pricing strategy consists of a structure and a level. The structure is either a uniform price or a form of price discrimination. Since details on developing these are presented in Paczkowski [2018], this chapter will only present highlights of issues and methods.

The place where the product will be marketed is a complicated issue because of online stores and online channels such as Amazon. It is also complicated by legalities, that is, contracts that may prohibit more than one (or a few) vendors from selling in a locale. I will discuss this in the third section.

The last two sections are a software review and summary.

5.1 Messaging/claims analysis

In this first section, I will discuss the analysis of messages or claims for the promotion of a new product. This is not to say the methods are only useful in this situation since promotion is ongoing. New messages have to be constantly developed and tested throughout a product's lifecycle. Since this book is about new products, the focus is only on messaging at this stage.

5.1.1 Stages of message analysis

Figure 5.1 illustrates four stages of message analysis:

1. creation;
2. testing;
3. deployment; and
4. tracking.

There are two ways to view the operationalization of these stages that are actually evolutionary. I refer to them as the *Old Messaging Paradigm* and the *New Messaging Paradigm*. These are illustrated in Figure 5.2 and Figure 5.3, respectively. In the old paradigm, there is no (or minimal) use of data at the *Creation* and *Deployment*

Stages of Message Development

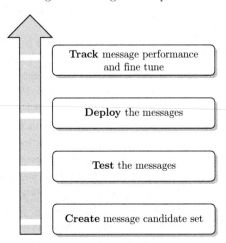

FIGURE 5.1 The four stages of message development.

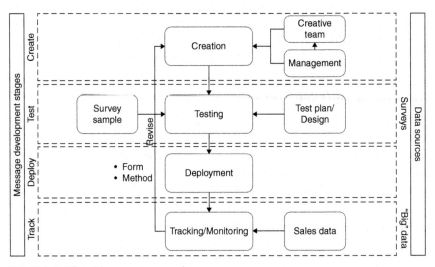

FIGURE 5.2 The old messaging paradigm.

stages and some use of data at the *Testing* and *Tracking* stages. Creation could be influenced by Message Tracking based on what did and did not work regarding sales and customer acquisition. It is, however, largely left to a creative team, perhaps influenced or directed by a management team, to "dream up" a message. The *New Messaging Paradigm*, Figure 5.3, is data intensive at all stages. This is largely a result of the Big Data and Social Media world in which we now live. These two have impacted all aspects of business, not just messaging. Both Big Data and Social Media

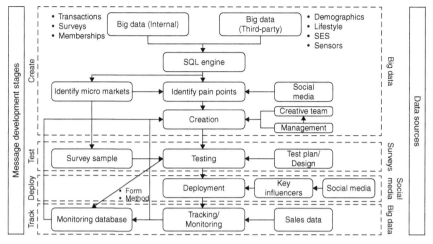

FIGURE 5.3 The new messaging paradigm.

were part of the idea generation process I discussed in Chapter 2. Both come to play again in messaging.

At the same time, the skill-sets of marketing practitioners have expanded, software has evolved to a more sophisticated level, and analytical tool sets have been developed to handle more challenging real-world problems. Statistical and econometric theory and machine learning techniques are in this last category. In the following subsections I will develop a perspective and methods for the four stages of messaging under the new data-intensive paradigm. The first stage, message creation, is discussed in the next subsection which is followed by approaches for the analysis of messages based on data.

5.1.2 Message creation

Where do messages come from? This is equivalent to the question: *"Where do new product ideas come from?"*. In a data-intensive world, Big Data from internal and external sources can be used in conjunction with social media data to identify *pain points* for customers. Pain points are customer problems that affect their daily lives. In terms of products, a new one (both new-to-the-world and an enhancement to an existing product) would alleviate, or at least ameliorate, the "pain." The message tells customers how the new product accomplishes this.

Internal data includes transactions data, product returns data, warranty data, call center logs, and so on. External data consists of socioeconomic and demographic data on customers and potential customers. Social media data consists of reviews, complaints, blogs, and so forth that emphasize issues. Combined, they can be used to identify issues that can be addressed by the new product. The creative team crafts messages explaining how their "pain" is addressed by the new product. This could be done for the entire market or micro markets (a.k.a., market segments).

5.1.3 Message testing

Once the initial messages are developed, they must then be tested with customers to uncover what works and what does not work. There are two quantitative ways to do this:

1. MaxDiff message testing; and
2. A/B message testing.

The messages could be qualitatively tested through focus groups but this has drawbacks. Focus groups require that key marketing personnel attend sessions to hear first-hand what customers have to say. They do not have to be physically present because of modern communication technology which allows them to remotely view sessions. Regardless if they view the sessions onsite or remotely, their time and attention must still be devoted to them, and this is time taken away from other business activities. In addition to this time cost, there are sample size and sample representation issues. Sample sizes are necessarily small making them unrepresentative of the market. As a result, it is difficult, if not impossible, to generalize findings to the entire market. See Vicsek [2010] for some discussion.

The two quantitative methods are discussed in the next subsections. The two subsections assume an initial set of messages, but this is for convenience. As I noted, creation and analysis are iterative.

MaxDiff analysis of messages/claims

Typically, the team responsible for message creation will develop several candidate messages. There is no rule or rule-of-thumb (*ROT*) about the size of the candidate set, but my experience has shown that an initial set of a minimum of five is sufficient. I have worked with clients, especially in the pharmaceutical industry, where 50–60 messages would be developed, each varying by a simple word. The reason for this large number is the sensitivity of customers (as well as physicians, regulators, and lawyers) to what is said about a drug. So the team has to be cautious regarding what is claimed.

The message analysis discussed here deals with the problem of identifying the best promotional message, claim, or slogan for a new product although the methodology could also be applied to messages at the corporate level. I restrict myself, however, to only the marketing function. The "best" is determined by customer ratings of proposed messages. There are many ways or dimensions to specify what a customer has to rate. I will confine myself to a *call-to-action* (*CTA*) at first but then expand to other dimensions later.

A *CTA* statement depends on the product and the type of action required. For instance, any of the following are viable candidate *CTA* statements:

- Likelihood to buy;
- Likelihood to recommend;

- Likelihood to prescribe;
- Likelihood to use; and
- Likelihood to ask or learn about.

CTA statements are usually rated on a Likert Scale, typically five points. A problem with a Likert Scale is that it is not clear whether or not customers use the whole scale (i.e., all five points) to evaluate the *CTA* or only a portion (e.g., they confine themselves to the top portion only) for all items they evaluate and regardless of whether or not their evaluation is relevant. This means results could be biased.

Suppose a marketing team developed seven potential advertising messages for a new product. It is certainly not practical to use all seven. Which is best? One way to determine the best is to survey customers and ask them to rate how likely they are to buy the product based on each message. This is a *CTA* statement. The issue right now is how to present the messages for evaluation. One way is to present them sequentially. This is inefficient and suboptimal since customers may respond differently to one message if they know a prior message may be better or worse. Alternatively, all seven messages could be presented at once and the customers could be asked to rank or sort them for their effectiveness in motivating them to buy. This could work if the number of messages is small, such as the seven in this example. Suppose, however, there are 60 as for the pharmaceutical example. A ranking task is clearly impractical. A compromise is to present a set of messages consisting of a minimum of two but being less than the full array of messages. This use of a set, called a *choice set*, is the basis for the message analysis I will describe. The use of a choice set is fundamental to an approach called *Maximum Differential Choice Analysis*, or *MaxDiff* for short. The concept of a choice set is the same as the one I described in Chapter 4 for discrete choice analysis. In fact, MaxDiff is in the same family of choice models as conjoint and discrete choice. It differs from conjoint and discrete choice analysis in that the items (messages in this case) are not varied by changing a level of an attribute; there are no attributes, *per se*. I will next describe the construction of the choice set and the approach. See Paczkowski [2018] for a discussion of the choice family.

Choice set construction

Each customer in a survey is shown a set of messages, not a single message, one set at a time. The sets are called *choice sets* because each customer is asked to select messages from each set. The sets are created using statistical design principles and procedures that lead to a *design matrix*. The design matrix is an array of rows and columns where the rows are the choice sets and the columns are the design elements (i.e., messages) comprising the choice sets. There are many design procedures that lead to a design matrix, some of which are discussed in Paczkowski [2018].

For most design procedures, the full set of design elements is represented in each row of the matrix but only in different arrangements. The design is how they are arranged. The elements could be discrete factors with levels, the minimum being two, such as "High" or "Low", "Present" or "Absent", "Red" or "Green".

TABLE 5.1 Full factorial design matrix for two discrete factors, each at two levels. The first column is the first factor and the second is the second factor. With only two factors at two levels each, there are only 4 (= 2 × 2) possible arrangements so there are only four rows to the matrix. Each row is an arrangement of the levels.

Low	Low
Low	High
High	Low
High	High

Suppose a simple case of two discrete factors, each at two levels: "High" and "Low". A design matrix showing all arrangements is show in Table 5.1.

Small design matrices such as this are easy to create and use with customers. Each row is a choice set so they are shown four sets. For each set, a customer has to state their preference for the first or second factor when each is set at the level specified in the matrix. For our example problem, however, which consists of seven messages, you run into a problem because customers have to judge seven elements in a set. This is far too many. It is better to have a subset of the seven in each row of the matrix, but yet with all seven still appearing equally in the entire matrix to ensure fairness (i.e., balance) to each message. A design called a Balanced Incomplete Block Design (*BIBD*) could be used.

A *BIBD* is a design procedure for creating a design matrix such that each factor measured at one level appears an equal number of times in the matrix and each row of the matrix has fewer than the total number of factors. For consumers studies, a rule-of-thumb (*ROT*) is that 2–5 factors should appear in each row with four being a typical number.[3] For our example, you could have seven messages with each choice set containing four. Such a design matrix is shown in Table 5.2. See Paczkowski [2018] for the *ROT*.

This arrangement implies that 28 messages (= 7 × 4) are shown in total. Since the example started with only seven messages, each message is obviously replicated

TABLE 5.2 *BIBD* design matrix example for seven messages in seven sets, each set with four messages. Each row is a choice set. Notice that each of the seven messages repeats four times throughout the design. Also, notice that each pair of messages (e.g., Message 6 and Message 3) appears the same number of times throughout the matrix: twice.

Message 6	Message 3	Message 7	Message 1
Message 1	Message 2	Message 5	Message 7
Message 5	Message 7	Message 4	Message 3
Message 7	Message 4	Message 6	Message 2
Message 2	Message 1	Message 3	Message 4
Message 4	Message 5	Message 1	Message 6
Message 3	Message 6	Message 2	Message 5

four times enhancing their exposure. The arrangement of the messages into the seven sets of four each is the design matrix, or simply the *design*.

A *BIBD* design must meet three requirements:

1. Each element must appear the same number of times as every other element.
2. Each pair of elements must appear the same number of times throughout the matrix.
3. An element cannot be duplicated in a single row of the matrix.

These conditions can be verified using an incidence matrix which shows the locations of each message. An incidence matrix corresponding to Table 5.2 is shown in Table 5.3. A pairwise matrix showing how many times a message pairs with another message is also helpful for assessing balance. A pairwise matrix for Table 5.2 is shown in Table 5.4

Six parameters define a *BIBD* design matrix:

TABLE 5.3 *BIBD* incidence matrix for Table 5.2. A "1" indicates that the message in the column header appears in that slot; "0" indicates that it does not appear. A quick perusal shows that each message appears four times in each column.

Block	Message 1	Message 2	Message 3	Message 4	Message 5	Message 6	Message 7
1	1	0	1	0	0	1	1
2	1	1	0	0	1	0	1
3	0	0	1	1	1	0	1
4	0	1	0	1	0	1	1
5	1	1	1	1	0	0	0
6	1	0	0	1	1	1	0
7	0	1	1	0	1	1	0

TABLE 5.4 *BIBD* pairwise matrix for Table 5.2. The matrix is obviously a square matrix that is symmetric along the main diagonal. Only the upper triangle is shown here. The main diagonal shows the number of times each message occurs and the diagonal cell entries are the respective column sums of the incidence matrix, Table 5.3. Also note that the off-diagonal cell entries are all equal.

Message	Message 1	Message 2	Message 3	Message 4	Message 5	Message 6	Message 7
Message 1	4	2	2	2	2	2	2
Message 2		4	2	2	2	2	2
Message 3			4	2	2	2	2
Message 4				4	2	2	2
Message 5					4	2	2
Message 6						4	2
Message 7							4

TABLE 5.5 This is a typical choice set presented to a customer. For our example problem, this is the first choice set in Table 5.2. All seven choice sets in Table 5.2 are shown to each customer.

Select the message you prefer the most and the one you prefer the least to motivate you to buy the product. Please select only two messages.

	Message 6	Message 3	Message 7	Message 1
Most Preferred	————	————	————	————
Least Preferred	————	————	————	————

1. t = number of messages (also called treatments);
2. b = number of *rows* or *blocks* or *choice sets* in the final matrix;
3. k = number of columns in the final matrix;
4. n = total number of messages shown = $b \times k$;
5. r = number of times each message repeats;
6. λ = number of pairs of messages.

A shorthand notation for a *BIBD* with these parameters is $BIBD(t, b, r, k; \lambda)$. The n is not needed in the notation since it is defined by other parameters. For the example in Table 5.2, you have $BIBD(t = 7, b = 7, r = 4, k = 4; \lambda = 2)$.

The construction of such a design matrix is not trivial. In fact, there are many situations in which a design matrix is not possible. In these cases, you have two options:

1. settle for a non-optimal design; or
2. change the number of messages until you get a *BIBD*.

A non-optimal design may not be terrible to work with and so should not be discounted. Changing the number of messages, especially reducing the number, may be an issue because the creative team and management have to approve the change.

Data collection

Each customer in a survey is shown a set of messages one set at a time. A possible choice set presentation is shown in Table 5.5. A customer is asked to select the message they most prefer and least prefer as motivating them to buy the product. This is the *CTA*. Since the most and least preferred messages are selected, the issue of how they interpreted a rating scale is eliminated.

Estimation

Since each customer is asked to make a selection from each choice set, the problem becomes a choice problem similar to the conjoint and discrete choice problems. In fact, MaxDiff is akin to the discrete choice so the estimation methods for discrete choice can be used, although with slight data coding changes usually handled automatically by software. Nonetheless, the estimation is the same. This means the

MaxDiff result is a set of estimated utilities, one for each message. These utilities are usually scaled to lie between 0 and 1 and sum to 1.0 so they can, therefore, be interpreted as probabilities. See Paczkowski [2018] about utility scaling.

Case study

A pharmaceutical company has a new allergy medication nearing market launch. The marketing and advertising teams developed seven messages to test before a marketing campaign is launched. The messages are:

1. FDA approved.
2. Take just once per day.
3. No side effects.
4. Available over the counter.
5. Noticeable results in 12 hours.
6. Available in pill or liquid form.
7. Requires taking with food.

A $BIBD(t = 7, b = 7, r = 4, k = 4; \lambda = 2)$ was created. This design matrix is the one in Table 5.2. A panel of consumers known to have the allergy the medication targets was recruited for an online survey. The questionnaire contained modules on the consumers' general health (e.g., how long they had the allergy; its severity; medications currently taken) and routine demographics. The new medication was described in a module in the middle of the questionnaire. The consumers were then asked the MaxDiff questions. They were shown the seven choice sets and for each one they were asked to select the message that motivates them the most and the least to buy the new medication for their problem.

There were two responses for each choice set: the most preferred and the least preferred. Since there are seven choice sets, there were 14 responses per respondent. This is a respondent's *response pattern*. The data for each respondent were recorded in the order Best/Worst for the first choice set, Best/Worst for the second choice set, and so on. The values recorded were the numbers, $1, \ldots, 7$, of the selected messages. The estimated utilities and scaled utilities, which are interpreted as probabilities or take rates, are shown in Figure 5.4.

The estimated take rates indicate that consumers prefer the message "*Take just once a day*" whereas "*Requires taking with food*" ranks last. The convenience of taking the medication just once per day is important and motivates them to buy the medication. The food requirement, however, is a deterrent to buying.

Extending the framework

While the message analysis framework described in the previous section will work, it may still be insufficient, not because of the approach but because it may be too restrictive. Consumers evaluate messages or claims on multiple dimensions, the importance of the dimensions varying among consumers. I will now discuss a multidimensional adjustment to this message analysis framework.

MaxDiff Model

MaxDiff Results

Marginal Utility	Marginal Probability		Data
0.1679	0.1680		Take just once per day
0.0603	0.1508		No side effects
0.0344	0.1470		Noticable results in 12 hours
0.0215	0.1451		Available over the counter
-0.013	0.1402		Available in pill or liquid form
-0.052	0.1349		FDA approved
-0.220	0.1140		Requires taking with food

Parameter Estimates

Term	Estimate	Std Error
Data[Available in pill or liquid form]	-0.012856851	0.0607891413
Data[Available over the counter]	0.021473314	0.0607979612
Data[FDA approved]	-0.051624300	0.0608220624
Data[No side effects]	0.060312742	0.0608316315
Data[Noticable results in 12 hours]	0.034413888	0.0608216669
Data[Requires taking with food]	-0.219612625	0.0611678204

AICc	3471.3747
BIC	3498.5599
-2*LogLikelihood	3459.2534
-2*Firth LogLikelihood	3424.6486

Converged in Gradient

Firth Bias-Adjusted Estimates

Likelihood Ratio Tests

Source	L-R ChiSquare	DF	Prob>ChiSq	
Data	19.616	6	0.0032*	

FIGURE 5.4 The MaxDiff utility estimates and scaled utilities are shown here. The scaled utilities lie between 0 and 1 and sum to 1.0 so they can be interpreted as probabilities or take rates. The bar chart shows the messages ranked by their take rates. There is some differentiation among these messages.

The issue for message assessment is the effectiveness of a message on a business metric such as sales. There are two ways to view effectiveness: *perceived effectiveness* before launch of the message and *actual effectiveness* after launch of the message. Perceived effectiveness addresses the question "*Will the message work?*" while actual effectiveness addresses the question "*Did the message work?*". For perceived effectiveness, the only way to determine whether or not a message will work is by asking customers to assess the message quality. In a simplistic manner, this was done with the MaxDiff procedure. It was simplistic because quality assessment was one-dimensional: people either liked or disliked the message, or it motivated

FIGURE 5.5 This illustrates an enhanced view of the key drivers for assessing message effectiveness, both perceived and actual by incorporating impact and attitude measures.

them or it did not motivate them, and so forth. Assessment, however, is not one-dimensional but multidimensional, with the message simultaneously appealing to different psychological factors. People could assess a message on its persuasiveness, its logic, its believability, just to name a few factors.

In general, assessment factors could be grouped into two categories: *impact measures* and *attitude measures*. See Dillard et al. [2007b] for a discussion. Impact measures assess the effect a message will have on taking an action such as purchasing a product; that is, the *CTA*. They "shape" opinion or judgment as noted by Dillard et al. [2007b]. Is the message persuasive, compelling, believable, or convincing enough that the individual will buy the product? Attitude measures assess the judgment or acceptance of the message. Is the message plausible, sound, logical, or novel enough that the individual will pay attention to the message and possibly then buy the product? The outcome of both impact and attitude measures is the same – product purchase – but the path is different. In both cases, the individual will perceive the message to be effective and therefore behave a certain way – buy. The connection between the impact and attitude measures and effectiveness is illustrated in Figure 5.6.

Table 5.6 shows a list of potential impact measures while Table 5.7 shows a list of potential attitude measures. These were gleaned from Dillard et al. [2007a] and Dillard et al. [2007b].

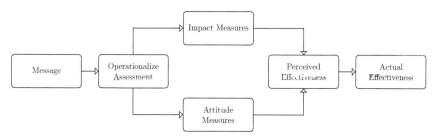

FIGURE 5.6 This illustrates the key drivers for assessing message effectiveness, both perceived and actual.

TABLE 5.6 Sample list of descriptors that could be used to measure the impact of a message.

Persuasive	Effective
Compelling	Convincing
Desirable	

TABLE 5.7 Sample list of descriptors that could be used to measure the attitude effect of a message. There is some overlap with the descriptors in Table 5.6.

Persuasive	Believable	Logical
Plausible	Sound	Motivating
Unique	Familiar	Memorable
Novel	Favorable	Friendly
Necessary	Good	Beneficial

Combinations of impact and attitude measures are sometimes used. Raghavarao et al. [2011] mention a study of Pennsylvania mushrooms involving nine message questions – which they refer to as brand concepts – and three scale questions: purchase intent, uniqueness, and believability. The purchase intent is the *CTA* while the uniqueness and believability are the attitude measures. Raghavarao et al. [2011] analyze only the purchase intent data using a method due to Landis and Koch [1977] that involves cumulative response proportions calculated from the responses on a five-point Likert scale ranging from 1 = *Very Unlikely to Purchase* to 5 = *Very Likely to Purchase*. The cumulative proportions are calculated for each brand concept although only four are maintained since the last is always 1.0. Let p_{ij} be the ith cumulative proportion for the jth concept, $i = 1, \ldots, 4$ and $j = 1, \ldots, 9$. The cumulative proportions are converted to logit values: $logit_{ij} = ln\left(p_{ij}/1-p_{ij}\right)$. Using appropriate dummy coding for the concepts, these logit values are modeled as a discrete choice model. See Raghavarao et al. [2011] for details.[4]

Another approach uses the MaxDiff framework. Suppose there are three measures as for the mushroom example: purchase intent, uniqueness, and believability. A customer is presented with a choice set of messages based on a *BIBD* and is asked to select the most preferred and least preferred message as before, but this time for each measure: once for purchase intent, once for uniqueness, and once for believability. If there are seven choice sets, a customer is asked to make 21 (= 3 measures × 7 sets) choices. Experience has shown that this task actually proceeds quickly. I have found it works for choice sets of seven to nine sets and up to five measures. The final data set has two columns (best followed by worst) for each set in the design times the number of measures. With seven choice sets and three measures, there are 2 × 7 × 3 = 42 columns of data, preferably with the first 14 for the first measure, the next 14 for the second measure, and the last 14 for the third measure. Take rates are estimated for each measure as described above. For our example, there are three sets of take rates with each set covering the seven messages. These could be arranged in one data table that has seven rows and three columns.

There are two ways to analyze the data table of take rates. The first is to plot the take rates for each column. The most common plot is a side-by-side bar chart. A better analysis is to recognize that the three measures are chosen to reflect the perceived effectiveness of the messages. One overall *perceived effectiveness index* (*PEI*) could be derived as the weighted average of the three measures, one weighted average for each message and one weight for each measure. The weights should sum to 1.0. This is a simple row weighted average for each message in the data table. The issue is the set of weights. There are four ways to derive them:

1. assign varying weights based on judgement;
2. assign a constant weight;
3. calculate the range of the take rates for each measure and then divide each range by the sum of the ranges; and
4. use the first principal component loading of the take rate table.

The first is obviously highly subjective and subject to challenge, especially if one person chooses the weights. A team of *SMEs* and *KOLs* could always decide on the weights, but this has the problem of assembling the right team. The second approach is a simple arithmetic average and is not insightful. The third is like the conjoint attribute importance method I described in Chapter 3. This has an intuitive appeal and is easily understood by management.

The principal component solution, outlined in the Appendix to Chapter 3, is more complicated because it involves knowing about principal components analysis (*PCA*), how to apply it, and how to interpret and use the results. Also, the method may be restricted by the number of messages relative to the number of observations. It is generally unclear what sample size should be used with *PCA*. Osborne [2004] and Shaukat et al. [2016] note that practitioners are divided between a sample size recommendation and a recommendation based on the ratio of sample size to number of items to use in the analysis, although most seem to gravitate to a ratio estimate. Osborne [2004] and Shaukat et al. [2016] note that ratio recommendations of 5:1 and 10:1 are common, although the latter due to Nunnally [1978] seems most commonly cited. See especially Shaukat et al. [2016] for citations on a number of recommendations. The focus on sample-item ratios is interesting since sampling theory *per se* does not concern itself with this ratio; the sample size to achieve a pre-specified precision, perhaps adjusted for the cost of collecting a sample, is the only issue. See Cochrane [1963] and Levy and Lemeshow [2008] for a good overview of sampling methodologies. The issue of sample size (or at least relative to the number of items) is generally important because, as noted by Osborne [2004], a large sample size tends "to minimize the probability of errors, maximize the accuracy of population estimates, and increase the generalizability of . . . results." For *PCA* with little or no guidance for sample size, Osborne [2004] further notes that overfitting can result which in turn results in "erroneous conclusions in several ways, including the extraction of erroneous factors or mis-assignment of items to factors."

This sample size issue (or a ratio issue) is important for using *PCA* with a multidimensional MaxDiff analysis of messages because the "sample" is actually the number of messages and the "items" are the dimensions. If there are 12 messages tested and three dimensions (e.g., purchase intent, uniqueness, and believability),

Message	Purchase Intent	Uniqueness	Believability	PEI
5	1	4	7	PEI_1

FIGURE 5.7 This *PEI* summary map shows the messages ranked ordered from "1" being highest ranked to "7" being lowest ranked for each measure. The whole table is sorted in descending order by the *PEI* value.

then the ratio of sample to items is only 4:1 which may be insufficient for good results.

I recommend the third method because of its simplicity and understandability.

Once the *PEI* is calculated for each message, they can be ranked in descending order by their *PEI* score. A bar chart could display the ranking. This shows which message is the overall "winner" in perceived effectiveness. The *PEI* scores could also be added to the take rate table as an additional column and the whole table sorted by the *PEI* score. A heatmap-like table could then be developed with the measures as rows and the *PEI* as columns. The table should be sorted in descending order by the *PEI*. It is helpful to know the rank order of each message on each measure so the cells of the table could contain the rank value of a message for a measure. An example is shown in Table 5.7 for a case of seven messages and three measures such as in the mushroom study. The advantage of this *PEI* summary table is that the best message is clearly indicated and the reasons for its rank are evident.

There is one further analysis that could be done based on the MaxDiff approach. The model I just described was estimated on an aggregate basis. This means the estimated utilities can be interpreted as averages of all the customers in the sample. Another way to estimate the utilities is at the individual level; that is, one set of utilities per customer in the sample. This estimation is obviously more complex. See Paczkowski [2016] and especially Paczkowski [2018]. One advantage of estimating at the individual level is that the resulting estimated utilities can be used in further analyses. One form of analysis is TURF which I described in Chapter 4. Paczkowski [2018] provides a detailed example of using estimated utilities in a TURF analysis.

I outlined a procedure for message testing that involved querying customers about different emotional aspects of a message. I referred to these as dimensions which could be, for example, believability, desirability, and memorability. A weighted average of the average utility scores, where the utilities were from MaxDiff estimations, could be calculated and this weighted score used to rank the messages. The advantage of this approach is that you can identify the drivers for the highest ranked message. For example, the highest ranked message based on the weighted average may also rank highest on believability and memorability.

Although useful, this procedure does not tell you why the message ranked high on, say, believability and memorability. What drove or motivated customers to rate these two dimensions high and, presumably, other dimensions low? Also, what motivated them to rate other messages the way they did? More information is needed to dissect the ratings.

A possible approach is to use demographic information along with other ratings to estimate a model of the mean utility scores for the messages. The demographic data are usually collected in a survey so they should be available. This data tells you about the nature of the people that may have driven them to rate the messages as they did. A simple approach is to profile the respondents by their individual ratings. Another is to estimate a MaxDiff model at the individual level using a Hierarchical Bayes estimation procedure and then profile the customers and their responses. Data visualization tools (e.g., boxplots) could be used to study the distribution of utilities by message and demographic characteristic. Another approach is to use a decision tree methodology with the utility scores as the dependent variable and the demographic variables as the independent variables.

A better approach, however, is to model the ratings as a function of the demographics and features or characteristics of the messages, characteristics that transcend the dimensions such as Believability, Desirability, and Memorability. These characteristics could be:

- terseness of the wording;
- average length of the message wording;
- tone (e.g., harsh, friendly, loving, threatening);
- style (e.g., simple, complicated);
- vocabulary;
- directness (e.g., blunt and to the point); and
- clarity and conciseness.

As noted by Sanders [1984]:

> The way in which messages are styled can amplify, dampen, or entirely cancel the public reactions of respondents to communicated information. Certain options of phrasing and syntax have this impact by constraining what can follow in the unfolding text or transaction with minimal risk of misinterpretation, and without undesired inductions about the character and traits of the respondent. Such stylistic options are a resource for strategic communication when conventions and protocols for structuring discourse do not apply or are rejected.

Also see Dillard [2014] on styles.

To learn about the effect of the message characteristics, you could ask the customers when they take the MaxDiff survey to rate each message on a list of characteristics such as the ones above. These characteristic ratings and the demographics could be used as independent variables in a regression model. In this case, however, there are multiple dependent variables; that is, each message dimension rating (e.g., on believability, desirability, and memorability) is a dependent variable. There would thus be a set of dependent variables. The goal is to uncover the relationship between a set of independent variables and a set of dependent variables.

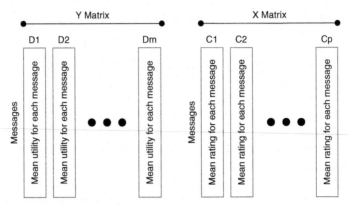

FIGURE 5.8 This illustrates a data format for using a *PLS* regression for estimating the effects of message characteristics ratings on message utility ratings. If there are N messages and m dimensions measured for each message (e.g., Believability, Desirability, and Memorability for $m = 3$), then the **Y** matrix has size $N \times m$. The cells of the matrix are the mean utility ratings. If there are p characteristics for the messages, then the **X** matrix has size $N \times p$. If demographics are included, then the mean utilities and characteristic ratings have to be grouped by logical combinations of the demographic variables which increases the N. For example, if income, measured as low/medium/high, and gender are included then there are six logical combinations. Mean utilities and ratings are grouped by these six combinations.

This is the structure for a partial least squares regression as outlined in the Appendix to Chapter 3. A data structure is illustrated in Figure 5.8.

This methodology could be used to uncover the key drivers for the messages while the MaxDiff approach outlined above reveals the top ranked message.

A/B *digital testing*

In the pre-Internet era, billboards, TV and radio spots, newspaper and magazine ads, and direct mail were the only means for promoting a message. Since the advent of the Internet, online digital ads are more dominant. This new form of promotion has introduced a new way to test messages online. This is *A/B* testing. The "*A*" and "*B*" refer to two variants of a message.

What is *A/B* testing?

A/B testing is a method to test:

- website landing pages;
- advertising and email messages;
- promotional offers;
- calls-to-action; and
- price points

to mention a few uses. The aim is to determine the impact on a key business metric, usually sales (click rates are also possible). In its simplest form, there are two steps:

1. Randomly assign each online store visitor to one of the two web pages, each with a variant of a message. Record the visitor's action. The visitor either made a purchase (i.e., converted) or not.
2. Arrange the data in a 2×2 table and then do a statistical test on the table to determine if there is a statistical difference in the metric, say sales.

The table might look like the one in Table 5.8. The number of "hits" is the number of consumers who visited the web page (the "visitor") and were exposed to a message. The *conversion rate* is the percent of exposed consumers who purchased the product because of the message. If h_i is the number of hits for message i, $i = A$, B, and $n_{i,Buy}$ is the number of the h_i consumers who purchased, then the conversion rate is

$$CR_i = \frac{n_{i,Buy}}{h_i} \times 100.$$

As an example, suppose you conduct an online study on your website for two weeks by randomly showing one message, A, to one group of visitors and another message, B, to another group of visitors during the same period. Suppose the total hits in the two-week period is 16,188. A summary table is shown in Table 5.9.

You can conduct a statistical test to determine if the proportion of online buyers is statistically the same for the two messages. If p_A is the proportion of web site visitors who convert who saw message A and p_B is the proportion given message

TABLE 5.8 This is a generic setup for an A/B test. The values $n_{ij}, i = 1, 2; j = 1, 2$ are the number of customers who saw the message for the respective row and column headers. The conversion rate is the percent of consumers who purchased (assuming a hit is equivalent to a consumer), given that they saw the message in that row margin so it is a marginal quantity.

Message	Hits	Buy	Not Buy	Conversion Rate
A	h_1	n_{11}	n_{12}	CR_1
B	h_2	n_{21}	n_{22}	CR_2

TABLE 5.9 Example A/B data.

Message	Hits	Buy	Not Buy	Conversion Rate
A	7,518	234	7,284	3.1%
B	8,670	504	8,166	5.8%

B, then the Null Hypothesis is

$$H_O : p_A = p_B = p$$

vs. the alternative that the proportions differ.[5] The proportion p is generally low. The statistical test is a chi-square test of significance. There are two possible tests: the *Pearson* and the *Likelihood-ratio Chi-square* Tests. These are reviewed in Appendix 3.A.

The two chi-square tests were conducted for the data summarized in Table 5.9. The results are shown in Figure 5.9 and Figure 5.10. The mosaic chart in Figure 5.9 simply shows that the overwhelming majority of site visitors did not buy so the

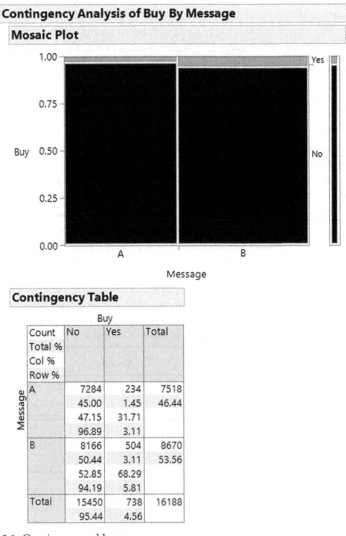

FIGURE 5.9 Contingency table summary.

Tests

N	DF	-LogLike	RSquare (U)
16188	1	34.719852	0.0116

Test	ChiSquare	Prob>ChiSq
Likelihood Ratio	69.440	<.0001*
Pearson	67.493	<.0001*

Fisher's Exact Test

	Prob	Alternative Hypothesis
Left	1.0000	Prob(Buy=Yes) is greater for Message=A than B
Right	<.0001*	Prob(Buy=Yes) is greater for Message=B than A
2-Tail	<.0001*	Prob(Buy=Yes) is different across Message

Odds Ratio

Odds Ratio	Lower 95%	Upper 95%
1.921212	1.640052	2.250572

FIGURE 5.10 Chi-square test results.

conversion rate was low. The contingency table at the bottom of the figure shows the relevant proportions. Figure 5.10 shows the two chi-square test results. From Figure 5.10, the Pearson Chi-square is 67.493 and the Likelihood-ratio Chi-square is 69.440. These are very large. For both tests, the p-values are below $\alpha = 0.05$, a traditional significant level, so the Null Hypothesis of equality is clearly rejected.

The test results in Figure 5.10 are based on the calculations in Appendix 3.A. This is standard in most elementary statistics textbooks. Another, more advanced approach is to use logistic regression to estimate a model fitting the *Buy/Not Buy* variable to the message indicator. Since the *Buy/Not Buy* variable is nominal with only two levels (*Buy* and *Not Buy*), OLS cannot be used to estimate parameters for three reasons:

1. OLS can predict any range of values, but this class of problems has only two, such as *Buy* and *Not Buy*;
2. OLS has a normally distributed disturbance term but this class of problems has a Bernoulli distribution; and
3. OLS has a constant variance under the Classical Assumptions for regression analysis but this class of problems has a nonconstant variance. See Gujarati [2003] for a review of the Classical Assumptions.

To see the Bernoulli disturbance for this problem, assume a linear in the parameters model is specified as

$$Y_i = \beta_0 + \beta_1 X_i + \epsilon_i$$

where Y_i has dummy coded values either 0 or 1. This is called a *Linear Probability Model*, or *LPM*. It assumes that $E(\epsilon_i) = 0$ so that $E(Y_i) = \beta_0 + \beta_1 X_i$. Now let

$$Pr(Y_i = 1) = p_i$$
$$Pr(Y_i = 0) = 1 - p_i.$$

Therefore,

$$E(Y_i) = 1 \times Pr(Y_i = 1) + 0 \times Pr(Y_i = 0)$$
$$= p_i.$$

This implies that

$$E(Y_i) = \beta_0 + \beta_1 X_i \quad \text{(a linear model)}$$
$$= p_i \quad \text{(a probability)}$$

so the mean (a linear function of X) must lie between 0 and 1, hence the name "linear probability model."

If the model is still $Y_i = \beta_0 + \beta_1 X_i + \epsilon_i$, then for $Y_i = 1$,

$$1 = \beta_0 + \beta_1 X_i + \epsilon_i$$

or

$$\epsilon_i = 1 - \beta_0 - \beta_1 X_i$$

with probability p_i since $Pr(Y_i = 1) = p_i$. For $Y_i = 0$,

$$\epsilon_i = -\beta_0 - \beta_1 X_i$$

with probability $1 - p_i$. The disturbance term can have only two values: $1 - \beta_0 - \beta_1 X_i$ with probability p_i and $-\beta_0 - \beta_1 X_i$ with probability $1 - p_i$ which means it is a Bernoulli, not a normal, random variable. This is not an issue since for large samples a Bernoulli random variable approaches a normally distributed random variable because of the Central Limit Theorem. See Gujarati [2003] for a discussion.

Now consider the variance of the disturbance given by

$$V(\epsilon_i) = E\left[\epsilon_i - E(\epsilon_i)\right]^2$$
$$= E(\epsilon_i^2)$$
$$= (1 - \beta_0 - \beta_1 X_i)^2 \times p_i + (-\beta_0 - \beta_1 X_i)^2 \times (1 - p_i)$$
$$= (1 - p_i)^2 \times p_i + (-p_i)^2 \times (1 - p_i)$$
$$= p_i(1 - p_i)$$

where the second line follows from $E(\epsilon_i) = 0$ and the fourth line follows from $E(Y_i) = \beta_0 + \beta_1 X_i = p_i$. The variance changes as X_i changes so the disturbance is heteroskedastic. This is not too bad since weighted least squares can always be used to make an adjustment. See Gujarati [2003] for a discussion.

The big issue is that the estimated value of Y_i, $\hat{Y}_i$, may not lie in the range $0 \le \hat{Y}_i \le 1$ so you may predict something that cannot physically happen. You need a new variable or a transformation of the dependent variable to ensure the right magnitudes. That is, you need a probability model with

$$0 \le p_i \le 1.$$

A *cumulative distribution function*, or *CDF*, defined as $Pr(X_i < x_i)$ will work. A model based on a *CDF* is

$$Pr(Y_i = 1) = p_i$$
$$= \frac{e^{\beta_0 + \beta_1 X_i}}{1 + e^{\beta_0 + \beta_1 X_i}}$$
$$= \frac{e^{Z_i}}{1 + e^{Z_i}}$$
$$Z_i = \beta_0 + \beta_1 X_i.$$

This is a *logistic distribution CDF*. For A/B testing, the X_i is message A and message B and Y_i is "Buy" and "Not Buy."

What happens when Z_i becomes large or small? Note that

$$Pr(Y_i = 1) = \frac{1}{1 + e^{-Z_i}}.$$

If $Z_i \to +\infty$, then $e^{-Z_i} = 0$ and $p_i = 1$. Similarly, if $Z_i \to -\infty$, then $p_i = 0$.

Finally, note that $\frac{e^{Z_i}}{1 + e^{Z_i}} + \left(1 - \frac{e^{Z_i}}{1 + e^{Z_i}}\right) = 1$ so the probabilities add correctly.

This model can be given an economic interpretation as

$$Pr(Y_i = 1) = \frac{e^{Z_i}}{1 + e^{Z_i}}$$
$$= Pr(\text{the probability someone chooses } option_1).$$

The numerator represents the influence of the independent variables and thus represents "choice". The "1" in the denominator represents "no choice". The factor $1 + e^{Z_i}$ represents the total choice option. The model is a choice model in the family of conjoint, discrete choice, and MaxDiff models but in this case the choice set has only two options.

The model can be written as

$$\frac{p_i}{1 - p_i} = \frac{\frac{e^{Z_i}}{1 + e^{Z_i}}}{1 - \frac{e^{Z_i}}{1 + e^{Z_i}}}$$
$$= e^{Z_i}.$$

The ratio $p_i/1 - p_i = e^{Z_i}$ is the *odds* of choosing $option_i$ from the choice set of two options. Odds come from sporting events and show the likelihood of an event happening. The odds of $3 : 1$ means the event is $3\times$ more likely to happen than not. The formula for any odds of an event happening is

$$Odds = \frac{\text{Probability of Event Happening}}{\text{Probability of Event Not Happening}} = \frac{p}{1 - p}.$$

TABLE 5.10 This is a summary of the relationship between probabilities and odds.

Probability of Event	Odds of Event
0 - 0.5	0 - 1
0.5 - 1	1 - ∞

Table 5.10 shows the relationship between probabilities and odds.

Taking the natural log of both sides of the odds, you get the "log odds", or

$$L = \ln\left(\frac{p_i}{1 - p_i}\right)$$

$$= \ln\left(e^{Z_i}\right)$$

$$= Z_i \ln(e)$$

$$= Z_i \quad \text{(Since ln and } e \text{ are inverses)}$$

$$= \beta_0 + \beta_1 X_{i1}$$

where L is called the *log odds* or *logit*.[6] This is a *logistic regression model*, a member of a large regression family. The unknown parameter, $\beta_k, k = 0, 1$ of the choice probability can be estimated using maximum likelihood (*ML*).

Although you can estimate the logit parameters, $\beta_k, k = 0, 1$, you would have difficulty interpreting them. The parameter β_1 shows the change in the log odds when its associated variable's value changes by one unit. This was not hard to understand for *OLS* because it is concerned with the change in Y for a change in X – the *marginal effect*. Now you have the change in the log odds. What does a change in log odds mean?

Assume a simple one-variable model for buying a product where X is discrete. Let X represent gender with the dummy coding: females = 0, males = 1. Then the log odds for females is

$$L_0 = \ln\left(\frac{p_0}{1 - p_0}\right)$$

$$= \beta_0$$

and the log odds for males is

$$L_1 = \ln\left(\frac{p_1}{1 - p_1}\right)$$

$$= \beta_0 + \beta_1.$$

Exponentiating both log odds and forming the ratio of males to females gives

$$\frac{e^{\ln\left(\frac{p_1}{1-p_1}\right)}}{e^{\ln\left(\frac{p_0}{1-p_0}\right)}} = \frac{\frac{p_1}{1-p_1}}{\frac{p_0}{1-p_0}}$$

$$= \frac{e^{\beta_0+\beta_1}}{e^{\beta_0}}$$

$$= \frac{e^{\beta_0} e^{\beta_1}}{e^{\beta_0}}$$

$$= e^{\beta_1}.$$

The exponentiation of β_1 is the odds of males buying the product to the odds of females buying the product. If the odds ratio is, say, 3, then the likelihood of males buying the product is 3× greater than the likelihood of females buying it.

The exponentiation rule is correct if dummy or *indicator variable* coding is used for the independent variable in estimation. Indicator coding uses "0" and "1" values for the coding where "0" represents the base. Recall that effects coding uses "-1" and "1" values where "-1" represents the base. The two coding schemes provide the same results, only the interpretations are different. Dummy coding shows the movement or difference from a base level while effects coding shows deviation from an overall mean. See Paczkowski [2018] for a thorough discussion of the two schemes. For the case considered here, the parameter estimate associated with indicator coding turns out to be twice the value of the parameter value based on effects coding. This means that if dummy coding is used, then the odds ratio is the exponentiated parameter; if effects coding is used, then it is the exponentiated parameter times 2 since $\frac{e^{\beta_0+\beta_1}}{e^{\beta_0-\beta_1}} = e^{2\times\beta_1}$. That is,

$$Odds\ Ratio = e^{\beta_1^{Indicator}} = e^{2\times\beta_1^{Effects}}.$$

The odds ratio also shows the degree of association between two variables, much like the correlation coefficient. This is summarized in Table 5.11.

A logit model was estimated for the *Buy/Not Buy* variable as a function of the message shown. The results are shown in Figure 5.11. The estimated parameter under effects coding is -0.3264781 while under indicator or dummy coding it is -0.652956. Notice that the indicator estimate is twice the effects estimate. The odds ratio using either (with the effects parameter multiplied by 2) is 0.52. This is interpreted as the odds of buying ("Yes") versus not buying ("No") when the message is "A" versus when it is "B." This means that someone is only half as likely to buy when the message is "A" as when it is "B". Notice also that $1/0.52 = 1.92$ which is the odds of buying when the message is "B" than when it is "A"; just the inverse. So someone is almost twice as likely to buy when message "B" is used rather than "A". This 1.92 odds ratio value is the same one shown in Figure 5.10.

TABLE 5.11 Odds ratio and association.

Odds Ratio Value	Interpretation
Greater than 1.0 (upper bound is infinity)	Positive association. The larger the value, the stronger the positive association.
Equal to 1.0	No association. The two variables are independent of one another.
Less than 1.0 (lower bound is 0)	Negative association. The smaller the value, the stronger the negative association.

The 95% confidence intervals are based on

$$e^{\ln OR \pm 1.96 \times se(\ln OR)}$$

where the standard error of the log of the odds ratio is

$$se(\ln OR) = \sqrt{\frac{1}{a} + \frac{1}{b} + \frac{1}{c} + \frac{1}{d}}$$

where "a", "b", "c", "d" are the frequency counts in the four cells of the contingency table. For our example, $a = 7284$, $b = 234$, $c = 8166$, and $d = 504$. The square root of the sum of the inverses is 0.080730. Therefore, the upper limit for the 95% confidence interval is $e^{\ln 1.921212 + 1.96 \times 0.080730} = 2.25057$ as shown in Figure 5.10 and Figure 5.11. The same calculation holds for the lower limit except for the use of a negative sign. See Agresti [2002] for a discussion of the confidence interval calculation.

Experimental designs

An experimental design was used for conjoint, discrete choice, and MaxDiff studies. One should also be used here. What is the design? There are two possibilities, both involving a random assignment to each message but with a twist. For both possibilities, a visitor is randomly assigned to one of two messages. Suppose, however, that a visitor returns to the website as they might for an online store. For the first approach, a record is kept of their visits and so if they were randomly assigned to message "A" on the first visit, then they are assigned to "A" on each subsequent visit. For the second approach, a visitor is randomly assigned to one of the two messages regardless of whether it is their first, second, or tenth visit. Each visit is a random assignment. It is not clear which is preferable. The first requires more record keeping and will then be more costly and onerous. It will, however, ensure that the visitor is not inconvenienced giving cause to become annoyed or angry at seeing different messages each time they visit the website.[7]

5.1.4 Message delivery

Messages have to be *delivered, deployed, dispersed,* or *spread* through the market to be effective. Basically, you have to "get the word out." At one time, this was easy.

Nominal Logistic Fit for Buy

Converged in Gradient, 6 iterations

Effects Coded Parameter Estimates

Term	Estimate	Std Error	ChiSquare	Prob>ChiSq
Intercept	-3.1116363	0.0403651	5942.4	<.0001*
Message[A]	-0.3264781	0.0403651	65.42	<.0001*

For log odds of Yes/No

Odds Ratios

For Buy odds of Yes versus No

Odds Ratios for Message

Level1	/Level2	Odds Ratio	Prob>Chisq	Lower 95%	Upper 95%
B	A	1.9212118	<.0001*	1.6400516	2.2505723
A	B	0.5205048	<.0001*	0.4443314	0.6097369

Normal approximations used for ratio confidence limits

effects: Message

Tests and confidence intervals on odds ratios are Wald based.

Indicator Coded Parameter Estimates

Term	Estimate	Std Error	ChiSquare	Prob>|t|
Intercept	-2.785158	0.045898	3682.3	<.0001*
Message[A]	-0.652956	0.08073	65.42	<.0001*

FIGURE 5.11 These are the logit model fit results.

Billboards, large print ads, TV and radio spots were the only forms of message dissemination. There was also the time-honored method of *word-of-mouth* (*WOM*). Basically, one person told something to someone who in turn told someone else and so on. This type of message dissemination was inherently dyadic: involving a relationship between two people. It works well in small, local markets but is more difficult to use and justify in large dispersed markets. In addition, the wider the market, the higher the probability the original message would become distorted and degraded.

In our modern, high-tech environment, these forms have diminished in importance, although they are certainly still used. They have been either replaced at worst or subordinated at best to more digital and social media methods. The traditional forms are less important to today's consumers who rely more on electronic, digital forms of communications. Most likely, this is due to the wider array of messaging channels such as chat rooms, emails, newsgroups, social media platforms, and so forth. See Christianson et al. [2008].

The various forms of social media are *networks* with complex interconnections and relationships. Marketing professionals, both academic and practitioners, and economists have been studying networks and their implications for a long time.

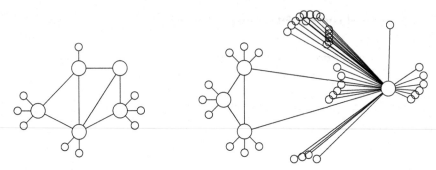

FIGURE 5.12 This shows two network hubs. See Leskovec et al. [2007] for a similar network chart.

Economists have mostly focused on the externalities generated by networks while marketers have focused on how to use them for practical purposes. See Mayer [2009] for a discussion of social networks in economics.

With the advent of social media, people in diverse disciplines have studied networks trying to understand their complexities and characteristics. One major feature is that social media networks are scale-free meaning network members are not homogeneously distributed. They are, instead, in clumps around central hubs or *centralities*. The example in Figure 5.12 shows clear groupings of people around a central person which is the hub. These hubs of people, because they touch so many others, can be influential both directly and indirectly. The collection of all hubs forms a set called the *Key Influencer Set* (*KIS*). The *KIS* contains all the people who have wide connections in the network and who, because of those connections, can greatly influence the thoughts, opinions, and behaviors of many others. They could be opinion leaders (*KOLs*), writers such as columnists and bloggers, early adopters, and so forth. Christianson et al. [2008] refers to a key influencer as someone who has a lot of social ties within a social network.

A message sent to one member of a *KIS* can be spread to many other people just as a biological or computer virus can be spread to many others – and spread exponentially. This is the basis for *viral marketing*: the spreading of a message through a network by taking advantage of the network's interconnections. Since the marketer has to send a message to only one person, the one who is a hub who then starts a chain reaction throughout the network, the costs of message deployment are greatly minimized. The deployment cost is the cost of contacting a hub person after which the marginal cost of deployment is zero. In addition, viral marketing is more effective because the influencers, those passing on the message, have credibility, are known entities (i.e., friends, coworkers, family members, recognized thought leaders, experts, etc.) and are viewed as believable, reliable, and trustworthy. A new product manager has every reason to want to use viral marketing: zero marginal cost, rapid dissemination of a message, and high credibility of those distributing the message. See Zhuang et al. [2013] for some discussion of viral marketing. See

Barabasi and Albert [1999] for a discussion about network scaling. The dispersion of a message from a hub via a social media network does not have the same message degradation issue as for the *WOM* dispersion in a small market because the social media dispersion is an electronic forwarding. Retweeting a tweet is the best example: the same tweet is spread and not changed as part of the forwarding.

Identifying a hub person, actually, identifying all members of a *KIS*, is a problem. A naive approach is to identify people meeting characteristics of someone most likely by a key influencer. Some characteristics are listed in Table 5.12. This is an interesting list but it does not lend itself to an operational method for identifying specific people. A higher level of aggregation of the characteristics of key influencers is shown in Figure 5.13 but this is also not useful for identifying specific people.

Identifying the *KIS*, as for the *WOM*, is not trivial. Zhuang et al. [2013] note that a naive, simplistic method is to scan a social media's membership records for those with the most connections. This is naive because many people would belong to the same subset of the network thus limiting their usefulness. A second approach is to look at all combinations of some people but the number of combinations would be huge making this computationally intractable. See Zhuang et al. [2013] for a brief comment.

Some social networks are huge to say the least with complex overlapping and interconnected relationships among their members. One person could be directly connected to 100 people, each of whom is directly connected to another 100

TABLE 5.12 This is a list of some characteristics of someone who might be classified as a key influencer or hub in a network. Partially based on Vollenbroek et al. [2014].

Active Mind	Trendsetter	Social Presence
Social Activity	Charismatic	Expertise
Communicative	Power	Shared Interests
Unique	Follow-up Activity	Innovative
Aware	Personal	Amount of Followers
Trustworthy	Early Adopter	Open-minded

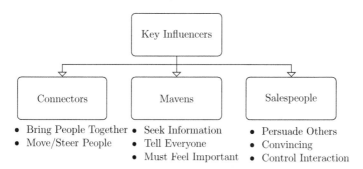

FIGURE 5.13 This is a higher level of aggregation. Based on Hoffman et al. [2016].

people, and so on. The number of pairs of connections is $\frac{N \times (N-1)}{2}$. For $N = 100$, the number of pairs is 4,950; for $N = 200$, it is 19,900. In 2016, LinkedIn had 500 million members, with 106 million active, in 200 countries. Its active user base has been estimated as 260 million in March 2017.[8] For N of this size, as it is for all social media networks, then the number of connections is astronomical. Despite this astronomical number, you have to identify only a small set of people, a key influential set (*KIS*), to start the epidemic.

Zhuang et al. [2013] propose selecting a *KIS* of M users by identifying those with the greatest number of connections that are not covered by other members of the set; that is, they are unduplicated. To do this, each member of the social network is first ranked by their number of connections. The one with the largest number is added to the *KIS*. That person and all his/her connections are then deleted from the main social media database. After the deletion, the now smaller database is sorted again by the number of connections each person has and the one with the largest number of connections is added to the *KIS*. That person and his/her connections are then deleted from the main social media database. This process is continued until either a target number of influencers M in the *KIS* is reached or the main database is depleted. In either case, the members of the *KIS* have the largest number of unique friends; they each reach the largest number of people without any duplication of coverage. This is the TURF analysis I described in Chapter 4.

Christianson et al. [2008] outline a system and methods (an "invention") for developing, testing, and tracking messages targeted to influencers for the *WOM* spreading of messages. The heart of the method is surveys with three key questions to get at *WOM*:

1. purchase intent;
2. message advocacy; and
3. message amplification.

The purchase intent question could be a 5-point Likert Scale question such as "*How likely are you to buy this product?*" A message advocacy question could ask how likely someone is to share information about the product. Message amplification measures "the potential *WOM* spread of the message."[9]. A question could ask how many friends or family members the respondent tells about the product. Christianson et al. [2008] suggest a question such as "*Of your 10 friends whom you talk with most often, how many of them would you tell about this idea?*".

For these questions, and others of their ilk, scores are calculated for the responses for each survey respondent. If five-point Likert Scales are used, simple means over all respondents can be calculated. Another approach is to assign weights to each point of the scales, the weights dependent on how consumers in past studies responded to similar questions and then eventually took the required action. For example, for purchase intent, if, as mentioned by Christianson et al. [2008] 100% of the people in past studies who said they would buy actually did buy and 50%

who said they are not likely to buy eventually did buy, then the weights of 1.0 and 0.5 can be applied to the responses for these response options. A weighted average index or score could then be calculated.

An interesting feature of the Christianson et al. [2008] method is the maintenance of a database of prior surveys, messages, and responses. This is the potential source for the weights mentioned above. It can also be the source for comparing results of a current study to those of past studies.

Other methods rely on principles from Graph Theory, a mathematical subdiscipline concerned with analyzing the properties of graphs, but not any graph. The graphs of Graph Theory are network graphs, such as the ones shown in Figure 5.12. There are (at least) four centrality identification methods that have been developed for such networks. Landherr et al. [2010] discussed these methods and reviewed their strengths and weaknesses. The four methods are:

Degree of Centrality (DC): the number of direct contacts of any one node in a network. The larger the degree, the wider the distribution of information. This is a simple method, one that is easily interpretable and is intuitive by nontechnical people.

Closeness Centrality (CC): the distance from one node to another. Nodes that are closer allow faster, more efficient distribution of information. Close friends, relatives, and associates are examples of close nodes while distant relatives or people you rarely contact are examples of distant nodes.

Betweenness Centrality (BC): the amount of intervening layers between two nodes in a network. The fewer the number of intervening layers between two nodes, the more direct and undistorted the information flow between the two nodes. Also, information distribution would be faster the fewer the layers the information has to flow through.

Eigenvector Centrality (EC): the degree of "well-connectedness" of two nodes. A node is well-connected if it is connected to other nodes that are themselves well-connected. Information distribution would be wider and faster for high EC.

Table 5.13 summarize these measures.

Another approach to determining the KIS is based on association rules, a methodology used in market research to determine the number of items that "go together" in a shopping cart. The set of items is called an *item set* or *market basket*. An example of an item set is hot dogs, hot dog buns, mustard, relish. These are four items someone planning a picnic typically buys. Erlandsson et al. [2016] argue that the methodology used to develop item sets can also be used to identify members of a KIS. See Erlandsson et al. [2016] for a discussion. Also see Qiao et al. [2017] for another approach based on entropy theory. There are many other approaches that are not documented in any professional literature because they are proprietary to consultants. These are basically black boxes that are most likely some form of one of the methods outlined here.

TABLE 5.13 Summary of centrality measures.

Centrality Measure	Characteristic
Degree of Centrality (*DC*)	Widespread of information
Closeness Centrality (*CC*)	Less degradation of information; faster, more efficient spreading of information
Betweenness Centrality (*BC*)	More direct distribution of information; less distortion; higher trust/greater willingness to forward information to next layer
Eigenvector Centrality (*EC*)	Widespread and fast

Once a *KIS* is identified, it has to be used in some process. A simple, naive viral marketing process is illustrated in Figure 5.14. Data on a social network (e.g., Facebook) is collected and then sent through a *KIS* engine that applies one of the above methods. A *KIS* is produced and then messages are sent to all members of the *KIS*. A more complex approach, illustrated in Figure 5.15, shows the process from Figure 5.14 on the right but with the "Deploy to Social Media" box moved and a Scoring Engine inserted. The left side of the figure shows a typical direct marketing process involving predictive modeling. This process is coupled with the *KIS* process because the *KIS* could be too large to be useful; only the most important members of the *KIS* have to be used. The process on the left takes the *KIS* as input, does the predictive modeling of the *KIS* members, and returns the model results to the Scoring Engine. Only a subset of the *KIS* is contacted. Basically, the whole process takes the social media database (which could be large as for LinkedIn with over a

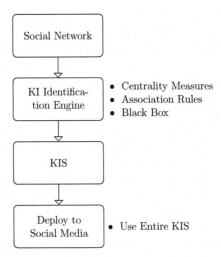

FIGURE 5.14 A simple application of a *KIS* involves sending messages to all members of the *KIS*.

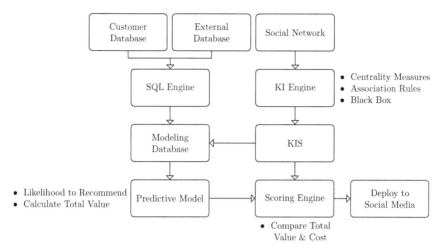

FIGURE 5.15 A more advanced application of a *KIS* involves sending messages to a smaller subset of the members of the *KIS*.

100 million active members as noted above) and targets a smaller portion, the really most influential social media members.

5.2 Price finalization

A second reason for a product failure is the wrong price point and price structure. The two combined define a pricing strategy. The price point is the actual number that goes on the product. The price structure is how that price point is presented to consumers. The structure could be simple: a uniform price in which the same price point applies to all consumers and is the same price point regardless of how much is consumed. This is the classic Economics 101 price from a supply and demand framework. Only one price is determined, the equilibrium price, that is the same for all buyers. In reality, there could be a different price point for different groups and different price points for the same group depending on how much is purchased. This is price discrimination.

Economists discuss three forms of price discrimination originally proposed by the British economist A.C. Pigou. See Pigou [1932]. They are simply referred to as *First Degree*, *Second Degree*, and *Third Degree Price Discrimination*. First Degree Price Discrimination occurs when the firm identifies a price, called the *reservation price*, that is applied to each unit of a good for each consumer in the market and charges that price. This is sometimes also referred to *personal pricing* by marketing experts because the pricing is unique to each person. This form of discrimination is often dismissed as impractical because it requires a lot of information on each consumer, basically their complete demand schedule, in order to develop an array of price points. Also, a computer infrastructure is required just to implement and track the prices and each consumer's individual purchasing behavior. Big Data and modern computer infrastructures make this somewhat doable and certainly attempts are currently underway to implement this form of price discrimination. But more has to be done. See Shiller [2013] for a discussion along with Paczkowski [2018].

Second Degree Price Discrimination occurs when the firm identifies or defines blocks of units of a good and charges a separate price for each block. The blocks represent or are defined by the amount purchased. The more blocks purchased, meaning the more units that are purchased, the lower the price for the marginal block. Everyone who purchases the same amount, that is they purchase in the same block, will see the same price schedule. This form of price discrimination is used by utility companies.

Third Degree Price Discrimination occurs when the firm segments the market and charges a different, but constant price for each segment based on price elasticities. The classic example is the price for a movie ticket. Senior citizens and students are considered to be more price elastic while everyone else is more price inelastic or has a lower degree of elasticity. Seniors and students are more elastic because the value of their time is lower which means they can search for another theater or do something else. Everyone else is less elastic because the value of their time is higher so they search less. Senior citizens and students are then charged a lower price and everyone else is charged a higher price. This is the form of price discrimination most commonly used. It is also the one typically found in an intermediate microeconomics textbook. See, for example, Ferguson [1972] and Gould and Lazear [1989]. Also see Paczkowski [2018].

Sometimes marketing and pricing analysts develop one part of a pricing strategy independent of the other part. It should not be done this way especially if you consider the case of Third Degree Price Discrimination. Separating the market into two or more groups and developing a price point for each should be done simultaneously so that they are consistent with one another.

The following two subsections consider ways to develop a single price point for a uniform pricing strategy (one price for all purchases by every consumer) and a price segmentation approach that determines the segments and price elasticities simultaneously. See Paczkowski [2018] for a thorough, in-depth discussion of these approaches as well as background on the forms of price discrimination.

5.2.1 Granger–Gabor analysis

There are many ways to develop a single price point. Conjoint and discrete choice models could be used with price as an attribute. I prefer that these approaches be used in the planning stage of a new product because they both involve other attributes that may not be settled upon before launch. At launch, however, most if not all of these attributes should be settled upon because production requirements have to be specified and responsibility for the new product shifts to the manufacturing division of the business. Production planning itself requires they be settled. The price point, however, is not part of production and could change up to the last minute before launch.[10] The Granger–Gabor pricing method could effectively be used to develop a single price point. This method is described next.

High-level background

The Granger–Gabor pricing method is a survey-based approach to developing a price point. It involves asking customers whether or not they would buy a product or service at a particular price point. Their response, either "*Yes*" or "*No*", is recorded. Another price point is presented and the same question is asked. Obviously, if a customer indicates that they would not buy the product at one price point, then, if they are rational, they would also not buy it at any higher price so only a lower price has to be asked. A lower price would be constantly presented and a response elicited until they said they would not buy, viewing the product as "cheap", or the lowest price point was reached. The end result is a series of yes/no responses and corresponding price points. The yes/no responses are dummy coded as 0 for "*No*" and 1 for "*Yes.*" An econometric model is then estimated and a price elasticity is determined. The elasticity is used in a simulator to estimate take rates for the different prices used in the study. The optimal price is the one that maximizes revenue or contribution for the product or service. See Paczkowski [2018] for more discussion of how this procedure works.

Two pieces of information are required for the Granger–Gabor method. First, the relevant target market must be known. This should have been developed in the earlier planning stages of new product development cycle. The second piece of information is a relevant price range to use in the iterative questioning I just outlined. This set of test prices comes from the earlier analytical work, primarily in the test phase. The van Westendorp method provided a price range which could be used with the Granger–Gabor method. Typically, however, the marketing and pricing teams develop a range often independent of other data that might be available.

The model basics: estimation and calculations

The input to the method is a data set consisting of an indicator variable of 0/1 values for the not buy/buy decisions and a column for the price points presented. Each customer has as many observations as the number of price points seen before stopping. The number will vary among the customers because each customer would stop at a different point. A logit model similar to the one presented above is estimated with the indicator variable as the dependent variable and the price variable as the independent variable. The model is

$$logit = \beta_0 + \beta_1 \times price.$$

The estimated parameters are used to calculate a take rate (i.e., the probability that a random customer would buy or take the product) for different price points. The estimated take rate is given by

$$\widehat{take} = \frac{e^{\hat{\beta}_0 + \hat{\beta}_1 \times price}}{1 + e^{\hat{\beta}_0 + \hat{\beta}_1 \times price}}.$$

Once the take rate is determined for a particular price point, it is multiplied by the size of the potential number of customers in the target market. This is the addressable market size. The product is the expected number of customers. Since the take rate is based on a particular price point, that price times the expected number of customers gives the expected revenue. These calculations are done for each price point in the range tested so that a table of price points, take rates, expected number of customers, and expected revenue is produced. The best price is the one for which expected revenue is highest (the maximum). See Paczkowski [2018] for an example.

5.2.2 Price segmentation

The Granger–Gabor method is good for determining a single price point for a uniform pricing strategy. As noted, however, a Third Degree Price Discrimination strategy is more the norm than the exception. This is a price segmentation strategy in which a different price is developed for different customer segments. Marketers are trained to think in terms of market segmentation as a strategy and develop different messages, perhaps even products, for the segments. Sometimes they also think of different price points so that the segmentation becomes more a price segmentation than not. The different price points, however, are usually developed **after** segments are developed, just the way messages, product variations, and so forth are developed after market segmentation. This is because they view segments as transcending all else in the market so they must be identified first before anything else can be developed. This is incorrect.

A segment consists of people who share similar characteristics such as buying patterns, demographic profiles, and attitude/interest/opinion (*AIO*) profiles. Their price responsiveness, that is, their elasticity, should be one of these characteristics because responsiveness is a feature of a person no different than their demographic makeup or *AIO* profile; it is part of them. These elasticities should be determined at the same time as the segments since they are fundamentally inseparable.

The classic way to segment the market is to use a two-stage process:

1. develop segments using a clustering technique such as hierarchical or k-means clustering; and
2. profile the segments using demographics, buying behaviors, or *AIO* measures.

Elasticities are then developed after the segments are defined and profiled.

A better approach is to simultaneously segment and profile the market where the segmentation includes a price variable. Segments are considered to be hidden or *latent* so this class of models is referred to as *Latent Class Models*. If a regression

TABLE 5.14 There are different types of latent variable models that are defined by the type of latent and indicator variables. Factor analysis is probably the best known because it is taught in standard multivariate statistics courses. It is defined for continuous latent (or factor) and indicator variables but is, nonetheless, often incorrectly used when the indicator is discrete. Source: Paczkowski [2018] and Collins and Lanza [2010].

		Latent Variable	
		Continuous	*Discrete*
Indicator Variable	Continuous	Factor Analysis	Latent Regression
	Discrete	Latent Trait	Latent Class

framework is used, the *Latent Regression Analysis* results. This is outlined in the next subsection. Various types of models are outlined in Table 5.14. See Paczkowski [2018] for an extensive discussion.

Latent regression approach

The *latent regression model* resembles an ordinary regression model except that it allows for a different set of parameters for the levels or classes of the latent variable. If the latent variable has only one level, then the two models are identical. As noted by Paczkowski [2018], the advantage of the latent regression model is that segments are identified at the same time as estimated parameters for those segments. The disadvantage is that the number of segments is undefined. You have to run multiple estimations to determine the best number, but this is no different than what is done for k-means clustering. This amounts to selecting the best number. See Paczkowski [2018] for a discussion and examples.

5.2.3 Pricing in a social network

The network concept introduced above stressed how people are interconnected and that this interconnectedness can be used for message deployment. The identification and exploitation of a *KIS* is the focal point of using a social network for messaging. The social network and the *KIS* can also be used for pricing and selling a new product. It operates by telling a potential customer that if they recommend the product they purchased to a friend, relative, associate, or coworker they will receive a cashback payment (i.e., reward) in the form of cash, gift card, coupons, or a discount on their next purchase. The seller thus influences the purchasing through the network.

As noted by Arthur et al. [2009], sellers try to monetize the information flow through a network, information that flows through the network for free via recommendations; that is, free publicity and advertising. It is not, however, solely this free flow of information they try to monetize; it is also the influence some people have as previously discussed. A cashback payment is basically a payment to an influencer for his/her recommendation and influence. The cashback is a form of a discount offer since the original price is reduced by the amount of the cashback. As a discount, this pricing strategy amounts to a Third Degree Price Discrimination strategy. See Narasimhan [1984] for a discussion about coupons as a form of price discrimination. In this framework, those who are more price elastic will take advantage of the cashback offer and pass on a recommendation (which is, of course, a message). The quality of the message is unknown to the seller at the time the cashback offer is accepted. Nonetheless, an offer is accepted and a recommendation is made. The party receiving the recommendation, the one contacted by the influencer, could choose to buy or not buy the product based on different stages of the discounted price and the strength of the influencer's recommendation. The latter is a function of the strength of the message sent by the influencer and the strength of the reputation of the influencer. A strong buy recommendation could be offset by a belief that the influencer is unreliable thus negating the recommendation.

The seller has an incentive to identify a *KIS* where the members of the set are viewed as highly likely to buy the product themselves, be highly likely to positively recommend the product to others, and be viewed as reliable, trustworthy, informed, and so forth, by members of the social network. The constituents of the *KIS* would thus be different from those of the messaging *KIS* who just have to be ones to forward a message and be reliable, etc. So the criteria for pricing and selling through an influencer on a social network are slightly broader and the problem is slightly more complex. See Arthur et al. [2009] for a discussion of the complexities.

5.3 Placing the new product

I do not discuss the Place component much because I believe placement is based on the targeted segments. For example, if college students are a target for soft drinks, then obviously college and universities are the places to investigate. Similarly, if senior citizens are a target for mobility devices such as walkers and motorized carts, then senior citizen centers and assisted living communities are places to explore. Once places are identified, then legalities enter the problem (e.g., contracts to place vending machines in student centers and lounges) and these are outside the scope of this book.

There are some considerations, of course, that go beyond legalities. Costs for placing a new product in particular markets is certainly one. Netflix, for example, estimates the costs associated with filming a new show in different locales. The costs they have to consider are for hiring extras, transportation of equipment, length of work day in the locale, just to mention a few. They then build a "hierarchical cost model" and estimate cost ratios for the components. They associate a prior distribution with these ratios that reflects their expertise and judgement for the costs in those areas. This amounts to a Bayesian approach. This forms the basis for deciding on a place for their production. See https://medium.com/netflix-techblog/studio-production-data-science-646ee2cc21a1 on Netflix's approach.

Not all companies are as advanced as Netflix. Most use judgement on deciding on a place for selling their product.

5.4 Software

General statistical software can be used do chi-square tests for A/B tests. Latent Regression estimation can be done in Latent Class Gold. JMP can be used for MaxDiff estimation.

5.5 Summary

This chapter is actually the first of two that are concerned with launching a new product. I am concerned with the messaging and final pricing in this one and forecasting sales in the other.

Messaging and pricing are just as important as the design which was the subject of most of the previous chapters. Pricing was mentioned a number of times in those earlier chapters but only with respect to preliminary pricing, primarily for business case development. The pricing discussed in this chapter is the "final" pricing. Pricing, however, is never finalized. Prices and price structures are always updated and refined based on market conditions. See Paczkowski [2018] for details of pricing research.

Messaging is new to this chapter so more attention was paid to this topic. Some simple and some complex ways to test messages were described. Like for pricing, however, message testing is an ongoing activity, but the methods I described here can be used beyond product launch.

Notes

1 There is earlier evidence of the mix concept in the 1940s. See https://en.wikipedia.org/wiki/Marketing_mix, last accessed on August 14, 2018.
2 A good summary of extensions as well as other approaches in given in the Wikipedia article on the Marketing Mix. See https://en.wikipedia.org/wiki/Marketing_mix, last accessed on August 14, 2018.
3 I typically recommend four.
4 Unfortunately, Raghavarao et al. [2011] did not provide a reference for the mushroom study and two of the authors have passed away since the book was published.
5 Note that $p_i = {}^{CR_i}/_{100}, i = A, B$.
6 The word *logit* is short for "logarithmic transformation". The logistic regression model is, therefore, often called a logit model. I tend to use the two terms interchangeably.
7 For some comments on these two approaches, see https://stats.stackexchange.com/questions/350919/experimental-design-in-a-b-tests, last accessed on November 7, 2018.
8 Based on https://foundationinc.co/lab/b2b-marketing-linkedin-stats/. Last accessed December 26, 2018.
9 Christianson et al. [2008, p. 6]
10 This is not completely true because a price message could be used as part of the launch campaign. Some lead time is needed to develop that promotional material.

6
LAUNCH II
How much will sell?

In Chapter 4, I described one way to forecast sales for a business case. Estimated take rates from a discrete choice study are applied to an estimate of the size of the target market to estimate expected total sales. This may be sufficient for a business case, but not at launch time for three reasons. First, once the product is launched, its performance must be tracked, as I discuss in Chapter 7, but part of tracking is assessing performance relative to objectives, otherwise you cannot tell if the product is doing well or not. Objectives are typically in terms of market share, return on investment (*ROI*), or sales growth. The sales force then becomes responsible for meeting these objectives. A forecast of units sold is the basis for these objectives.

The second reason for a forecast is that the manufacturing division of the business must produce the product so it needs to know how much to produce and how to plan for that production. Raw material must be ordered, factories must be retooled or new ones built, and personnel must be hired and trained or robots must be designed, built, and installed. Not only does this all require a lead time, but also the scale for this new capacity must be known. How much factory space is needed? How many new robots are required?

The third reason for a forecast is that final pricing has to be set but price points depend in part on expected sales; that is, demand. If sales are projected to be weak during an initial period after launch, then a low price point reflecting a penetration pricing strategy is required. On the other hand, if sales are projected to be extremely strong, especially because of early adopters, then a high price point is needed. More formally, in the former situation, demand is elastic so a low price point is needed while demand is inelastic in the latter situation thus dictating a high price point. All of this requires a sales forecast prior to launch. See Paczkowski [2018] on elasticities and pricing analytics and Nagle and Holden [2002] on pricing strategies.

In this chapter, I will discuss some of the mechanics and issues associated with developing a forecast. This will be done in eight sections. The first section

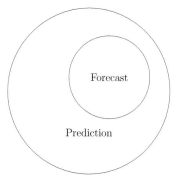

FIGURE 6.1 This Venn diagram illustrates the relationship between a forecast and a prediction. Predicting is a general concept with forecasting as a special case. This diagram shows that all forecasts are predictions but not all predictions are forecasts.

distinguishes between forecasting and predicting. They are not the same although they are nonetheless closely related. Forecast development responsibility is briefly mentioned in the second section. Since a demand forecast is based on a time series, it is helpful to define a time series. I do this in the third section. Data issues, which determine the possible type of forecast, are discussed in the fourth section. The fourth section provides some detail on forecast methods applicable for the amount and type of data available. Forecast methods and forecast error analysis are discussed in Sections 5 and 6, respectively. Sections 7 and 8 are for software and a summary. A technical appendix of the forecasting methods rounds out this chapter.

6.1 Predicting vs. forecasting

Let me first clear up confusion between the words "prediction" and "forecasting." The two terms have similar meaning in that they refer to producing a number for an unknown case or situation. Basically, they both fill in a "hole", something that is missing, in either our data or understanding. In this sense, they are the same. They differ, however, regarding the nature of the hole. Forecasting is concerned with time series data so it is concerned with saying something about what will happen in the future. The data "hole" is a future time period, a hole that should be obvious. Predicting, however, is concerned with an unknown case which could be in the future or it could be now under different situations. So you forecast this year's sales but you predict what sales would be under different price points. The relationship is illustrated in Figure 6.1.

6.2 Forecasting responsibility

Sometimes, sales forecasts are developed by different organizations. A forecasting department and the sales department, for example, might independently develop

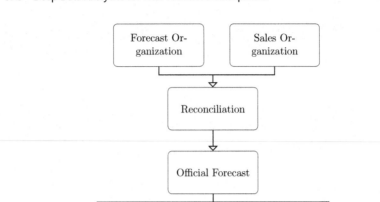

FIGURE 6.2 Forecasting requires a process just as the overall *NPD* requires a process. This flowchart illustrates how a forecast, developed by a forecasting organization which is responsible for developing and maintaining a forecast, is reconciled with views held by the sales organization. The resulting reconciled forecast is shared with other organizations that depend on it for their operations.

forecasts but the business can only use one. These diverse forecasts must be reconciled to produce one official forecast that guides manufacturing, sales, procurement, capacity planning, and pricing. A stylized sales forecasting reconciliation process is outlined in Figure 6.2.

6.3 Time series and forecasting background

Regardless of how a forecast is developed, a time series is needed. Let $Y_1, Y_2, \ldots, Y_T$ be a time series from period $t = 1$ to period $t = T$ where T is the most recent, last period before the forecast begins. A forecast is made in period $t = T$ for period $t = T + 1$ based on, or conditioned on, all the past history in the time series. For one method, described below, the history is of no consequence; just the last data point counts. This is obviously a naive method. Technically, the conditioning should be explicitly stated but I will drop reference to it for simplicity in what follows.

A forecast for a future period is referred to as a "step ahead." A forecast for one period into the future is a "1-step ahead" forecast; a two-period forecast is a "2-step ahead" forecast; a forecast $h = 1, 2, \ldots$ periods into the future is an "h-step ahead" forecast. A forecast made at $t = T$ for the next period outside the history of actual observations is denoted as $Y_T(1)$. This is a 1-step ahead forecast for period $t = T + 1$ made in period T (conditioned on the past). The h-step ahead forecast, $Y_T(h)$, is the h-period ahead forecast made in period T. The set of values $\{Y_T(1), Y_T(2), Y_T(3), \ldots, Y_T(k)\}$ is a *forecast profile*. When a new value, Y_{T+h}, becomes available in period $T + h$, this value is referred to as an *actual*. There is a forecasted value for period $T + h$, $Y_T(h)$, and an actual value, Y_{T+h}.

6.4 Data issues

Forecasting in general is difficult regardless of the responsible organization or the extent of a reconciliation process. The newness of a product compounds the difficulty because of the lack or sparsity of data. By definition, the product is not yet available to generate sales data. Nonetheless, there may still be data that can be used as I will discuss shortly. There are several methods available to forecast for products with some data history. These include *econometric models, Autoregressive Integrated Moving Average (ARIMA)* models, *simple trending*, and *smoothing techniques* such as *exponential smoothing*. Which one is used depends on the level of sophistication of the business analysts, the amount of data available, and the influence of seasonality and external economic patterns (e.g., the business cycle). See Wei [2006] and Hyndman and Athanasopoulos [2018] for discussions of general forecasting methods. Even for these methods, sample size is an issue since the historical data may still be insufficient. Mik [2019] and Hyndman and Kostenko [2007] note that a sample size of 16–17 months is necessary for ARIMA and exponential smoothing models to produce adequate and acceptable forecasts. Mik [2019] also notes that when seasonality is present, even more data are required. These sample sizes may not be, and often are not, possible for new products.

The type and amount of historical data depends on the nature of the new product. Not all new products have the same form of "newness." Kahn [2006], reported in Mik [2019], listed seven types of new products based on their combination of embedded technology and market focus. Table 6.3 summarizes the combinations

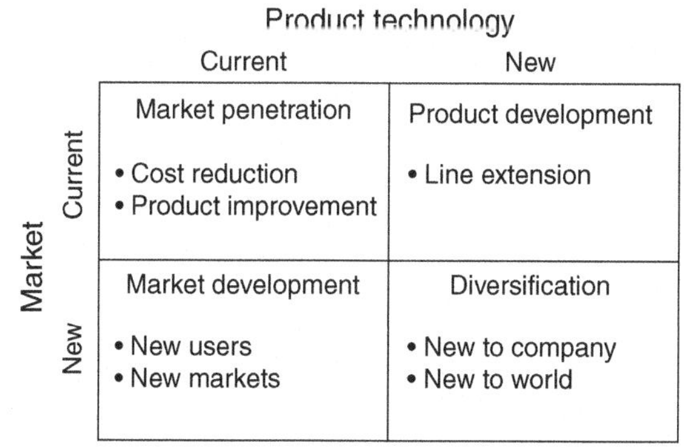

		Product technology	
		Current	New
Market	Current	Market penetration • Cost reduction • Product improvement	Product development • Line extension
	New	Market development • New users • New markets	Diversification • New to company • New to world

FIGURE 6.3 Definitions of new products based on Kahn [2006].

and the seven types of "newness." To simplify my discussion, however, I will only distinguish between two types: new-to-the-world (*NTW*) and not new-to-the-world (*NNTW*). The former are revolutionary items that have never been seen before in any form and people have no inkling they are about to be introduced to the market. In fact, these products create new markets. The Apple iPad, iPod, and iPhone are excellent examples of *NTW* products that had never been seen before and resulted in the creation of new markets which were eventually populated with a host of similar products. *NNTW* products, like the ones that followed the three Apple products, are basically variations of a theme of something that already exists. There is a change of some kind that warrants a new marketing strategy, production effort, sales and marketing campaign, and so forth. *NNTW* products could be completely new to the firm, that is, a new line it had never developed or marketed before, or an extension to an existing line. Some categorizes of *NNTW* products are:[1]

- new to the firm;
- new to a product line;
- an enhancement to an existing product; and
- a repositioning of an existing product.

For forecasting, the type is not important; the amount of data available for it is the important factor. I will discuss two cases in the next subsection followed by forecasting methods available for each case.

6.4.1 Data availability

There are two cases of data availability: no data are available and some data are available.

Case I: no data available

New-to-the-world products are the only type of new product in this category. Since they are completely new, historical sales data, whether internal or external (i.e., competitive) are unavailable and there are no *analog products*. An analog product is one that already exists and has characteristics, functions, form, and features similar to the new product, but yet differs from the new product in at least one significant way. The analog would have a sales history that could be used, albeit with caveats because it is only an analog. The lack of an analog, however, makes forecasting the *NTW* product difficult since there is literally nothing to work with. Another way to forecast, perhaps using judgement only, is needed.

Case II: some data available

A lack of data of any form and quantity for *NNTW* forecasting, is unrealistic. Some data should be available for these products, although they may not be what most analysts consider useful or sufficient. For example, if a market test was conducted to determine selling potential and identifying product issues (e.g., usability) then sales data collected during the test could be used for forecasting when the product is ready for launch. If a clinic was conducted, then sales data would not be available since sales were not made, but a discrete choice experiment could be part of the clinic and the estimated take rates from the experiment could be used as I described above. In fact, a clinic is not necessary since discrete choice experiments could be conducted outside, or independent, of clinics. Several choice studies could be conducted and results averaged to yield a more robust set of take rates.

Data may be available for competitive analog products. These data may be difficult to obtain, but most large companies have competitive assessment and tracking groups that can develop estimates of sales and market share as well as collect price data. *Web crawlers*, also known as *spiders* and *spiderbots*, crawl the world wide web looking for information. Crawlers could be used to gather data and message data but crawling for sales data may be more difficult if not impossible because sales data are generally not publicly available. See Lemahieu et al. [2018] for some discussion about web crawlers. Also see the Wikipedia article at https://en.wikipedia.org/wiki/Web_crawler on web crawlers.

Data for internal products in the same or similar line are definitely available. Data for internal analog products can be combined in some fashion. Baardman et al. [2017] note that one method used by practitioners involves convening a team of experts, perhaps *SMEs* and *KOLs*, to identify which products should be combined if the product line is sufficiently large. A simple averaging of the data for the selected products yields the needed series. They refer to this as a "cluster-then-estimate" approach: subjectively form a cluster of products that seem appropriate for the new product and then use the average sales data for forecast model estimation for the new product. This is a simplistic approach but an easily explained and intuitive one.

Baardman et al. [2017] proposed a method that involves a different form of clustering of analog products that involves simultaneously building a cluster and fitting a forecasting model to the cluster. They call their method "cluster-while-estimate." The models are standard regression models. These models, and other modeling approaches that can be used in new product forecasting, will be discussed in Section 6.5. Baardman et al. [2017] note an issue with their approach: its complexity. There are potentially a large number of parameters that have to be estimated since one model is needed to cluster the products and another is needed to produce a forecast. They note that this problem is "NP-hard and practically intractable."[2] However, they developed an algorithm that makes the problem more tractable and thus practical to use. See Baardman et al. [2017] for details.

6.4.2 *Training and testing data sets*

A best practice to follow, when possible, is to split historical time series data into two parts for model estimation: training and testing data sets as I mentioned in Chapter 2. The training data set contains historical data used to "train" a forecasting model. Training means estimation. Since a time series is the basis for a forecast, typically either the first $^2/_3$ or $^3/_4$ is used for training. Other terminology for this data set includes "with-in sample", "initialization period", and "calibration period" data set.

The testing data set is the remaining historical data reserved to "test" the results of the forecasting model using forecast accuracy measures such as the ones I describe below. I also discuss forecast accuracy testing in Chapter 7, but the difference between the testing I describe there and here, even though the same statistics are used, is the focus. In Chapter 7, the focus is actual market performance relative to the forecasted performance. Here, the focus is on how well a forecast model predicts the future before that future is known. The only way to judge this is with a surrogate for the future. This is the testing data set. Other terminology for the testing data set includes "test period", "validation period", and "holdout-sample period" data set.

Notice that the division into two data sets is not based on random sampling. It can not be; random sampling will result in nonsequential data in both data sets. In other words, random sampling will produce gaps in a time series because some of the time periods will be (randomly) assigned to one of the two data sets. We prefer "gapless" time series. The method for splitting to preserve the time sequence involves picking a period and declaring all data before it to be training data and all other data to be testing data.

Also common is dividing the data such that only a few observations at the end of the series are held back for testing. This depends on how far out you want to forecast. If you want to forecast only 1 or 2 steps ahead, then only hold back 1 or 2 of the last observations. If your data set is small, then it is not practical to hold out too many – fit might be jeopardized if too many are withheld from the training data set. Hold out only a few of the precious observations. Some people use all the data for training a model. Then what is used for testing accuracy? The only possibility is future actuals which may take too long to come in, but more importantly there is no way to develop confidence in the forecast.

Figure 6.4 shows how a time series is divided.

I discuss forecast accuracy below and again in Chapter 7.

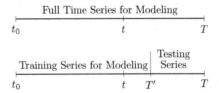

FIGURE 6.4 Period t_0 is the starting time for the data set and T is the ending time. The original data set spans this entire time interval. T' is an arbitrarily set period for dividing the original data into two parts. The first part from t_0 to T' is the training data set and the remainder from $T' + 1$ to T is the testing data set.

6.5 Forecasting methods based on data availability

Without historical or analog data, non-modeling methods have to be used to develop a forecast. Judgement can certainly be used, and often is. This involves management contributing their opinions as well as experts, *SMEs* and *KOLs*, providing their input sometimes in a panel setting. The Delphi method is an alternative way to get their input. This involves using a questionnaire rather than talking to the experts in person. As noted by Levenbach and Cleary [2006], there are criticisms of this approach that include the true level of expertise of the panel, the clarity of the questionnaire, and the reliability of the forecasts based on the survey results. Also see Hyndman and Athanasopoulos [2018] for other discussions of judgement-based forecasts.

There are more opportunities for forecast modeling when there is some data. The possibilities depend on the amount. I will divide the possibilities into two classes: naive and sophisticated.

6.5.1 Naive methods

There are two naive methods. One is actually called a *naive forecasting model* and the other is a *constant mean model*. Both are naive because they rely on simplistic assumptions. Yet both have proven useful in applications.

Naive forecasting model

A naive forecasting model uses the current period's actual value for the 1-step ahead forecast

$$Y_T(1) = Y_T.$$

This is sometimes called the *Naive Forecast 1*, or *NF1*. See Levenbach and Cleary [2006]. A naive h-step ahead forecast is a repetition of the one-step ahead forecast since nothing else is known beyond period T so $Y_T(h) = Y_T, \forall h \geq 1$. For this model, $V[Y_T(h)] = h\sigma^2$. This is a *random walk* model. See the Appendix for details.

A problem with a naive forecast is that each time a new actual value becomes available, a new forecast must be generated. This is not so onerous because modern software can easily make the adjustments.

Another problem occurs when there is a change from the penultimate to last observation in a series. If there was a drop that brought you to the last actual, then it is reasonable to believe the drop will repeat so the first future value should be lower than the last actual value. This change in the actuals is not considered in the *NF1*, just the last value is used, so the forecast will be wrong from the start. The change in the actuals is handled by modifying the naive procedure to be

$$Y_T(1) = Y_T + p(Y_T - Y_{T-1})$$

where p is the proportion of the change from period $T - 1$ to T you wish to include. This is *Naive Forecast 2* (*NF2*). There is also a *Naive Forecast 3*, or *NF3*, that accounts for seasonality. Seasonality may be a problem for a new product forecast but it depends on the nature of the product and the length of the available time series. See Levenbach and Cleary [2006] for some discussion.

New actuals will become available for a new product once the product is launched so *NF1* or *NF2* can only be used for a short period of time. The length of the time depends on the sales generating process. Once a sufficiently long set of actuals is developed, a different, more sophisticated forecasting method should be used and *NF1* and *NF2* dropped.

Constant mean method

Another naive procedure, if more historical data are available, is to average the most recent values and use the average for the forecast. This is a *constant mean model*. See Gilchrist [1976]. This model assumes that

$$Y_t = \mu + \epsilon_t, t = 1, 2, \ldots, T$$

where $\epsilon_t \sim \mathcal{N}(0, \sigma^2)$ and $COV(\epsilon_t, \epsilon_{t-j}), \forall t, j$ is *white noise*. The actual value in period $T + h$ is

$$Y_{T+h} = \mu + \epsilon_{T+h}.$$

The h-step ahead forecast based on data up to time T is $Y_T(h) = \mu + \epsilon_{T+h}$, but since you do not know the future disturbance term when the forecast is made, you have to use its expected value which is zero. Therefore, the h-step ahead forecast is merely $Y_T(h) = \mu$. Since you also do not know the mean μ, you substitute the unbiased estimate of μ which is the sample mean, $\bar{Y} = 1/T \sum_{t=1}^{T} Y_t$. An estimate of the h-step ahead forecast is then $\hat{Y}_T(h) = 1/T \sum_{t=1}^{T} Y_t$.

6.5.2 Sophisticated forecasting methods

The *NF1* and constant mean models are useful when small amounts of data are available, which is the typical case. If only one data point is available, then the *NF1* and constant mean models are identical; they diverge otherwise. In situations where more data are available, perhaps from analogs, then more advanced methods can be used. These include *ARIMA* modeling which is actually a family of methods, trend analysis, econometric analysis with key driver variables (e.g., real GDP), and smoothing techniques such as exponential smoothing. Exponential smoothing is a member of the *ARIMA* family. The *ARIMA* family is summarized in the Appendix to this chapter. Modeling possibilities based on data availability are summarized in Figure 6.5.

Smoothing methods

The basic structure for a constant mean was developed above. This model, however, is only good for short periods. It is unlikely that the mean will be constant from one *locality in time* to another. A locality is a period of time, say the first 5 months,

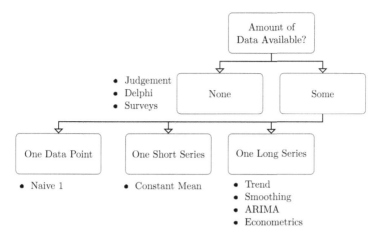

FIGURE 6.5 This decision tree will help you select a forecasting methodology based on data availability.

the second 5 months, etc. This is also sometimes referred to as a *window*. The mean, μ, is often viewed as a slowly varying quantity. I will consider situations in which the mean changes later.

In the constant mean model, averaging over all the data has the effect of reducing random variation, leaving an estimate of μ. If an estimate of μ is required in only one locality of the data, then you can average the data for that locality and ignore the rest. But this is unlikely. You will typically be interested in many localities. A *moving average* is the most popular technique for handling many localities because of its simplicity. It is based on averaging a sliding window of values over time resulting in a *smoothing* of historical data in which the effects of seasonality and randomness are eliminated or reduced. This method is good for short-term forecasts of one or two steps ahead. As long as no trending is expected in the immediate future and no seasonality is present, this is an effective, readily understood, and practical method.

Like any average, moving averages are based on weighted data, but the weights for a simple average are all constant at $1/n$, where n is the number of values being averaged in a window. Clearly, these weights are positive and sum to 1.0. You could use any window size. The larger the n, the greater the smoothing. The n-term moving average is

$$\overline{Y_{t,n}} = \frac{Y_t + Y_{t-1} + \ldots + Y_{t-(n-1)}}{n}$$

$$= \frac{1}{n}\sum_{i=0}^{n-1} Y_{t-i}.$$

A 1-step ahead forecast made at $t = T$ based on a simple moving average is found by setting the forecast equal to the value of the moving average at $t = T$

$$Y_T(1) = \overline{Y_{T,n}}.$$

It is the last smoothed value based on the last n actuals – you can not do any more calculations because there is no more data. The h-step ahead forecast, $Y_T(h)$, based on a simple moving average is a repetition of the one-step ahead forecast: $Y_T(h) = Y_T(1)$ for $h \geq 1$.

For forecasting short-term demand based on weekly or daily data, the most recent historical period is usually the most informative. So you want to weight the most recent values in a window more heavily. The weighted n-term moving average is

$$\overline{Y_{t,n}} = \frac{w_1 Y_t + w_2 Y_{t-1} + \ldots + w_n Y_{t-(n-1)}}{n}$$

$$= \frac{1}{n} \sum_{i=0}^{(n-1)} w_{i+1} Y_{t-i}.$$

The w_i weights are positive and must sum to 1.0.[3] The 1-step ahead forecast, $Y_T(1)$, based on a weighted moving average, is $\overline{Y_{t,n}}$ as above. The h-step ahead forecast, $Y_T(h)$, is the h-step ahead forecast given by a repetition of the one-step ahead forecast:

$$Y_T(h) = Y_T(1)$$

for $h \geq 1$.

The one-step ahead forecast based on the simple moving average can be written as

$$Y_T(1) = Y_{T-1}(1) - \frac{Y_{T-n}}{n} + \frac{Y_T}{n}.$$

Suppose you only have the most recent observed value, Y_T, and the one-step ahead forecast for that same period, $Y_{T-1}(1)$, made in the previous period, $T-1$. The value Y_{T-n} is unavailable because it is outside the window, but you could use an approximate value, the most likely being the one-step ahead forecast from the preceding period, $Y_{T-1}(1)$. The updated formula is now

$$Y_T(1) = Y_{T-1}(1) - \frac{Y_{T-n}}{n} + \frac{Y_T}{n}$$

$$= Y_{T-1}(1) - \frac{Y_{T-1}(1)}{n} + \frac{Y_T}{n}$$

$$= \frac{1}{n} Y_T + \left(1 - \frac{1}{n}\right) Y_{T-1}(1).$$

Let $\alpha = 1/n$. Then you have a general form of an equation for forecasting by the method of *exponential smoothing* or *exponential averaging*

$$Y_T(1) = \alpha Y_T + (1-\alpha) Y_{T-1}(1).$$

You only need the most recent observation, Y_T, the most recent forecast for T, $Y_{T-1}(1)$, and a value for α, the weight placed on "today."

You need $0 < \alpha < 1$. It can be specified or estimated. The α is typically specified by the user rather than estimated from data. Experience has shown that good values for α are between 0.05 and 0.3. As a general rule, smaller smoothing weights are appropriate for series with a slowly changing trend, while larger weights are appropriate for volatile series with a rapidly changing trend. You can "estimate" α by repeatedly trying different values for α (typically $0.1, 0.2, \ldots, 0.9$), checking some error statistic such as *mean square error* (*MSE*), and then choosing that value of α that gives the best value for the statistics (e.g., minimum *MSE*). This is a *grid search*.

This discussion of moving averages and exponential smoothing follows Wheelwright and Makridakis [1980]. Also see Levenbach and Cleary [2006].

Linear trend method

Consider the model

$$Y_t = \beta_0 + \beta_1 t + \epsilon_t.$$

Without the $\beta_1 t$ term, you have the constant mean model. For the model with the $\beta_1 t$ term, you have a simple linear regression model with a time trend variable capturing an underlying trend in the data. The variable is $t = 1, 2, \ldots, T$. This variable is interval scaled, meaning you can change variable definition by adding a constant and results invariant to change. For example, you can add 1900 to t and estimation is unaffected.

The 1-step ahead forecast, $Y_T(1)$, is obtained by substituting the time $t = T + 1$ into the fitted model

$$Y_T(1) = \hat{\beta}_0 + \hat{\beta}_1 \times (T + 1).$$

The forecast error for $Y_T(1)$ is

$$\begin{aligned}
e_{T+1} &= Y_{T+1} - Y_T(1) \\
&= [\beta_0 + \beta_1(T+1) + \epsilon_{T+1}] - [\hat{\beta}_0 + \hat{\beta}_1 \times (T+1)] \\
&= \beta_0 - \hat{\beta}_0 + (\beta_1 - \hat{\beta}_1) \times (T+1) + \epsilon_{T+1}.
\end{aligned}$$

Observe that $E(e_{T+1}) = 0$ since $E(\hat{\beta}_0) = \beta_0$ and $E(\hat{\beta}_1) = \beta_1$. Therefore, $E[Y_T(1)] = Y_{T+1}$, so the forecast is unbiased. The *MSE* is

$$\begin{aligned}
MSE &- E(e_{T+1}^2) \\
&= Var(e_{T+1}) \\
&= Var(\hat{\beta}_0) + (T+1)^2 \, Var(\hat{\beta}_1) + \sigma^2 \\
&= \sigma^2 \left(\frac{1}{T+1} + \frac{(T+1)^2}{\sum t^2} + 1 \right).
\end{aligned}$$

Econometric methods

The linear trend method is a special case in the econometric family of models. The larger, more general family includes explanatory variables such as prices, competitive factors, real GDP, and so forth. Forecasting is more complicated because separate forecasts of these other explanatory variables are needed. The linear trend is simpler for forecasting because you just have to extend the time variable to however far into the future you want to go. You cannot simply do this with a larger econometric model.

ARIMA methods

ARIMA is an acronym for *AutoRegressive Integrated Moving Average*. This is a family of models that has as special cases some of the models I discussed above. In fact, an econometric model is also a special case of an even wider *ARIMA* model called a *transfer function model*. The basics of an *ARIMA* are discussed in the Appendix to this chapter.

6.5.3 Data requirements

The actual method used depends on data availability. There are no hard and fast rules for how much data you need for any method, just rules-of-thumb.

To quote Hyndman and Athanasopoulos [2018]:

> *We often get asked how few data points can be used to fit a time series model. As with almost all sample size questions, there is no easy answer. It depends on the number of model parameters to be estimated and the amount of randomness in the data. The sample size required increases with the number of parameters to be estimated, and the amount of noise in the data.*
>
> *Some textbooks provide rules-of-thumb giving minimum sample sizes for various time series models. These are misleading and unsubstantiated in theory or practice. Further, they ignore the underlying variability of the data and often overlook the number of parameters to be estimated as well. There is, for example, no justification whatever for the magic number of 30 often given as a minimum for ARIMA modelling. The only theoretical limit is that we need more observations than there are parameters in our forecasting model. However, in practice, we usually need substantially more observations than that.*

6.6 Forecast error analysis

The previous sections focused on models or methods using the training data set portion. Recall that a portion of the time series data set was reserved, if possible, for testing. There are many ways to test a forecast, but they all basically rely on the use of measures using the *forecast error* at time t defined as

$$\text{Forecast Error}_t = \text{Actual}_t - \text{Forecast}_T(t)$$

where *Actual*$_t$ is the actual value in the testing data set and *Forecast*$_T(t)$ is the forecasted value in the testing data set. The forecasted value is based on the training data that ended at time T. The error measurement is illustrated in Figure 6.6. Forecast

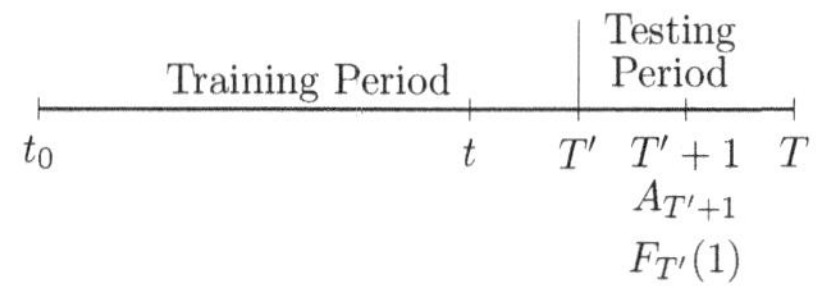

FIGURE 6.6 This time line illustrates the values used for measuring forecast accuracy during model development. The training period, as described earlier, extends from t_0 to T' and the testing period from T' to T. At time $T' + 1$, the known actual is $A_{T'+1}$ and the one-step ahead forecast into the testing period at this point in time is $F_{T'}(1)$. The error at $T' + 1$ is the difference $A_{T'+1} - F_{T'}(1)$.

error is sometimes called the *out-of-sample error* because it is based on data not used in the training (i.e., outside that data or sample).

There are a number of forecast error statistics, each based on the forecast error: $A_{T'+1} - F_{T'}(1)$. Some analysts calculate an error for each step ahead into the testing period and then graph these errors, perhaps with a bar chart. The goal is to see pattern in the errors. I do not recommend this because patterns may be difficult to discern. I recommend any one of the following:

Percentage Error $PE_{T'+t} = 100 \times \dfrac{A_{T'+t} - F_{T'}(t)}{A_{T'+t}}$

Mean Error $ME = \dfrac{\sum_{i=1}^{h} \left(A_{T'+i} - F_{T'}(i) \right)}{h}$

Mean Percentage Error $MPE = 100 \times \dfrac{\sum_{i=1}^{h} \left[\dfrac{\left(A_{T'+i} - F_{T'}(i) \right)}{A_{T'+i}} \right]}{h}$

Mean Absolute Percentage Error $MAPE = 100 \times \dfrac{\sum_{i=1}^{h} \left| \left[\dfrac{\left(A_{T'+i} - F_{T'}(i) \right)}{A_{T'+i}} \right] \right|}{h}$

Median Absolute Percentage Error $MdAPE = $ Median value of $\left| \dfrac{A_{T'+i} - F_{T'}(i)}{A_{T'+i}} \right|$;

$i = 1, 2, \ldots, h$

Mean Square Error $MSE = \dfrac{\sum_{i=1}^{h} \left(A_{T'+i} - F_{T'}(i) \right)^2}{h}$

Since the testing period only extends for time T' to time T, then the steps ahead, h, can only go as far as time T, so $1 \leq h \leq T$.

The *ME* and *MPE* are useful supplements to a count of the frequency of under- and over-forecasts, the *ME* gives the average of the forecast errors expressed in the units of measurement of the data and the *MPE* gives the average of the forecast errors in terms of percentage and is unit-free. The Root Mean Square Error (*RMSE*), the square root of *MSE*, is a popular measure.

See Levenbach and Cleary [2006] for these statistics and some application examples. They also discuss the difference between model fit error and forecast error. The former applies to the data used for training and the latter for testing. The distinction should be clear.

I defined these error measures in terms of the training and testing data sets. The same measures are used when the full forecast is developed beyond period T. I mention this in Chapter 7.

6.7 Software

There are many software packages that handle time series models. JMP, SAS, Stata, R, and Python are excellent options. Hyndman and Athanasopoulos [2018] provide an excellent treatment of R for time series analysis and forecasting.

6.8 Summary

This is a very long and complex chapter. The forecasting methods outlined here are sophisticated enough that many of them warrant their own book. This is especially true of the *ARIMA* family of models. Nonetheless, new product development requires a sales forecast before launch so these methods should be studied and considered.

6.9 Appendix

This appendix summarizes a general class or family of time series models used for forecasting. Three models mentioned in this chapter, Naive 1 (*NF1*), constant mean, and exponential smoothing, are special cases of an *ARIMA* specification. The first subsection reviews two operators commonly used in time series analysis and that are used in this Appendix. The remaining sections review various models using these estimates.

6.9.1 Time series definition

Following Parzen [1962], let a set of data values measured at discrete equidistant points in time be S. Values collected or measured in real-time are definitely possible, but most applications rely on discrete measurements. We write the set as $S = \{1, 2, 3, \ldots, T\}$, where T is the number of observations. An observation is a *realization* at time t of an underlying process. This realization is denoted as Y_t. The set of observations $\{Y_t, t \in S\}$ is a *time series*. This is simply written as $Y_1, Y_2, \ldots, Y_T$. See Parzen [1962] for the definition.

6.9.2 Backshift and differencing operators

The *backshift operator* is a convenient tool to use when dealing with time series models. Another operator, the *differencing operator*, is related to the backshift operator. I present a high-level overview of both of them in this section.

Denote a time series of T observations as $Y_1, Y_2, \ldots, Y_T$. The *backshift operator* (B) when applied to a time series produces a new series of lagged values: $BY_t = Y_{t-1}$. B can be applied successively. For example,

$$B^2 Y_t = B(BY_t)$$
$$= B(Y_{t-1})$$
$$= Y_{t-2}.$$

The exponent for B means to repeatedly apply the backshift in order to move backward a number of time periods equal to the "power", but the exponent is not a power; it just indicates the amount of backward shift. In general, based on reapplication of the basic definition you have

$$B^k Y_t = Y_{t-k}.$$

Observe that $B^0 = 1$ so that $B^0 Y_t = Y_t$. B^0 is the *identity operator*. Also note that if c is a constant, then $B^k c = c$ since a constant cannot be shifted by definition.

The *differencing operator*, ∇, gives the change in Y_t from the previous period: $\nabla Y_t = Y_t - Y_{t-1}$. The differencing and backshift operators are related. Notice that

$$\nabla Y_t = Y_t - Y_{t-1}$$
$$= Y_t - BY_t$$
$$= (1 - B)Y_t.$$

Therefore, $\nabla = 1 - B$ by equating "coefficients". The ∇ operator can also be applied successively. For example,

$$\nabla^2 Y_t = \nabla(\nabla Y_t)$$
$$= \nabla(Y_t - Y_{t-1})$$
$$= \nabla Y_t - \nabla Y_{t-1}$$
$$= Y_t - Y_{t-1} - Y_{t-1} + Y_{t-2}$$
$$= Y_t - 2 \times Y_{t-1} + Y_{t-2}.$$

6.9.3 Random walk model and naive forecast

A random walk model is

$$Y_t = Y_{t-1} + \epsilon_t$$

where the error term is white noise: $E(\epsilon_t) = 0$, $V(\epsilon_t) = \sigma^2$, and $COV(\epsilon_t, \epsilon_{t-j}) = 0, \forall t, j$. Starting from some base number, Y_0, the series evolves as

$$Y_0 = Y_0$$
$$Y_1 = Y_0 + \epsilon_1$$
$$Y_2 = Y_0 + \epsilon_1 + \epsilon_2$$
$$\vdots$$
$$Y_T = Y_0 + \epsilon_1 + \epsilon_2 + \dots + \epsilon_T.$$

The last value, Y_T, is the evolution of all the past white noise terms. This is the basis for how the stock market operates. See Malkiel [1999] for the classic treatment of the stock market and random walks.

If ϵ_t is white noise following a normal distribution, $\epsilon_t \sim N(0, \sigma_\epsilon^2)$, then Y_t is also normally distributed by the reproductive property of normals. This property states that a linear combination of normally distributed random variables is itself normally distributed. See Dudewicz and Mishra [1988] for the reproductive property.

Using the backshift operator, B,

$$Y_t = Y_{t-1} + \epsilon_t$$
$$= BY_t + \epsilon_t$$
$$= (1-B)^{-1}\epsilon_t.$$

Since $(1-B)^{-1} = 1 + B + B^2 + \dots = \sum_{i=0}^{\infty} B^i$, then

$$Y_t = \epsilon_t + \epsilon_{t-1} + \dots$$
$$= \epsilon_t \sum_{i=0}^{\infty} B^i$$

which can be truncated to going back to a finite past for practical purposes. Note that Y_0 is so far back (i.e., the infinite past) that it can be ignored. The infinite series $\sum_{i=0}^{\infty} B^i$ must converge to some value, K. Otherwise, the series explodes which is impractical. More importantly, if the series diverges, the $E(Y_t) = 0 \times \infty$ which is an indeterminate form. Nelson [1973] notes that this is a condition that must hold.

Assume that the infinite sum is truncated at time T. Then you have

$$Y_t = \epsilon_t \sum_{i=0}^{t} B^i.$$

The mean and variance are then (note that $\sum_{i=0}^{t} B^i$ converges because it is a finite sum)

$$E(Y_t) = 0$$
$$V(Y_t) = t\sigma_\epsilon^2.$$

Notice that the variance gets bigger the further out in time you go.

Suppose you use the random walk model to forecast. What form will those forecasts take and how are they derived? Let $X = \dots, Y_{T-1}, Y_T$ be given. Note for what follows that the actual Y_{T+1} is a random variable. By the random walk formula, $Y_T(1) = Y_T + \epsilon_{T+1}$. Y_T is known so it is not a random variable, but ϵ_{T+1} is an unknown random variable. Therefore, the one-step ahead forecast, $Y_T(1)$, is a random variable. You can describe the probability distribution of the one-step ahead forecast, $Y_T(1)$, conditioned on its past history. Its expected value is

$$E[Y_T(1) \mid X] = E(Y_T + \epsilon_{T+1} \mid X)$$
$$= E(Y_T \mid X) + E(\epsilon_{T+1} \mid X)$$
$$= Y_T + E(\epsilon_{T+1} \mid X)$$
$$= Y_T.$$

The expected number in the next period is just the current number. I will now drop the X to simplify notation, but remember that the forecasts are conditioned on this history.

The variance of $Y_T(1)$ is

$$V[Y_T(1)] = V(Y_T + \epsilon_{T+1})$$
$$= V(Y_T) + V(\epsilon_{T+1})$$
$$= 0 + V(\epsilon_{T+1})$$
$$= \sigma_\epsilon^2.$$

Remember that Y_T is an actual, so it is nonstochastic and thus has no variance.

If ϵ_t is white noise following a normal distribution, then

$$Y_T(1) \sim N(Y_T, \sigma_\epsilon^2)$$

by the reproductive property of normals. A 95% confidence interval is simply

$$Y_T \pm 1.96 \times \sigma_\epsilon.$$

Now extend the forecast to two-steps ahead. Then

$$E[Y_1(2)] = E[Y_1(1) + c_{1+2}]$$
$$= E(Y_T + \epsilon_{T+1} + \epsilon_{T+2})$$
$$= E(Y_T) + E(\epsilon_{T+1}) + E(\epsilon_{T+2})$$
$$= Y_T + E(\epsilon_{T+1}) + E(\epsilon_{T+2})$$
$$= Y_T.$$

The variance is

$$V[Y_T(2)] = 2 \times \sigma_\epsilon^2.$$

The forecast is just the current value, Y_T, and the variance is twice σ^2. The forecast for h-steps ahead is still Y_t and the variance is $h \times \sigma_\epsilon^2$. Using the reproductive property of normals, then $Y_T(h) \sim \mathcal{N}(Y_T, h\sigma_\epsilon^2)$ and a 95% confidence interval is $Y_T \pm 1.96 \times \sqrt{h}\sigma_\epsilon$. The confidence interval expands in proportion to the square root of the number of steps ahead.

6.9.4 Random walk with drift

Consider the random walk model

$$Y_t = Y_{t-1} + \epsilon_t + \delta$$

where δ is a constant. This is the *random walk with drift* model where δ is the *drift parameter*. Starting at Y_0 as before, through successive substitution you get

$$Y_0 = Y_0$$
$$Y_1 = Y_0 + \epsilon_1 + \delta$$
$$Y_2 = Y_0 + \epsilon_1 + \epsilon_2 + 2 \times \delta$$
$$\vdots$$
$$Y_t = Y_0 + \epsilon_1 + \epsilon_2 + \ldots + \epsilon_t + t \times \delta.$$

The series keeps drifting by δ.

Using the backshift notation, you have

$$Y_t = BY_t + \epsilon_t + \delta$$
$$= (1-B)^{-1}\epsilon_t + (1-B)^{-1}\delta$$
$$= \epsilon_t \sum_{i=0}^{\infty} B^i + \delta \sum_{i=0}^{\infty} B^i.$$

Truncating the summations to t periods, yields

$$Y_t = \epsilon_t \sum_{i=0}^{t-1} B^i + \delta \sum_{i=0}^{t-1} B^i$$
$$= \epsilon_t \sum_{i=0}^{t} B^i + t \times \delta.$$

Note that $\delta \sum_{i=0}^{t-1} B^i = \delta \times (1 + B^1 + B^2 + \ldots + B^{t-1})$ where the expression in parentheses has t terms. The second line then simplifies as shown.

The mean and variance are then

$$E(Y_t) = t\delta$$
$$V(Y_t) = t\sigma_\epsilon^2.$$

The 1-step ahead forecast is $Y_T(1) = Y_T + \delta + \epsilon_{T+1}$ with $E[Y_T(1)] = Y_T + \delta$. It is easy to show that $E[Y_T(h)] = Y_T + h \times \delta$. The variance is $V[Y_T(h)] = h \times \sigma_\epsilon^2$. So the drift affects the level and not the variance of the forecast.

6.9.5 Constant mean model

For the constant mean model,

$$Y_T(h) = \frac{1}{T}\sum_{t=1}^{T}(\mu + \epsilon_t)$$

$$= \mu + \frac{1}{T}\sum_{t=1}^{T}\epsilon_t$$

so that $E[Y_T(h)] = 0$ since $E(\epsilon_t) = 0, \forall t$. The h-step ahead forecast is unbiased. The variance of this forecast is

$$V[Y_T(h)] = V(\mu) + \frac{1}{T^2}\sum_{t=1}^{T}V(\epsilon_t)$$

$$= \frac{\sigma^2}{T}.$$

See Gilchrist [1976] for this demonstration.

The forecast error is

$$e_{T+h} = Y_{T+h} - \hat{Y}_T(h)$$

$$= \mu + \epsilon_{T+h} - \mu - \frac{1}{T}\sum_{t=1}^{T}\epsilon_t$$

$$= \epsilon_{T+h} - \frac{1}{T}\sum_{t=1}^{T}\epsilon_t$$

so $E(e_{T+h}) = 0$. The mean square error (MSE) of the forecast is

$$MSE = V[Y_{T+h} - Y_T(h)]$$

$$= V[Y_{T+h} + V[Y_T(h)]$$

$$= \sigma^2 + \frac{\sigma^2}{T}$$

$$= \frac{T+1}{T}\sigma\epsilon^2.$$

You can now write a 95% confidence interval statement as

$$Y_T(h) \pm 1.96\sqrt{\frac{T+1}{T}}\sigma\epsilon.$$

An unbiased estimate of σ_ϵ is the sample standard deviation of the historical data. See Gilchrist [1976] for discussion of this model.

6.9.6 The ARIMA family of models

I will now consider a broad, general class of models that are sometimes called:

- stochastic time series models;
- time series models;
- Autoregressive Integrated Moving Average (*ARIMA*) models; or
- Box–Jenkins models

although *ARIMA* is the most common reference. In this class of models, the random element, ϵ, plays a dominant role rather than being just an add-on error (i.e., disturbance) to a strictly deterministic model. The *ARIMA* model is actually a family of models with different members of the family (cousins, if you wish) that themselves define more specific cases. The *ARIMA* model has parameters the specification of which define these family members. The parameters are p, d, and q which I will specify below.

Consider the model

$$Y_t = \phi Y_{t-1} + \epsilon_t$$

where ϵ_t is white noise. If $\phi = 1$, then this is a random walk. From backward substitution, you get

$$Y_t = \epsilon_t + \phi \epsilon_{t-1} + \ldots + \phi^t Y_0.$$

So Y_t is a weighted sum of past white noise terms and the initial value of Y. Using our backshift operator, you have

$$Y_t = (1 - \phi B)^{-1} \epsilon_t$$
$$= \epsilon_t + \phi \epsilon_{t-1} + \ldots.$$

If $t \to \infty$ and $|\phi| < 1$, then you have an infinite sum that must converge. That is, $\sum_{i=0}^{\infty} \phi^i B^i = K$ where K is a finite (but perhaps large) constant.

A general form for our model of practical value is

$$Y_t = \phi_1 Y_{t-1} + \ldots + \phi_p Y_{t-p} + \epsilon_t.$$

This has the form of a regression model with p explanatory variables. It is called an *autoregressive model* of order p or an $AR(p)$ model. Using the backshift operator, B, you can write

$$Y_t = \phi_1 Y_{t-1} + \ldots + \phi_p Y_{t-p} + \epsilon_t$$
$$= \phi_1 B Y_t + \ldots + \phi_p B^p Y_t + \epsilon_t$$

where the parameter p defines the order of the process. You could also write

$$\Phi(B) Y_t = \epsilon_t$$

where

$$\Phi(B) = 1 - \phi_1 B - \ldots - \phi_p B^p.$$

The polynomial $\Phi(B)$ is called the $AR(p)$ *operator*.

Suppose you now write a new model

$$Y_t = \epsilon_t + \theta_1 \epsilon_{t-1} + \ldots + \theta_q \epsilon_{t-q}.$$

This can be rewritten as

$$Y_t = B^0 \epsilon_t + \theta_1 B^1 \epsilon_t + \ldots + \theta_q B^q \epsilon_t$$
$$= (1 + \theta_1 B^1 + \ldots + \theta_q B^q) \epsilon_t$$
$$= \Theta(B) \epsilon_t.$$

This is a moving average of order q ($MA(q)$) model and $\Theta(B)$ is the $MA(q)$ operator. The parameter q defines the order of this process. This is a *linear filter* that takes the white noise series and transforms it to Y_t. The "moving average" name is misleading since the weights do not necessarily sum to 1.0, so do not confuse this with what you know from above.

You can extend the model to include both AR and MA components to capture lingering effects and temporary shocks, respectively. The model is

$$Y_t = \phi_1 Y_{t-1} + \ldots + \phi_p Y_{t-p} + \epsilon_t + \theta_1 \epsilon_{t-1} + \ldots + \theta_q \epsilon_{t-q}.$$

This mixed model is called an *autoregressive moving average model* of order p and q, or simply $ARMA(p, q)$, and is conveniently written as

$$\Phi(B) Y_t = \Theta(B) \epsilon_t$$

so that

$$Y_t = \Phi^{-1}(B) \Theta(B) \epsilon_t$$
$$= \Psi(B) \epsilon_t.$$

All econometric models should have a constant term unless economic theory strongly says otherwise – and it typically does not. The inclusion of a constant term also holds for time series models. An $ARMA(1, 1)$ model, for example, is

$$(1 - \phi B) Y_t = \mu + (1 + \theta B) \epsilon_t.$$

Most often, the level is removed by subtracting the mean μ so you have $\widetilde{Y}_t = Y_t - \mu, \forall t$. This way, $E(\widetilde{Y}_t) = E(Y_t) - \mu = 0$. Therefore, there are no changes from what you already learned. An estimate of μ is, of course, the sample mean, $\overline{Y}$.

Suppose you have a nonstationary time series. That is, it has a randomly occurring shift in its level. You require a model whose behavior is not influenced by the level of the process. You can often eliminate the effect of the changing level by *differencing*. This is where the differencing operator, ∇, is used. For example, consider a random walk given by $Y_t = Y_{t-1} + \epsilon_t$. This model can be written as $Y_t = BY_t + \epsilon_t$ or $(1 - B) Y_t = \epsilon_t$. The first term is equivalent to ∇Y_t so $\nabla Y_t = \epsilon_t$.

Using the differencing operator and removing the level, our basic mixed model is expanded to be

$$\Phi(B) \nabla^d \widetilde{Y}_t = \Theta(B) \epsilon_t$$

TABLE 6.1 This is a list of common time series and forecasting models derived from a general ARIMA model. Seasonal variations are also possible but these are not relevant for new product forecasts. Source: https://stats.stackexchange.com/questions/23864/what-common-forecasting-models-can-be-seen-as-special-cases-of-arima-models.

Model	ARIMA Specification
Constant Mean	ARIMA(0, 0, 0) with constant
Random Walk or Naive (*NF1*)	ARIMA(0, 1, 0)
Random Walk with Drift	ARIMA(0, 1, 0) with constant
Simple Exponential Smoothing	ARIMA(0, 1, 1)
Holt's Exponential Smoothing	ARIMA(0, 2, 2)
Damped Holt's	ARIMA(0, 1, 2)

where $\Phi(B)\nabla^d$ is the *generalized autoregressive operator*. This model is called the *autoregressive integrated moving average model of order p, d, and q*, or simply *ARIMA(p, d, q)*. This is a general family since different values for the parameters define different types of models. Table 6.1 shows some key family members that typically arise in practice. As the table shows, the naive and constant mean models are special cases. Also, the classic random walk model is equivalent to the naive model and is also a special case of the $ARIMA(p, d, q)$ model.

For more details on this class of models including seasonal variations, see Wei [2006], Montgomery et al. [2008], and Nelson [1973]. Also see the original treatment in Box et al. [1994]. For implementation of many time series models in R, see Hyndman and Athanasopoulos [2018].

Notes

1 See https://marketing-insider.eu/categories-of-new-products/.
2 NP-hard problems are a complex topic in theoretical computer science and are concerned with the time needed to solve a problem. The time is a polynomial of the input size, hence the "P". See www.quora.com/What-does-NP-hard-mean for a good explanation.
3 If they are positive and do not sum to 1.0, then the weighted moving average must be divided by the sum of the weights which forces them to sum to 1.0.

7

TRACK

Did you succeed?

Effective post-launch product tracking requires a tracking system. One possibility is displayed in Figure 7.1. There are two main branches. One is based on transactions data: orders, revenues, returns, margins, and so forth. This is what most managers typically think about when tracking a product's performance. The second branch is based on the plethora of text data businesses collect and house from customer comments, online reviews, etc.; all the text data I discussed in Chapter 2 for clues for new product ideas. The same data can be used to discover sentiments and opinions regarding the newly launched product. This holds, incidentally, for both new and existing products, but my focus is on new ones.

Tracking a product, whether new or existing, is not a simple issue. Creating or studying a report showing the number of units sold, perhaps the number returned,

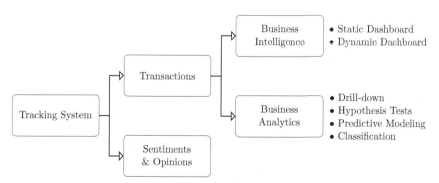

FIGURE 7.1 This illustrates the key components and their relationships in a post-launch product tracking system. The objective of this system is to collect and organize market transactions data to determine if the new product is meeting objectives.

and the net revenue earned, which is what most managers believe is "tracking," only skims the surface of what is needed and possible. A tracking analysis must go much deeper to determine root causes for weaknesses in sales. Root causes could be by:

- marketing region;
- sales rep; and
- customer classification (e.g., loyal and satisfied customers).

Not to be overlooked are the different components of the marketing mix. The price points and price structure may be inappropriate for the target markets despite the pre-launch research described in the previous chapters; excessive use of discounts offered by the sales force may be stimulating sales but hurting net revenue; marketing messages, although adequately tested, may still not resonate with customers; website online purchasing tools (e.g., shopping carts) may be poorly implemented; and the list goes on. It is definitely important to identify which of these is the culprit hurting sales or even causing sales to be more than expected. If sales are not up to expectations, as determined by the choice models and simulations I described in Chapter 4 or the sales forecasts I described in Chapter 6, then corrective actions are needed and needed before the new product gains a negative appraisal in the market from which it might be unable to recover.

There are thus three parts to new product tracking post-launch, although these could, as I mentioned above, be applied to all existing products that have been in the market for some time. These are:

1. analysis of what has happened to the product and what is currently happening to it;
2. what will happen if some aspect of the product and its marketing is changed; and
3. assessing customer sentiments and opinions about the product.

The first is the domain of Business Intelligence, the second is Business Analytics, and the third is Sentiment Analysis and Opinion Research. I will describe each branch of Figure 7.1 and their subdivisions in the following sections.

This chapter is divided into four sections corresponding to the two main branches of Figure 7.1. In the first section, I discuss the types of analysis possible with transactions-type data. This includes data visualization, predictive modeling, and forecast error analysis. The forecast error analysis differs from the one I described in Chapter 6 because this error analysis is based on actual market data as opposed to the testing data set. The second section focuses on sentiment analysis and opinion mining, a newer area with a lot of currently active research. The third and fourth sections are software review and summary, respectively.

7.1 Transactions analysis

In this section, I will cover some material on analyzing transactions data, although the word "transactions" is inaccurate. The data in the top branch of Figure 7.1 may consist of any type of data such as field representatives' time logs, financial data, personnel data, and so forth. The types of analysis – Business Intelligence or Business Analytics – are the same. For this section, "transactions" refers to numerical data of any sort for any part of the business. The only fact that matters for this branch of Figure 7.1 is that text data for sentiment analysis and opinion mining is not included. They are handled in the second branch.

Transactions data are drawn from a number of different data tables or databases such as those listed in Figure 7.2. These tables could comprise a data store, data warehouse, data lake, or data mart. Elements of these tables are pulled into a *Data Consolidator* that appropriately transforms the data and loads them into a data mart.

A data store is the storage location closest to the source. It is temporary storage before the data are cleansed and loaded into the data warehouse which is a more encompassing and inclusive storage location for data. A data warehouse has a wide variety of types of data: financial, personnel, transaction, and so forth, all, of course, organized by topical and functional areas. A data lake is a variation of a data warehouse in that, like a warehouse, it stores a variety of data but these data are in their

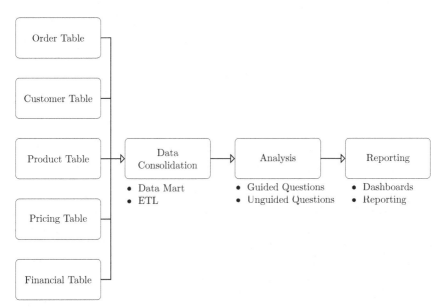

FIGURE 7.2 This flow chart illustrates the processing of data from some source elements, a data store for example, to a consolidator that creates a data mart for a functional area. End-user analysts can access the data mart using a query system to address questions which are either guided by management's issues or unguided ad hoc questions. A report of some sort usually results as an end product.

"native format" and can be structured and unstructured. They may come from social media, blogs, emails, sensors, and so forth. The costs of maintaining these data in a lake are lower than for a warehouse because the storage arrangements are less restrictive. The data lake, however, has other costs beyond those associated with maintenance. The primary cost is the level of preprocessing that has to be applied to the data from a lake that will be used in an analytical process. Since the data in a lake are unprocessed, by definition, and direct from their source, they will first have to be processed, cleaned, checked, and wrangled (i.e., merged with other data) before they could be used in the analytical process. See Lemahieu et al. [2018] on processing costs and Kazil and Jarmul [2016] for insight into the concept and complexities of data wrangling.

A data mart is an extract from one of these three storage media that puts the data closer to the end-user. It is more functionally oriented meaning the data are for a functional area. For example, there could be a finance data mart, a marketing data mart, and a personnel data mart. Analysts in the marketing department use their marketing data mart for their work and do not use (or even have access to) the finance data mart. There are several reasons for having a data mart as listed by Lemahieu et al. [2018]:

- they provide focused content for the end-users;
- they provide more focused and efficient end-user queries because there are fewer layers of data to navigate;
- they are closer to the end-users which minimizes network congestion; and
- they allow pre-defined reporting tools that are functionally oriented.

As noted by Lemahieu et al. [2018], because of the existence and use of data marts, which can be quite large and complex in their own right, the data warehouse they draw from is sometimes called an *enterprise data warehouse* to distinguish it from a data mart.

The data store is probably the furthest from the end-user but the closest to the source while the data mart is the opposite. All four have query capabilities allowing any user access to data although the data mart's query capabilities are more in line with the abilities of the end-users it serves since they generally are less sophisticated in this regard than IT professionals who manage the other data bases. See Lemahieu et al. [2018] for discussion on data storage. Also see the succinct online article by Baesens summarizing these storage concepts.[1]

The process of extracting data from multiple sources, appropriately transforming them, and loading the transformed data into a more convenient data table is referred to as the *Extract-Transform-Load* process (*ETL*). This is a standard way of viewing the manipulation of large amounts of data with the goal of making them more accessible and consolidated for the end-user. Once the data have been consolidated, they are ready for the analytical applications. See Lemahieu et al. [2018] for some discussion of the *ETL* process.[2]

7.1.1 Business intelligence vs. business analytics

There are numerous key decisions that have to be made at all stages of the new product development process. This has been emphasized throughout the preceding chapters. These decisions affect not only the definition of the product but also its launch and future marketing. In addition, key decisions are made throughout the process regarding the continued efforts on the product development and launch itself. This is the business case process which results in a simple *Go/No-Go* decision. At each critical decision point, information is needed. With no or little information, decision makers have to guess or "approximate" the impact of their decision. This approximation, however, comes at a high cost because they could be wrong, and probably will be wrong, so big mistakes will happen. These mistakes are costly, perhaps in terms of lost opportunities, lost revenue, lost sales, lost market share, or a lost business. This should be evident.

As information is gained about customers, markets, and competitors, then decision makers would not guess as much and the costs of their decisions would fall. But not to zero! Even with a large amount of information, decisions could still be wrong so they would still incur a cost of guessing or approximating. This is especially true in a world with Big Data – but that is another story. Nonetheless, the costs of approximating will fall the more information you have and use.

Some people believe information is discrete or, better yet, binary: you either have it or you do not. But it is not discrete. It is continuous, running from **Poor** to **Rich** Information as I noted in Chapter 1. Poor Information is raw data, or perhaps some simple summary statistics such as means and proportions. This type tells you something, but not much. Rich Information, on the other hand, provides insight. It tells you something you did not know. It is insightful, useful, and actionable. Poor information is none or little of this.

Figure 7.3 is a modification of Figure 1.6 to show the type of analyses available along the *Information Continuum*. All too often, analyses are at the shallow end, restricted to means, proportions, and pie and bar charts which results in Poor Information. Analyses at the deep end, such as predictive modeling, resulting in Rich Information are needed.

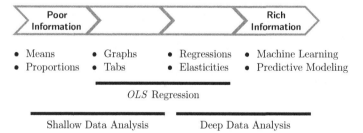

FIGURE 7.3 Here are examples of Poor and Rich Information. Actually, the sources for them which are some form of data analysis. The sources on the left are *Shallow Analytics* while those on the right are *Deep Analytics*.

Rich Information has two variations:

1. What **did** happen or what is **currently** happening on the one hand.
2. What **will** happen under different conditions on the other hand.

The way you get both variations is somewhat the same; they both rely on statistical and data visualization methods. Yet, they are fundamentally different. The former, as I noted above, is the domain of Business Intelligence while the latter is the domain of Business Analytics. These are the two splits in the Transaction branch of Figure 7.1.

A further distinction is possible. More formally, Business Intelligence relies on simple statistics and data visualization to say something about what *did* happen or what is *currently* happening with the business and its markets. Dashboards are popular management tools, not analysts' tools, for summarizing this Poor Information. Due to their layouts and infographics orientation, they convey a sense of authority and empowerment to management. Business decisions, by their nature, are forward looking so, in my opinion, dashboards with Business Intelligence summaries and graphics are of limited use.

Business Analytics, in the hands of skilled analysts, relies on scientific data visualization and complex predictive modeling to extract Rich Information from data. Scientific data visualization differs from the infographics type of visualization in that it is more penetrating. Infographics are meant to have a "wow" impact as they often have more glitz than substance. They tend to have a lot of chart-junk. Scientific data visualization is meant to provide Rich Information with clear, insightful presentation of data unencumbered by glitz and chart-junk. It also supports and complements predictive modeling, which is forward looking. It is this forward-looking aspect that is needed for business decisions. See Tufte [1983] for a discussion of chart-junk.

Business Intelligence and Business Analytics, although they have a separate focus, nonetheless complement and support each other. Business Intelligence, perhaps through a dashboard, may indicate a problem, say about pricing. Business Analytics would then be employed by the analysts, perhaps *Data Scientists*, to delve into the nature of the pricing problem and the implications for key business metrics if prices, both structure and levels, were to be changed. The same holds if a dashboard indicated a competitive change or an economy change (e.g., real GDP slows or the stock market has a precipitous decline) while Business Analytics would enable an analyst to assess the implications. The important point is that Business Intelligence and Business Analytics work together to reduce the cost of approximation: you know more and have richer information.

7.1.2 Business intelligence dashboards

There are two dimensions to a dashboard: focus and interactivity. Focus is meant to summarize internal operations or external market forces. Interactivity refers to the ability of the business manager to do something with the dashboard's contents, the display itself. A static dashboard allows no interactivity. A business manager has to go elsewhere in the organization to learn more about what is displayed. A dynamic dashboard is fully interactive allowing that manager to learn more through point-and-click and drill-down. Drill-down is the process of disaggregating data, going from one level of detail in a data structure to a higher level of detail. For example, it is the process of going from sales in a marketing region to the individual cities that comprise the region. The regions are the low level of detail and the cities are the high level of detail. Both dimensions are discussed in the next subsections. See Lemahieu et al. [2018] for an explanation of drill-downs as well as roll-up, slicing, and dicing of a data set.

Dashboard focus

Dashboards have been a common part of the business environment for some time, especially since the penetration of IT into business. They are supposed to show the current state of a business so that decision makers can understand the state of their business and have insight into where they may have to take action. There are two types of dashboards: operations performance and market performance. The former is concerned with the way the different operations of the business are currently performing and perhaps how that performance has been changing over time. The performance is that of the different parts of the business. Recognizing that any business is not just a "business" but the sum of many interacting parts, it becomes clear that each of those parts must function well and in concert with other parts. The trite saying *"like a well-oiled machine"* is applicable here. If one part malfunctions, is not meeting targets, or is inefficient, then other parts dependent on it will also malfunction and the business could then be in jeopardy. A performance dashboard tells management how all the parts are functioning. This type of dashboard is internally focused.

A market performance dashboard is externally focused. It is concerned with how the business is performing in the market: how much is being sold; how much is being returned and why; how revenue, both gross and net, is changing over time; how the business's product is selling by marketing region and customer classes; and the list goes on. Market insight gained by these dashboards is as important as that gained about the internal operations of the business. A business could function internally as a *"well-oiled machine"* but be losing sales or market share and not meeting sales and financial objectives. Its market performance will impact shareholder equity which could affect its ability to raise capital to further grow the business and, which is the focus of this book, innovate and develop new products. Management needs this type of dashboard as much as it needs an operations one. Since this book is not concerned with business operations, I am only concerned with the market-oriented dashboard and its follow-up issues and implications. I will classify the market-oriented dashboard as providing Business Intelligence, although it has to be stressed that the operations dashboard also provides Business Intelligence. See Eckerson [2010] for a thorough discussion of dashboards.

Dashboard interactivity

Whether internally or externally focused, a dashboard supplies information. Where this information lies on the Poor–Rich Continuum depends on the dashboard construction. See Few [2006] for the effective design of dashboards. The level of the information, how deep managers are allowed to go into the data, and the types of analysis they can do is another issue addressed by levels of interactivity. At one extreme, there is no interactivity so what managers see is what they get. The dashboard is static, to be updated only when the dashboard provider (i.e., the IT department) repopulates its data fields and regenerates tables and graphs. There may be a daily schedule for doing this, but nonetheless it is not the managers viewing the dashboard who do it. Any question or concern they have at the moment of viewing the dashboard will have to be addressed by someone else at a later time. This delay is not without a cost. If the new product is not performing well as indicated by the static dashboard, then any delay in learning why may result in the product failing. In short, time is of the essence.

A fully interactive dashboard allows managers to click on an image on the display and drill down for more penetrating insight; i.e., Rich Information. They could, for example, click on a bar of a bar chart to see further displays and reports on the data behind the bar. This allows them to learn more and make better use of their time to gain information. There is, of course, a limit to how far they can drill down, but however far they can go is better than what is possible with a static dashboard. The highly interactive dashboard is dynamic, changing at the control of the user.[3]

7.1.3 The limits of business intelligence dashboards

Both types of dashboards, operations and market, static and dynamic, provide business intelligence. They tell management what did happen or what is currently happening. These are important, but they beg the question management would eventually ask: "*What do we do with this intelligence?*" In short, they need to know two more pieces of information:

1. the root cause of any problem revealed by the dashboard; and
2. what can be done to correct the problem.

The first requires a drill-down to reveal further insight which could be provided by a dynamic dashboard. Even with this type of dashboard, however, deeper analysis may still be needed beyond what managers are able to or should do. Everyone has two personal restrictions. The first is his or her knowledge of advanced statistical, econometric, data visualization, and machine learning methods to be able to go further. After all, people do specialize in areas and a business manager's specialization is in running the business, not doing analytical work. At the same time, a manager, like everyone else, has a time constraint: you have only 24 hours in a day regardless of who you are. If you allocate your time to doing analytical work, then that is time taken from running the business; there is a time misallocation.

The second piece of needed information, the solution to the problem, requires predictive modeling allowing what-if or scenario analysis. This is also a specialty, probably more so than many forms of data analysis most managers think about. Some examples will be described below.

The following sections will illustrate some deep drill-down capabilities and predictive modeling that could be done. This only skims the surface, but it at least illustrates possibilities. This will be done using a case study.

7.1.4 Case study

A leading household furniture manufacturer sells to locally owned, boutique retailers throughout the U.S. which is divided into four marketing regions consistent with U.S. Census regions. The company has 43 products in six product lines consistent with the major rooms in a house: Den, Dining Room, Kids' Room, Kitchen, Living Room, Master Bedroom. Each product line is divided into a product class such as Chairs, Tables, and Baker's Racks for the Kitchen product line. Four types of discounts are offered at the discretion of sales force: Order Discount, Special Competitive Discount, Dealer Discount, and a Pickup Discount.

The product manager for living rooms has a problem with a new product: living room blinds (a.k.a., window treatments) with a remote voice control system that runs through a controller such as Alexa. Basically, the window blinds will open and close or rise and fall by voice commands. The product is one of the first in its class so there are few competitors. In terms of the Chapter 6 classification of new products I used, this is a not-new-to-the-world (*NNTW*) product.

The product manager keeps track of the product's performance via a dashboard; this is Business Intelligence. The dashboard has displays of unit sales, gross revenue, returns, and net revenue (revenue based on unit sales less returns). These metrics are shown as bar charts with metric targets overlaid on the charts to indicate if targets are met or not. She has noticed that sales and revenue are not performing as expected so she has asked the Data Science group to investigate. Specifically, she needs information on:

1. Sales patterns by:
   - Marketing Region
   - Customer Loyalty
   - Buyer Rating: basically, a good or poor customer.
2. An estimate of price elasticity based on sales as opposed to what she has from the pre-launch studies.
3. Tests for statistical differences among the four discounts that are offered.

She has also requested a tool for predicting sales to a specific customer based on the customer's characteristics. She needs this information so she can decide what to do to fix what she perceives is a marketing problem, not a product design problem.

7.1.5 Case study data sources

As for all the components of the new product development process I described in this book, data are needed. Data are the driving force for everything a business must do. To quote W. Deming: "*In God we trust. All others must bring data.*"[4] The data sources are both internal and external.

Internal business data are the most common data used, not only in a dashboard but also for drill-down to root causes and predictive modeling. This internal data comes from a number of different sources or databases, perhaps consolidated in a data mart, such as and certainly not limited to:

- orders;
- products;
- pricing;
- marketing;
- customer; and
- many others.

The external databases are too numerous to mention. At the least, the data analyst should have access to one (or several) that provides demographics on households and business firmographics, detail that includes household income, age distribution, education distribution and socioeconomic classification for households and revenue and number of employees for businesses.

The business analyst for the Case Study compiled a data dictionary for an initial analytical database she will use to address the product manager's requests. A data dictionary contains "metadata" which are data about the data. Metadata can be anything that documents the data. They are information about the distinct data elements such as[5]:

- means of creation;
- purpose of the data;
- time and date of creation;
- creator/author/keeper of the data;
- placement on a network (electronic form);
- where the data were created;
- what standards were used to create the data; and
- so forth.

I will restrict the metadata to:

- variable name;
- possible values or value ranges;
- source; and
- mnemonic.

The mnemonic is the label used in data files and statistical and modeling output. The data dictionary for the Case Study is shown in Table 7.1. A customer background data dictionary, reflecting data from the customer database, is shown in Table 7.2. The customer data will be merged or joined with the basic orders data based on a common identifier which is the *CID*.

7.1.6 Case study data analysis

A basic data analysis should be done before any complex analysis such as estimating a regression model. There are two parts or stages discussed here in what could be interpreted as a chronological order but which are really done in any order. The two parts are an examination of descriptive statistics and data visualization.

The basic descriptive statistics include:

- count of the observations;
- mean;
- standard deviation;
- minimum value;
- 25th percentile or first quartile ($Q1$);
- 50th percentile or median (or $Q2$);
- 75th percentile or third quartile ($Q3$); and
- maximum value.

The last five are known as the *Five Number Summary*, a robust set of statistics unaffected by distribution skewness. Although unaffected, they help determine skewness and symmetry of the data distribution:

1. Symmetric: $(75\% - 50\%) = (50\% - 25\%)$
2. Right-Skewed: $(75\% - 50\%) > (50\% - 25\%)$
3. Left Skewed: $(75\% - 50\%) < (50\% - 25\%)$

The descriptive statistics for the discounts are shown in Table 7.3.

A correlation is also helpful. Recall that a correlation shows association, not cause and effect. This distinction is important because you could have disastrous results if the wrong interpretation is placed on a correlation. Also, correlation is only between pairs of variables; never more than two. A correlation value varies between -1.0 and $+1.0$. A whole set of pairwise correlations could be calculated but these are then shown in a *correlation matrix*. A correlation matrix for the discounts is shown in Table 7.4.

TABLE 7.1 This is a basic data dictionary for the Case Study showing the order detail for customers of living room blinds.

Variable	Values	Source	Mnemonic
Order Number	Nominal Integer	Order Sys	Onum
Customer ID	Nominal Integer	Customer Sys	CID
Transaction Date	MM/DD/YYYY	Order Sys	Tdate
Product Line ID	Five house rooms	Product Sys	Pline
Product Class ID	Item in line	Product Sys	Pclass
Units Sold	Units/order	Order Sys	Usales
Product Returned?	Yes/No	Order Sys	Return
Amount Returned	Number of units	Order Sys	returnAmount
Material Cost/Unit	USD cost of material	Product Sys	Mcost
List Price	USD list	Price Sys	Lprice
Dealer Discount	% to dealer (decimal)	Sales Sys	Ddisc
Competitive Discount	% for competition (decimal)	Sales Sys	Cdisc
Order Size Discount	% for size (decimal)	Sales Sys	Odisc
Customer Pickup Allowance	% for pickup (decimal)	Sales Sys	Pdisc
Total Discount	% discount	Sum of discounts	Tdisc
Pocket Price	USD	$LPrice \times (1 - TDisc)$	Pprice
Net Unit Sales	Net units/order	$Usales - returnAmount$	netUsales
Log of Net Unit Sales	Log net sales	$log(netUsales)$	log_netUsales
Log of Unit Sales	Log sales	$log(Usales)$	log_Usales
Log of Pocket Price	USD	$log(Pprice)$	log_Pprice
Revenue	USD	$Usales \times Pprice$	Rev
Contribution	USD	$Rev - Mcost$	Con
Contribution Margin	%	Con/Rev	CM
Net Revenue	USD	$(Usales - returnAmount) \times Pprice$	netRev
Lost Revenue	USD	$Rev - netRev$	lostRev

A second step in data analysis is *data visualization*. This is the latest "buzz phrase" – everyone talks about data visualization. It is really just looking at your data using graphs. The graphs, however, could be somewhat complex and hopefully informative – that they convey Rich Information. Graphs are generally more informative than tables. Small tables, like a 2x2, may be sufficient for presentations, but they usually cannot provide the Rich Information needed by decision makers. Larger

TABLE 7.2 This is a basic customer data dictionary for the Case Study. It shows the customer features that could eventually be used with the sales data to provide a complete picture of the customers and their orders. The *Buyer Rating* is based on the sales force evaluations of ease of doing business with that customer while the customer satisfaction is based on an annual satisfaction study.

Variable	Values	Source	Mnemonic
Customer ID	Nominal Integer	Customer Sys	CID
State of Business	Two-character state code	Customer Sys	State
ZIP Code of location	Five-digit ZIP (Character)	Customer Sys	ZIP
Marketing Region	Four Census Regions	Customer Sys	Region
In Loyalty Program	Yes/No	Customer Sys	loyaltyProgram
Buyer Rating	Poor, Good, Excellent	Customer Sys	buyerRating
Buyer Satisfaction	Five-Point Likert	Customer Sys	buyerSatisfaction

TABLE 7.3 The descriptive statistics for the four discounts are for the Case Study. The variable *Tdisc* is the total discount as the sum of the four discounts. It was added to the data set of the two primary data sets merged into one. Notice that the dealer discount (*Ddisc*) is right-skewed. Also note that the sample size differs slightly. The full data set has 70,270 records. This indicates that there are some missing data.

	count	mean	std	min	25%	50%	75%	max
Ddisc	70262	0.12	0.04	0.04	0.09	0.12	0.16	0.22
Cdisc	70261	0.07	0.02	0.04	0.05	0.07	0.09	0.10
Odisc	70266	0.05	0.01	0.02	0.04	0.05	0.06	0.08
Pdisc	70268	0.04	0.01	0.02	0.03	0.04	0.05	0.06
Tdisc	70270	0.28	0.05	0.02	0.24	0.28	0.32	0.43

TABLE 7.4 This is the correlation matrix for the four discounts. The total discount was not included because, as the sum of discounts, it will be highly correlated with the four discounts and so it will not provide any new information.

	Ddisc	Cdisc	Odisc	Pdisc
Ddisc	1.000000	-0.000919	0.001962	-0.003748
Cdisc	-0.000919	1.000000	0.002217	0.000396
Odisc	0.001962	0.002217	1.000000	0.002888
Pdisc	-0.003748	0.000396	0.002888	1.000000

tables are needed, but we have difficulty seeing patterns in large tables so they have a drawback. Generally, visuals are superior to tables of numbers because we are visual creatures. We can see, for example, patterns in graphs much faster and more easily than in large tables. See Cleveland [1993] and Cleveland [1994] for thorough accounts of data visualization. Also see Tufte [1983] for the authoritative treatise on effective data visualization. It is worthwhile also to look at Wickham [2009] for useful discussions and implementations in R of the Grammar of Graphics due to Wilkinson [2005].

I cannot oversell visual displays either. Not all visuals are created equal or are the best for revealing Rich Information. There are visual display issues, such as colors and excessive use of 3-D, that counter the benefits of visualization.[6] Nonetheless, you cannot do effective Business Analytics **without** data visualization.

To say you need to create graphs to visualize data is insufficient. A logical question to ask is: "*What do I look for in graphs?*" I have my own list of "clues" to look for in graphs that tells you about the underlying processes generating the data and data issues you need to note.

1. Distributions
    *   Symmetry/skewness.
2. Relationships
    *   Correlations or causality statements between two or more variables.
3. Trends
    *   Developments or changes over time (e.g., a tracking study).
4. Patterns
    *   Groupings of objects as in market segments.
5. Anomalies
    *   Outliers or unexpected values.

These are not in any special order. In fact, after a while you will unconsciously, almost instinctively, look for them as soon as you produce a graph. I will discuss these one at a time in the following sections.

Examine distributions

First on my list is an examination of the distribution of the data. The distribution is where the data are centered and how they are spread out from that point. Two display tools that reveal the distribution are the *histogram* and the *boxplot*. Both are introduced in a basic statistics course with the histogram being introduced first, almost within the first week, followed by the boxplot a few weeks later after summary statistics are introduced.

The histogram, although a basic almost elementary graph for **one** variable, has a major issue – the size, and therefore the number, of bins to display where the bins are represented by bars. Changing the size of the bins can dramatically change how the histogram is interpreted and, therefore, what kind of Rich Information it will provide. Most statistics packages have their own algorithm for determining bin sizes. One rule is the *Freedman–Diaconis* rule for bin width:

$$h = 2 \times \frac{IQR(x)}{n^{1/3}}$$

where h = bin width, IQR = Interquartile Range (= Q3 - Q1) for variable x, and n is the number of observations. The number of bins is then

$$k = \frac{Max\ x - Min\ x}{h}.7$$

You can set your own bin size in most data visualization software, but the default is usually sufficient. The Python package, Seaborn, uses this rule. Another rule is *Sturges' Rule* for determining the number of bins:

$$k = 1 + log_2 n$$

where n is the sample size. See the short note by Hyndman [1995] about issues with these rules.

The shape of the histogram indicates the shape of the data's distribution. There are three possibilities. The distribution could be:

1. symmetric – the most desirable;
2. right-skewed; or
3. left skewed.

A distribution is symmetric if the right and left sides of the histogram are approximately mirror images of each other. A distribution is skewed to the right if the right side of the histogram extends much farther out than the left; there is a long right tail. A distribution is skewed to the left if the left side of the histogram extends much farther out than the right; there is a long left tail. Skewness is an issue because skewed data impacts many summary statistics, especially the mean or average. Three possible shapes are shown in Figure 7.4. The lower right is almost uniform while the lower left is almost normal. The one on the lower left is the most desirable.

Because of the bin issue, and also since a histogram is for a single variable, a better plot is the boxplot because it does not have this issue. This creative display shows the Five Number Summary mentioned earlier and it can also show the effect of a second, qualitative variable. Figure 7.5 shows the anatomy of a boxplot.

Examine relationships

The best way to examine and discover relationships between two or more quantitative variables is with a scatter plot. This shows combinations of values of the variables as points and all the points will show a relationship, if one exists. Figure 7.6 illustrates possibilities.

There is something to notice about the one in the lower left of Figure 7.6: there are a lot of data points! Maybe there is something hidden inside this graph, some Rich Information, hidden because there are too many data points. I will comment on this shortly.

When you see a nonlinear relationship, such as the one on the upper right of Figure 7.6, you could make it linear with a log transformation. The log actually does two things:

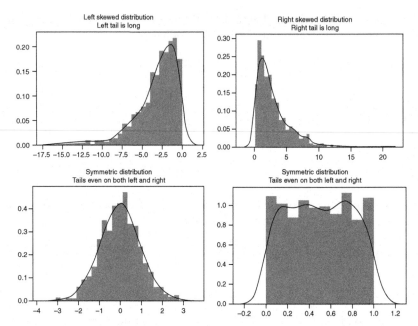

FIGURE 7.4 Three possible shapes for a histogram. The top left is left skewed; the top right is right-skewed; the two bottom ones are symmetric. The bottom left histogram is normal while the bottom right is uniform.

1. Straighten, or linearize, a curve
   - Linear relationships are easier to work with.
   - Linear relationships make it easier to handle probability distributions.
2. Stabilize variances
   - Make the distributions more evenly spread.
   - Remove extreme skewness.

Demonstrations of these two properties are in the Appendix to this chapter.

Figure 7.7 shows the distribution of the net unit sales for the Case Study. Net sales are total, or gross, unit sales less returns. Notice that net sales are highly right-skewed which distorts the impression of the data. Any statistical analysis is jeopardized by this skewness. Transforming the data with the natural log normalizes the data so when you model net unit sales you should use a log transformation. Figure 7.8 shows the same data but on a natural log scale. The distribution is now fairly normal. As a recommendation, use the natural log of one plus the argument, or $\ln(1 + x)$, rather than $\ln x$ to avoid cases where $x = 0$ since $\ln 0$ is undefined, which is meaningless, but $\ln 1 = 0$ so you have a meaningful number. For the Case Study, it is possible that net sales could be zero if the entire order was returned. This is, in fact, the case as shown by the Five Number Summary in Table 7.5.

Log transforming data also produces a nice, useful economic interpretation: the estimated coefficient in an *OLS* model is an *elasticity*! This is demonstrated in the

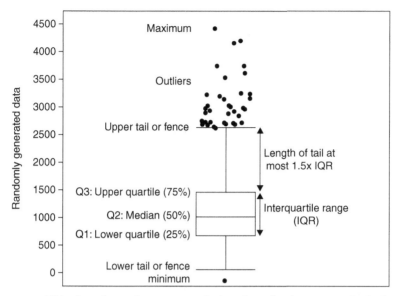

FIGURE 7.5 This chart shows the anatomy of a boxplot. The distance inside the box is the Interquartile Range (*IQR*). The upper and lower fences are at most 1.5 times the *IQR*. Data points outside the fences are outliers.

TABLE 7.5 Five-number summary of net unit sales. Notice that the minimum is zero which justifies adding 1 to the log transformation of net sales as discussed in the text. Since Q3 − *Median* > *Median* − Q1, then net sales are right-skewed.

Minimum	Q1	Median	Q3	Maximum
0	15	24	36	338

Appendix. Also see Paczkowski [2018] for a discussion of this demand function, elasticities, and the log transformation.

Since one objective from the product manager is to estimate a price elasticity, you should graph net unit sales and the Pocket Price. I observed earlier that net unit sales were right-skewed but that using a log transform shifted the distribution to a more normal one. The log of net unit sales as well as the log of pocket price should therefore be used. This is a common transformation in empirical demand analysis because the slope of a line is the elasticity. A scatter plot of the log of net sales versus the log of the pocket price is shown in Figure 7.9. The data cloud is dense because of the number of data points plotted, hence it is difficult to see any clear pattern. A regression line was overlaid on the graph but the line is barely discernible. This is a case of *Large-N*. See Carr et al. [1987] for a discussion of *Large-N* problems.

A *Large-N* case results in a dense scatter plot making it difficult to see patterns. Options for handling this situation are:

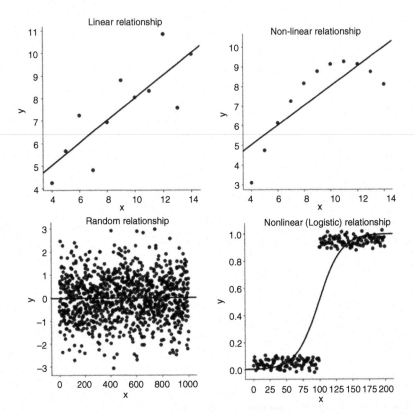

FIGURE 7.6 This chart shows some examples of relationships revealed by a scatter plot. The upper left is the most desirable because it is the easiest to work with. The one on the lower left is the least desirable because there is no discernible pattern. The data for the top row are from the data set know as Anscombe's quartet. See https://en.wikipedia. org/wiki/Anscombe%27s_quartet. The data for the bottom row were randomly generated.

1. select a random sample of the data;
2. use a contour rather than a scatter plot; and
3. use a hex bin plot.

Sampling is powerful for reducing the *Large-N* problem and allowing you to do cross-validation. Cross-validation means that you could draw several samples and use each one as a check against the others. You should see the same relationships, more or less, but not dramatic differences. There are two issues with sampling:

1. because you are sampling, you might not have the best view of the data, so outliers and the mode may be hidden;

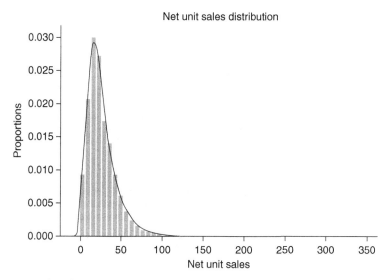

FIGURE 7.7 This chart shows the distribution of net unit sales without a log transformation.

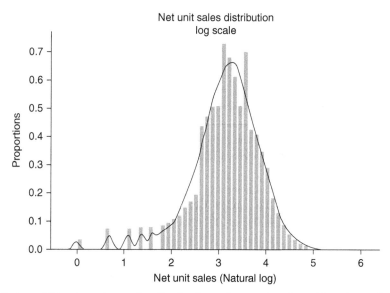

FIGURE 7.8 This chart shows the distribution of net unit sales with a (natural) log transformation.

2. you may actually introduce modes and outliers that are not really there, but appear to be there by luck of the draw of the sample.

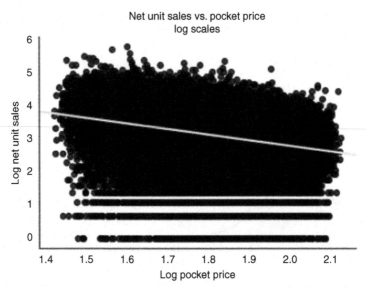

FIGURE 7.9 This chart shows the relationship between the log of net unit sales and the log of the pocket price.

See Carr et al. [1987] for a discussion of using random sampling with *Large-N* data. These are problems with any sampling, whether for graphs, which is our concern, or for surveys, or clinical trials, and so forth. Figure 7.10 shows the same data but based on a sample size of $n = 500$. The negative relationship between net sales and pocket price is clear.

An alternative is a contour plot which shows contours of the data. Different densities are shown with shaded areas as in Figure 7.11. A drawback to contour plots is the *hyperparameters* defining the plot. Different hyperparameter values give different impressions. See Dupont and W. Dale Plummer [2005] for a discussion and examples.

The hex bin plot is sometimes better because it involves drawing small hexagonal shapes, the coloring or shading of the shapes indicating the number of data points inside the hexagon. These shapes are less affected by hyperparameters and so are more robust. This is a much more effective way to visualize *Large-N* data. A hex bin plot is shown in Figure 7.12.

The product manager for the Case Study wanted some insight into discounts by marketing regions. Boxplots will help reveal any differences. Figure 7.13 shows the distribution of total discounts by region. Notice that discounts are lowest in the Southern Region while the Midwest has a large number of low discounts. Also, the dispersion of discounts in the Southern Region is small relative to that in the other three regions. Let me drill down to verify the differences for the Southern Region. You can use Tukey's pairwise *Honestly Significant Difference* (*HSD*) test for this which I mentioned in Chapter 2. The test adjusts for the fact that multiple pairwise tests

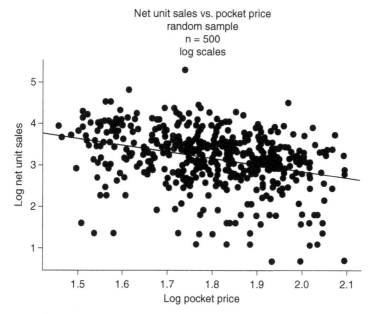

FIGURE 7.10 This chart shows the relationship between the log of net unit sales and the log of the pocket price using a random sample of $n = 500$ data points.

are conducted which increases the probability of making a false decision. In fact, the usual standard for a hypothesis test is $\alpha = 0.05$; this is the probability of falsely rejecting the null hypothesis. When multiple tests are conducted, this probability becomes $1 - (1 - \alpha)^k$ where k is the number of pairwise tests. If $k = 1$, then this simplifies to α. If there are n units to test, then there are $k = {}^{n \times (n-1)}/_2$ tests. For the region problem, $n = 4$ so there are $k = 6$ pairwise comparison tests. Results of a Tukey *HSD* test of total discounts by region are shown in Table 7.6. Summary statistics are shown in Table 7.7 to help interpret Table 7.6. These results confirm the observation made from the boxplots in Figure 7.13. See Paczkowski [2016] for a discussion of Tukey's *HSD* test.

A further step in the tracking analysis by region is to drill down on the components of total discounts for the Southern Region. Figure 7.14 shows boxplots of the components for the Southern Region. Notice that the dealer discount tends to be the largest while the order discount has the most variation. These discounts could affect sales and revenue.

Examine patterns

As rules-of-thumb, look for clumps, or darkly shaded areas, or dispersion of the data, all depending on the type of graph you are using.

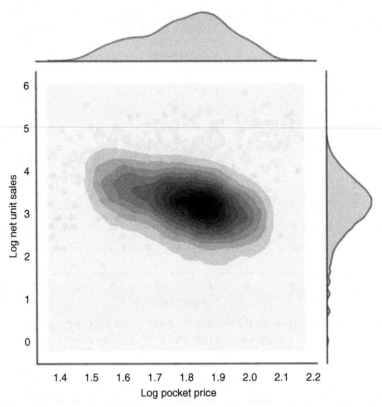

FIGURE 7.11 This chart shows the relationship between the log of net unit sales and the log of the pocket price using a contour plot. Smooth histograms, called *kernel density plots*, are shown on the two margins of the graph to emphasize the distributions. You can see that the distributions are almost normal.

Examine anomalies

Finally, look for anomalies, or outliers. These are suspicious points, some of which could be innocuous, while others could be pernicious leading to the wrong information; in other words, Poor Information. A boxplot is a great tool for showing outliers as in Figure 7.16. The points above the upper fence are all considered to be outliers. In this case, there are many of them. There is also one point slightly below the lower fence so there is only one low outlier. It is the mass at the top that is the issue in this example. These are cases that should be checked because they have the potential to adversely affect any statistics and modeling.

7.1.7 Predictive modeling

Now that you have your data and you have visually examined them, you have to turn your attention to predictive modeling to address the product manager's business

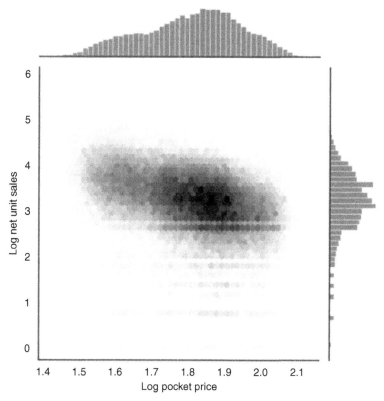

FIGURE 7.12 This chart shows the relationship between the log of net unit sales and the log of the pocket price using a hex plot. Histograms are shown on the two margins of the graph to emphasize the distributions. You can see that the distributions are almost normal.

problems. Recall that she wants to know the price elasticity for living room blinds now that actual market data are available but she also wants to know the effect of changing the price level. The latter is a more complicated problem. See Paczkowski [2018] for a thorough discussion regarding price modeling.

Every process has steps that should be followed. Predicting is no different. The steps for predictive modeling are:

1. split the data into training and testing data sets;
2. train a model with the training data set; and
3. test the trained model with the testing data set.

These steps hold even for forecasting the future, but that is not our focus here. Forecasting has its own complex issues, but the framework is the same. I will discuss

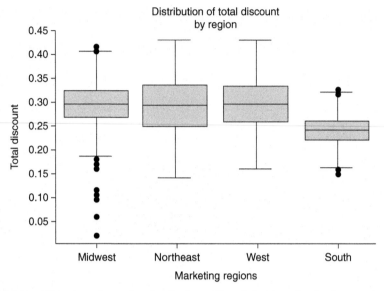

FIGURE 7.13 This chart shows the distributions of total discounts by the four marketing regions.

TABLE 7.6 These are the test results for differences in mean total discounts by marketing regions. The difference in the means is Group 2 – Group 1. The columns labeled "Lower" and "Upper" are the confidence limits around the mean difference. Notice that the Null Hypothesis is rejected for all combinations of the Southern Region and the other three (the last row of the table should be reversed to be consistent with the other Southern comparisons). Also notice that the difference in the means for the Southern Region is negative in all cases.

Group 1	Group 2	Mean Difference	Lower	Upper	Reject Null?
Midwest	Northeast	-0.0038	-0.0053	-0.0024	True
Midwest	South	-0.0549	-0.0561	-0.0537	True
Midwest	West	-0.0003	-0.0014	0.0008	False
Northeast	South	-0.0511	-0.0526	-0.0496	True
Northeast	West	0.0035	0.0021	0.0049	True
South	West	0.0546	0.0535	0.0558	True

these three general steps in the following subsections for predicting. Forecasting methods were already discussed in Chapter 6.

Training and testing data sets

It is best practice to divide a data set into two parts for prediction purposes:

TABLE 7.7 These are the summary statistics to help interpret Table 7.6.

Region	Count	Mean	Std. Dev.	Min	Q1	Median	Q3	Max
Midwest	19565	0.294990	0.040023	0.023	0.267	0.295	0.323	0.414
Northeast	8704	0.291163	0.056135	0.139	0.249	0.293	0.334	0.431
South	15831	0.240060	0.028707	0.149	0.220	0.240	0.260	0.325
West	26170	0.294682	0.048876	0.158	0.258	0.294	0.331	0.431

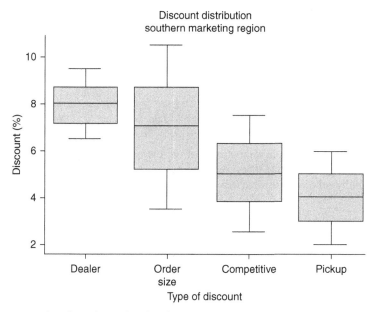

FIGURE 7.14 This chart shows the distributions of the components of the total discount for the Southern Region.

1. a training data set; and
2. a testing data set.

The former is used for model estimation while the latter is used for model testing. This is best practice to ensure optimal modeling. When a model is estimated, we say that it *learns* what the estimates should be from the data we give the estimation procedure. In essence, the model is trained by the data. Actually, the model is trained by a dependent variable in the sense that this variable guides how the parameters are estimated. It supervises the training so this is sometimes called supervised learning. There is, of course, unsupervised learning, but that is another issue.

Once a model is trained, it has to perform; that is, predict. You need to check those predictions, but you cannot do that with the same data used in the training since the model already saw or knows that data. This is where the testing data come

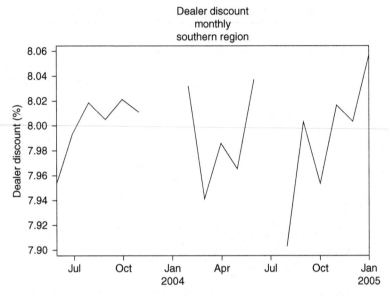

FIGURE 7.15 This chart shows the trend of the mean monthly dealer discount for the Southern Region. Notice that several months are missing discounts and that the last few months indicate an upward trend.

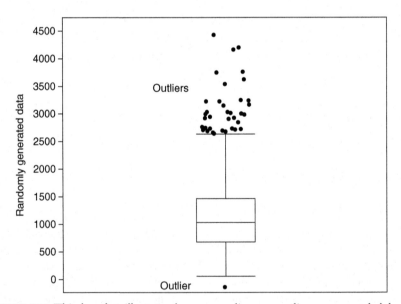

FIGURE 7.16 This boxplot illustrates how anomalies, or outliers, are revealed by a boxplot. The data for this graph are simulated.

in. This data set is a new one the model has not seen. If the model is good, it should be able to predict the testing data, albeit with some random variation or noise. A rough rule-of-thumb is to split your data into 3/4 training and 1/4 testing. Another is 2/3 training and 1/3 testing. It all depends, of course, on the size of your original data. Basically, you need a larger portion in the training data set because learning is more challenging and data intensive.

If time is not a characteristic of the data, then simple random sampling could be used to divide a data set into training and testing parts. However, if time is involved, then a split cannot be based on random sampling as I noted in Chapter 6 and the method I described there must be used. If the data are a panel data set consisting of both cross-sectional and time series dimensions, then it is best to randomly sample on the cross-sectional dimension and preserve the time series for those units.

Training a model

Let me now discuss training a model with the training data set. The framework you select for predictive modeling depends on the nature of the dependent variable, the variable that guides the training. There are several cases or possibilities.[8] For one case, the dependent variable is *continuous*; this is just *OLS*. For another case, the dependent variable is *binary*; this is where logistic regression is used. Both are members of a regression family, which is large. There is actually a third case that can handle either a continuous or discrete dependent variable but it does so by fitting constants to the data. This is also a member of the regression family. In a sense, these are all cousins. Regardless of the specific family member, a regression model fits:

- straight lines: this is *OLS*;
- curves: this is logistic regression[9]; and
- constants: this is decision trees.

These three cases are discussed in the following subsections.

Case I: Training a model with a continuous dependent variable

Technically, this is the model for an *OLS* regression. A model is

$$Y_i = \beta_0 + \beta_1 X_{i1} + \beta_2 X_{i2} + \ldots + \beta_p X_{ip} + \epsilon_i$$

where:

Y_i is the dependent variable for the ith observation, $i = 1, 2, \ldots, n$;

β_0 is the intercept;

$\beta_j, j = 1, 2, \ldots, p$ are the slopes;

$X_{ij}, j = 1, 2, \ldots, p$ are the independent variables; and

ϵ_i is the random disturbance: $\epsilon_i \sim \mathcal{N}(0, \sigma^2)$.

Y_i is continuous and our goal is to estimate the parameters or slopes to say something about Y_i which could, for example, be net unit sales. There should be an intercept, β_0, but I usually do not care about this since it just places the line or plane or hypersurface. The slopes, however, are important since they show the effects of the independent variables. These slopes are intimately related to the dependent variable which is why I refer to the model as being trained by the dependent variable.

Once the model is trained, you have to examine it statistically. This means you have to test the effects. You use an F-test for this purpose. You also have to check the relationship among the independent variables for multicollinearity, using the variance inflation factors (*VIF*). See Gujarati [2003] and Paczkowski [2018] for a discussion of *VIF*. There are other checks you need to do, but these will suffice for here.

In general, a model is trained following four steps:[10]

1. define a formula (i.e., the specific model to estimate);
2. instantiate the model (i.e., specify it);
3. fit the model; and
4. summarize the fitted model.

For the Case Study, a model for unit sales is

$$Usales_i = e^{\beta_0} \times Pprice_i^{\beta_1} \times e^{\beta_2 Midwest_i + \beta_3 Northeast_i + \beta_4 South_i} \times e^{\epsilon_i}$$

where the focus is on the pocket price and marketing regions. Notice only three regions are specified. Since *Region* is categorical, you must create dummy variables for it. There are four marketing regions corresponding to the four U.S. Census Regions so only three dummies should be created. The *Western* region is omitted to avoid the dummy variable trap. This region is the last in alphanumeric order and was arbitrarily selected as the base. Although omitted in the model specification, it is still present as the intercept. The intercept is the *Western* region and the estimated parameters for the other three regions show differences from the *Western* region which is the base. See Paczkowski [2018] and Gujarati [2003] for discussions about dummy variables, their interpretation, and the dummy variable trap.

This model is an inherently linear model meaning it can be linearized by taking the natural log of both sides. The earlier histogram analysis showed that net sales are highly right-skewed but that the distribution for the log transformation is more symmetrical. This is why it is preferred. In addition to being inherently linear, this model is also a constant-elasticity (or isoelastic) model. The price elasticity is the estimated parameter, β_1. See Paczkowski [2018] for a discussion of this type of model and elasticities. Also see the Appendix to this chapter for the constant elasticity demonstration.

Applying the natural log to both sides of the model yields

$$\ln Usales = \beta_0 + \beta_1 \ln Pprice_i + \beta_2 Midwest_i + \beta_3 Northeast_i + \beta_4 South_i + \epsilon_i. \quad (7.1)$$

Once a model is specified, it must be *instantiated*, which simply means the estimation methodology must be specified for the model just stated. Since an *OLS* model is considered in this section, instantiation means that *OLS* must be specified. In addition to specifying the methodology, the data used with that model is also specified. This will be the training data set.

Response Log[Usales]

Summary of Fit

RSquare	0.175914
RSquare Adj	0.175867
Root Mean Square Error	0.508186
Mean of Response	3.276517
Observations (or Sum Wgts)	70269

Analysis of Variance

Source	DF	Sum of Squares	Mean Square	F Ratio
Model	4	3873.524	968.381	3749.734
Error	70264	18145.905	0.258	**Prob > F**
C. Total	70268	22019.429		<.0001*

Indicator Function Parameterization

Term	Estimate	Std Error	t Ratio	Prob>|t|
Intercept	6.0781107	0.023506	258.57	<.0001*
Log[Pprice]	-1.45438	0.012224	-119.0	<.0001*
Region[Midwest]	0.0039274	0.004806	0.82	0.4138
Region[Northeast]	-0.000203	0.006293	-0.03	0.9743
Region[South]	-0.103613	0.005122	-20.23	<.0001*

FIGURE 7.17 Regression summary for the linearized model, (7.1).

Next, the model is fit; that is, the unknown model parameters are estimated using the training data set. In some software, once the model is fit, a summary report is displayed which is the last step; in other software products, you have to call a summary function. Regardless, a summary of the fit is displayed.

Estimation results for the Case Study are shown in Figure 7.17. The estimated price parameter is -1.5 which indicates that the demand for the new product is highly elastic. This should be expected since window treatments is a highly competitive business. In addition to blinds, there are also shades and drapes. In addition, this new product is a high-tech product that is voice activated which means that its appeal in the market may be hindered by the low-tech (i.e., old-fashioned) blinds currently in the market. If sales are suffering as the product manager's dashboard and business intelligence systems indicate, lowering the price may be necessary. This elasticity helps justify this strategy.

Why lower the price rather than raise it? I show in the Appendix to this chapter and in Paczkowski [2018] that the total revenue elasticity with respect to a price

Effect Tests

Source	Nparm	DF	Sum of Squares	F Ratio	Prob > F
Log[Pprice]	1	1	3655.6262	14155.20	<.0001*
Region	3	3	135.1536	174.4459	<.0001*

Effect Summary

Source	LogWorth		PValue
Log[Pprice]	2802.448		0.00000
Region	111.960		0.00000

FIGURE 7.18 Regression effects summary shows that the regions are significant. The price and region effects tests F-ratios are calculated as the respective sum of squares (SS) divided by the error SS in the ANOVA table. The SS are the difference in the ANOVA model SS when the effect is omitted. So the Region SS is the ANOVA model SS including and excluding the region variable. The Effects Summary report plots the p-values from the Effects Test report. These p-values are scaled using the negative of the log to the base 10 of the p-value. This transformation is called a log-worth which is $log_{10}(p-value)$. See Paczkowski [2016] for a discussion of the log-worth and its applications.

change is $\eta_P^{TR} = 1 + \eta_P^Q$ where η_P^Q is the price elasticity for unit sales with respect to the price. For this problem, $\eta_P^Q = -1.5$ so $\eta_P^{TR} = -0.5$. If price is lowered 1%, then revenue rises 0.5%. Clearly a price increase results in revenue declining.

The regression results also indicate that regions vary in significance. An effects test (an F-Test) shows that regions as a whole are significant. The test results are shown in Figure 7.18.

The analysis could be taken a step further by estimating the interaction between price and region. There may be a regional price elasticity differential that could lead to an enhanced price discrimination strategy. The result of interacting price and region is shown in Figure 7.19. The effects are summarized in Figure 7.20. Notice that the interactions are insignificant.

Testing a model

Once a model is trained, you should test it against the pristine testing data set. Recall that this is a data set the model did not see during its training. The estimated, trained coefficients could be applied to the testing data to predict values for the dependent variable. For the Case Study, first recognize that net unit sales are in natural log terms. You will convert back to net unit sales in "normal" terms by exponentiating the log term. The same holds for the price variable. Once this is done, an "r2_score" can be calculated to check the fit of actual vs. predicted values.

Response Log[Usales]

Summary of Fit

RSquare	0.175929
RSquare Adj	0.175846
Root Mean Square Error	0.508193
Mean of Response	3.276517
Observations (or Sum Wgts)	70269

Analysis of Variance

Source	DF	Sum of Squares	Mean Square	F Ratio
Model	7	3873.845	553.406	2142.829
Error	70261	18145.583	0.258	**Prob > F**
C. Total	70268	22019.429		<.0001*

Indicator Function Parameterization

Term	Estimate	Std Error	t Ratio	Prob>|t|
Intercept	6.1029081	0.037795	161.47	<.0001*
Log[Pprice]	-1.467392	0.019764	-74.25	<.0001*
Region[Midwest]	0.0038606	0.004808	0.80	0.4220
Region[Northeast]	-0.000481	0.00635	-0.08	0.9396
Region[South]	-0.103688	0.005131	-20.21	<.0001*
Region[Midwest]*(Log[Pprice]-1.911)	0.0288667	0.029813	0.97	0.3329
Region[Northeast]*(Log[Pprice]-1.911)	1.492e-6	0.038415	0.00	1.0000
Region[South]*(Log[Pprice]-1.911)	0.0242158	0.034954	0.69	0.4884

FIGURE 7.19 Regression summary of price and region interaction. An adjustment is made to the interaction term to avoid potential bias. This output was produced using JMP. See the JMP documentation for the adjustment.

The r2_score function "computes R^2, the coefficient of determination. It provides a measure of how well future samples are likely to be predicted by the model. The best possible score is 1.0 and it can be negative (because the model can be arbitrarily worse). A constant model that always predicts the expected value of y, disregarding the input features, would get a R^2 score of 0.0."[11] For the Case Study, the score is 0.138 which is not very good.

You can graph the actual vs predicted values. Sometimes, however, the number of data points is too large to plot so a random sample may be needed. This is our situation for the Case Study. The data visualization methods described earlier could be used for this problem.

You can also predict unit sales for different settings of the pocket price variable. This is *scenario* or *what-if* analysis. Since the pocket price is a function of the discounts given by the sales force, you might want to have separate equations for pocket price with different discounts. Recall that pocket price is the list price less

Effect Tests

Source	Nparm	DF	Sum of Squares	F Ratio	Prob > F
Log[Pprice]	1	1	3114.7593	12060.57	<.0001*
Region	3	3	134.3789	173.4416	<.0001*
Region*Log[Pprice]	3	3	0.3215	0.4150	0.7422

Effect Summary

Source	LogWorth		PValue
Log[Pprice]	2419.059		0.00000
Region	111.311		0.00000
Region*Log[Pprice]	0.129		0.74223

FIGURE 7.20 Regression effects summary for the price-region interaction.

TABLE 7.8 This is a tally of those who purchased each of the three window treatments. There were 372 (= 179 + 193) customers who did not purchase any of the three products but are in the data set because they purchased some other product in the company's product line.

	Drapes			Shades		
Blinds	No	Yes	Total	No	Yes	Total
No	179	178	357	193	164	357
Yes	161	618	779	155	624	779
Total	340	796	1136	348	788	1136

discounts. A simple program could be written to use discounts as inputs and return pocket prices which are then used as inputs to the estimated model.

Case II: Training a model with a discrete dependent variable

For the Case Study, the product manager wants to know the determinants or key drivers for a customer buying or not buying the new window blinds product. She is particularly interested in knowing the likelihood of buying blinds if window drapes and/or shades are purchased. To address her questions, you create a data table that has for each unique customer ID (*CID*) the total number of blinds, drapes, and shades purchased by each customer since the introduction of the new blinds. There were 1,136 unique customer IDs. An indicator variable was created for each product that was 1 if the total order was greater than zero and 0 otherwise. A tally is shown in Table 7.8.

The data were split into training and testing data sets. The training set had 761 records and the testing data set had 375; the total for the two is the original 1,136.

A logit model was specified for the blind purchases. The model is for the probability that any customer either buys or does not buy the new living room blind as a function of several factors:

- whether or not drapes were ordered (0/1 coding);
- whether or not shades were ordered (0/1 coding);
- Marketing Region (dummy coded);
- Loyalty Program membership (0/1 coding);
- Buyer Rating (dummy coded);
- Customer Satisfaction Rating (*T2B* coded);
- population size of store location;
- median household income of store location;
- number of housing units of store location;
- number of occupied housing units of store location;
- ratio of occupied to total housing units; and
- credit rating (*T2B*).

Since there is a variable that measures the ratio of occupied to total housing units, only this ratio was used. This means 10 of the twelve variables listed were used to fit a model.

A logit regression model was fit to the training data with the blinds as the dependent variable. Estimation results are shown in Figure 7.21 and Figure 7.22. The odds ratios for drapes and shades, the two significant variables, are shown in Figure 7.23.[12]

Case III: Training a model with constants

Now let me consider what happens when you have constants to model. This is where decision trees come in. So let me discuss this class of models which are also in the regression family. See Beck [2008] for a discussion of decision trees as a regression family member.

Decision trees are used when the dependent variable is continuous or discrete; it is versatile. There are also independent variables as with *OLS* and logistic regression. These variables, however, are used to "cut" the dependent variable into groups by fitting constants to the dependent variable. This cutting up of the dependent variable amounts to creating smaller and smaller groups of the dependent variable and therefore the sample. The dependent variable is thus partitioned so the trees are sometimes called *partition trees*. Trees are graphed upside down with the root at the top and branches flowing down. There are "leaves" and it is these leaves that show or summarize the partitioning of the dependent variable.

For terminology, when the dependent variable is discrete with classes or groups the tree is called a *classification tree*; otherwise, it is a *regression tree*. The contents of the leaves, also called *nodes*, vary depending on the software. The leaves generally look like the one displayed in Figure 7.24. In this example, the dependent variable is buy or not buy the new blind, which is discrete, so the tree is a classification

Nominal Logistic Fit for Blinds

Effect Summary

Source	LogWorth		PValue
drapes	7.592		0.00000
shades	7.376		0.00000
hh_income	0.973		0.10640
sat_t2b	0.370		0.42703
region	0.318		0.48072
credit_score	0.247		0.56674
population	0.212		0.61343
h_units_ratio	0.122		0.75425
buyer_rating	0.073		0.84525
loyalty_program	0.066		0.85876

Converged in Gradient, 4 iterations

Whole Model Test

Model	-LogLikelihood	DF	ChiSquare	Prob>ChiSq
Difference	53.44196	16	106.8839	<.0001*
Full	400.65241			
Reduced	454.09437			

RSquare (U)	0.1177
AICc	836.172
BIC	913.246
Observations (or Sum Wgts)	724

Lack Of Fit

Source	DF	-LogLikelihood	ChiSquare
Lack Of Fit	707	400.65241	801.3048
Saturated	723	0.00000	**Prob>ChiSq**
Fitted	16	400.65241	0.0077*

FIGURE 7.21 This shows the logit regression model fit statistics for the training data.

tree. The purchase of a shade is a key driver. The node has a sample size of 534 customers. The G^2 value is the Likelihood-ratio Chi-square value discussed in Chapter 5 and the log–Worth is the transformed p-value for this chi-square. Recall that the logistic model estimates a probability. So does the classification tree. The predicted probabilities are 0.223 for *Not Buy* (the 0 value) and 0.777 for *Buy* (the 1 value). Since the predicted probability is larger for *Buy*, then the predicted class for all those in this node is *Buy*.

See Paczkowski [2016] for a discussion of decision trees using the JMP software and how to interpret the output.

Nominal Logistic Fit for Blinds

Converged in Gradient, 4 iterations

Parameter Estimates

Term	Estimate	Std Error	ChiSquare	Prob>ChiSq
Intercept	0.77723775	0.6391008	1.48	0.2239
drapes[0]	-0.5296101	0.0950161	31.07	<.0001*
shades[0]	-0.5181265	0.0942583	30.22	<.0001*
loyalty_program[0]	0.02758299	0.1553822	0.03	0.8591
buyer_rating[1]	0.11542465	0.2227829	0.27	0.6044
buyer_rating[2]	-0.038002	0.1517073	0.06	0.8022
sat_t2b[0]	0.0738741	0.0932787	0.63	0.4284
credit_score[1]	-0.3660202	0.2947375	1.54	0.2143
credit_score[2]	0.29487014	0.2078826	2.01	0.1561
credit_score[3]	0.0724488	0.1585478	0.21	0.6477
credit_score[4]	-0.0609384	0.1716031	0.13	0.7225
region[Midwest]	0.04100776	0.1754999	0.05	0.8152
region[Northeast]	0.29598572	0.2745632	1.16	0.2810
region[South]	-0.2323354	0.162585	2.04	0.1530
population	-2.8967e-6	5.7196e-6	0.26	0.6125
h_units_ratio	0.23556258	0.7500558	0.10	0.7535
hh_income	-7.2257e-6	4.5372e-6	2.54	0.1113

For log odds of 1/0

FIGURE 7.22 This shows the logit regression model fit estimates for the training data.

7.1.8 New product forecast error analysis

If a sales forecast was produced prior to launch, then it should be monitored in conjunction with sales data. The problem for forecast tracking is how the sales forecast was produced. If a judgement, naive, or constant mean method was used, then forecast tracking is most likely pointless – the forecast will be off simply because poor methods were used. Recall that a forecast has to be developed for planning purposes and this is probably as far as it should go when these methods are used. If analog product histories were combined either through simple averaging (e.g., "cluster-then-estimate" approach) or a more complex method (e.g., "cluster-while-estimate" approach), better forecasting methods could have been used and a forecast has more power and credibility. The forecast should be tracked and updated as new data become available. The updating is important because there are implications for all the business domains impacted by the original forecast. The issue is how to assess forecast accuracy.

Forecast accuracy and model fit are often confused. They are two different parts of an overall modeling process that, although separate and distinct, are nonetheless

Nominal Logistic Fit for Blinds

Converged in Gradient, 4 iterations

Parameter Estimates

Term	Estimate	Std Error	ChiSquare	Prob>ChiSq
Intercept	0.77723775	0.6391008	1.48	0.2239
drapes[0]	-0.5296101	0.0950161	31.07	<.0001*
shades[0]	-0.5181265	0.0942583	30.22	<.0001*
loyalty_program[0]	0.02758299	0.1553822	0.03	0.8591
buyer_rating[1]	0.11542465	0.2227829	0.27	0.6044
buyer_rating[2]	-0.038002	0.1517073	0.06	0.8022
sat_t2b[0]	0.0738741	0.0932787	0.63	0.4284
credit_score[1]	-0.3660202	0.2947375	1.54	0.2143
credit_score[2]	0.29487014	0.2078826	2.01	0.1561
credit_score[3]	0.0724488	0.1585478	0.21	0.6477
credit_score[4]	-0.0609384	0.1716031	0.13	0.7225
region[Midwest]	0.04100776	0.1754999	0.05	0.8152
region[Northeast]	0.29598572	0.2745632	1.16	0.2810
region[South]	-0.2323354	0.162585	2.04	0.1530
population	-2.8967e-6	5.7196e-6	0.26	0.6125
h_units_ratio	0.23556258	0.7500558	0.10	0.7535
hh_income	-7.2257e-6	4.5372e-6	2.54	0.1113

For log odds of 1/0

FIGURE 7.23 This shows the odds ratios for drapes and shades for the logit regression model fit for the training data.

shades(1)

Count	G^2	LogWorth
534	566.56019	4.2698152

Level	Rate	Prob	Count
0	0.2228	0.2230	119
1	0.7772	0.7770	415

FIGURE 7.24 General composition of a decision tree node.

connected. A model that fits the training data very well may produce very good forecasts if the trends and patterns in the training data are stable and repeatable. But there is no guarantee that they will be. In addition, a model may forecast well into a testing period, but then may not do well outside this period. Conditions in the economy could suddenly change (e.g., a new tax policy is enacted) that could cause a radical change in the time series underlying the forecast. Or a new competitor could enter the market and completely change market dynamics. A model, on the other hand, that had a terrible fit to the training data or poor error performance in the testing data would most likely produce a forecast that was equally terrible.

Model estimation must be judged using the basic criteria applied to all models. This includes R^2 (where applicable), F-statistics, p-values, and so forth as part of a modeling strategy. A model that does poorly on these statistics should be discarded in favor of one that does well. Once a good model is selected, then a separate check for forecast accuracy should be done using the testing data as I described in Chapter 6. But the model may still not forecast well outside the testing period. You still must check its performance against actual values when they become available. The forecast error for an h-step ahead forecast, $F_T(h)$, is the difference $A_{T+1} - F_T(1)$. This differs from the definition in Chapter 6 by the use of the last value in the full time series sample, T, and not $T' < T$ for a testing period. All the error measures in Chapter 6 can be used with this slight adjustment. See Levenbach and Cleary [2006] for the measures and some examples. In addition, see Jr. [2015] for modeling strategies and model fit criteria. Finally, see Chatfield [2000] for a discussion of model uncertainty and forecast accuracy.

7.1.9 Additional external data – text once more

Tracking, root cause, and what-if analyses are not the sole analyses that must or should be done post-launch. In the modern social media age, customers do write online reviews. In the case of a business-to-business (*B2B*) business, those customers will be other businesses that buy at wholesale. Most likely they will not write reviews but rather go directly to their sales rep to voice an opinion. Their customers, the end-user consumers who are the ultimate customers, will, however, write reviews. It was an analysis of these that was the basis for some new product ideas described and discussed in Chapter 2. These same reviews, and the same text analysis described in Chapter 2, should be studied post-launch to determine if there are any problems. This is in the domain of Sentiment Analysis and Opinion Mining which I will discuss in the next section.

7.2 Sentiment analysis and opinion mining

Section 2.3 focused on methods for extracting key words, phrases, and topics from text data for the purpose of identifying ideas for new products or improvements to existing ones. Another form of text analysis goes a step further and uncovers people's *sentiments* or *opinions* about a concept, which is a product in our case. A sentiment is a negative, neutral, or positive view. In many instances, just a polarity – negative or positive – is used. Examples are:

1.   "*This is a great product. You must own one.*"
     - This is a positive sentiment.

2. "*I can't live without it!*"
    *   This is a positive sentiment.
3. "*I have mixed feelings about this product.*"
    *   This is a neutral sentiment.
4. "*I really regret buying this!!*"
    *   This is a negative sentiment.
5. "*Don't waste your money on this.*"
    *   This is a negative sentiment.

Some sentiment analysis methodologies also consider emotions rather than sentiments, but the concept is the same. See Sarkar [2016, p. 342] for some discussion. Also see Zhang and Liu [2017] for a more detailed discussion of sentiment analysis.

Market researchers have, of course, always captured consumers' sentiments about a product through customer satisfaction surveys. They typically asked three questions:

1. How satisfied are you with the performance of this product?
2. How likely are you to recommend this product to someone else?
3. How likely are you to switch to another product within the next six months?

These questions are obviously looking for sentiments or opinions. A numeric scale for them is usually a Likert five-point scale which the market researchers transform to top-two box, middle box, and bottom-two box.[13] These are positive, neutral, and negative sentiments, respectively.

One form of analysis of these three questions is based on a Venn Diagram such as the one in Figure 7.25. The scores for the three satisfaction questions are converted to top-two box ratings (*T2B*), which are 0/1 values, and then simple proportions are calculated as the average of these 0/1 values for each of the eight possible intersections of the questions corresponding to the three Venn circles. A tabular report based on these proportions, similar to the one shown in Table 7.9, is also possible.

The difference in this analysis from the focus of this section is that text data are used in our current discussion, not a numeric scale.

7.2.1 Sentiment methodology overview

Sentiment analysis is based on a *lexicon*, a special dictionary that classifies words and phrases as negative/neutral/positive sentiments. There is a wide array of lexicons. See Sarkar [2016] for a discussion of some of them.

Sentiment analysis is done by tokenizing the words of a document (after preprocessing the text to delete stop-words, correct spelling, removing punctuation, changing case, and so forth) and then passing the tokens through a lexicon. The document as a whole is classified for its sentiment following some procedure. See Sarkar [2016] for Python code for accomplishing this. Values representing the sentiment of each document are returned and used in statistical analysis. For example,

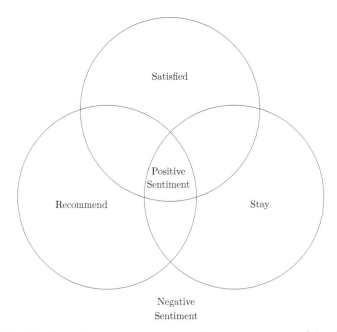

FIGURE 7.25 This Venn diagram shows one possible summarization of the three customer satisfaction questions in a typical customer satisfaction study. In terms of sentiment analysis, the intersection of the three circles shows a positive sentiment; the customers in this intersection are loyal to the product. Those outside all three circles, have a strong negative sentiment. Customers at other intersections have varying degrees of neutral sentiment.

FIGURE 7.26 These are the sequence of steps for feature opinion analysis.

simple frequency counts could be calculated. If the proportion unfavorable is larger than the favorable, then the product has a problem.

A problem with sentiment analysis as usually applied is that it does not explicitly say what is wrong with the product. It does not say which aspect – feature or attribute – is an issue, only that something is wrong. In order to pinpoint a specific problem, one that can be addressed by the R&D staff, you still have to read through the texts. Several researchers have proposed a methodology for extracting features or attributes referenced in product reviews. The opinions of these features are then classified. Quantitative measures are created that can be used in statistical and machine learning applications to further understand opinions of product features, but the opinions are pinpointed to specific features. See de Albornoz et al. [2011], Morales et al. [2008], and Plaza et al. [2010] for discussions.

TABLE 7.9 This is a tabular form of the Venn diagram in Figure 7.25. The counts (corresponding percentages) should add to the total sample size (100%). For this example, $n = 1000$. There are 683 in the *T2B* for Satisfaction; 877 for Recommend; and 548 for Stay. All others were in the bottom boxes with 66 in the bottom box for all three questions. These 66 are the strongly negative sentiment. This example is based on fictitious data.

Sentiment	Count	Percent
Strongly Positive	430	43.0%
Somewhat Positive	314	31.4%
Satisfied & Recommend	198	19.8%
Satisfied & Stay	39	3.9%
Recommend & Stay	78	7.8%
Somewhat Negative	190	19.0%
Satisfied Only	16	1.6%
Recommend Only	171	17.1%
Stay Only	4	0.4%
Strongly Negative	66	6.6%

There are several steps in the process which are illustrated in Figure 7.26. The first step, of course, is to compile a corpus of product reviews from internal logs, social media, or product review websites as I discussed in Chapter 2. Each review is a document in the corpus. The sentences in each document are preprocessed and then sentence-tokenized. The words in each sentence are then tokenized. The reason for this second tokenization is to allow you to refer back to the original sentence from where the word came. Each tokenized word is assigned a "sense or meaning" using *WordNet*. See Miller [1995] and Fellbaum [1998] for background on *WordNet*.

WordNet is a lexical database that classifies words into a hierarchy of more abstract words and concepts. It maps words to their synonyms thus allowing a grouping of words. In this regard, some have equated *WordNet* to a combination dictionary and thesaurus. The important use for this application is the hierarchy of concepts that is formed. This hierarchy can be visualized as an inverted tree with the root, representing the most general abstract concept, at the top of a graph with branches flowing down from the root. Each branch can be split into new branches, the split points, called *nodes*, being a next lower (and less abstract) concept or word. This split continues until the original word is reached. At this point, the branches terminate at a final node. There will be as many final branches and terminal nodes as there are words originally submitted to the *WordNet* program. In our case, the tokenized words from a single sentence are used so there are as many terminal nodes as there are words in that sentence.

A hierarchy of general concepts contained in *Wordnet* is shown in Figure 7.27. The root, an "entity", is at the top and an "organism" is at the bottom.

Using *WordNet*, the tokens or words can be classified as nouns, verbs, adjectives, and adverbs. de Albornoz et al. [2011] note that only nouns, but not proper nouns,

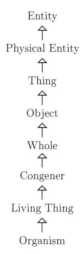

FIGURE 7.27 This illustrates the lexical hierarchy on *Wordnet*. Notice that the highest element in the hierarchy is an *Entity* which could be a physical entity or an abstract entity.

are useful for product features. These nouns are processed through the WordNet database and *WordNet* concepts are returned. The concepts are extended with their hypernyms. *Hypernyms* are words that have a more general, broader meaning than the word under consideration. For example, canine is a hypernym for dog since a canine could be wolf, jackal, fox, or coyote as well as a domesticated dog.[14] There are also *hyponyms* which are the opposite of hypernyms; they have a more specific meaning. Dog is a hyponym for canine.

If your focus is on hypernyms, then the flow of a tree is upward to more abstract concepts. If your focus is on hyponyms, then the flow is downward to more specific concepts. In Figure 7.27 and Figure 7.28, I chose to move up the trees to more abstract concepts.

For "blinds", the hypernym is "protective covering." For a robotic vacuum cleaner, the hypernym for "robot" is "automaton", a more general concept involving any mechanism, including a person, that is self-operating.[15] At an even more general level, a blind and an automaton are each a physical "entity", something that exists, whether it be living or not such as an abstract idea or an abstract entity.[16] A graph for the words "dog", "blind", "robot", and "vacuum" is shown in Figure 7.28.

Following de Albornoz et al. [2011], a graph can be created for each sentence in a product review and then all the graphs are merged. The edges of the graph are weighted, the weights being a function of how far a concept is from the root. Those concepts that are further have more specificity and so are weighted more than those that are close to the root. These weights are used to calculate the *salience* or *importance* of each concept. The salience of a concept is "the sum of the weights of the

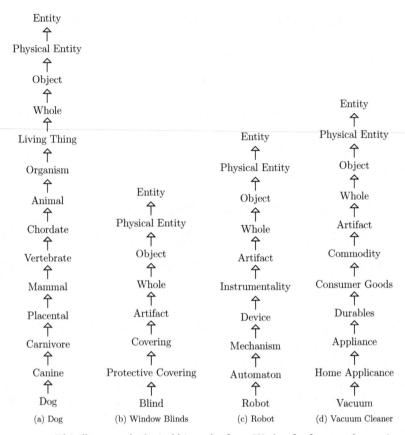

FIGURE 7.28 This illustrates the lexical hierarchy from *Wordnet* for four words mentioned in this book.

edges that have as source or target the given vertex."[17] The weights are multiplied by the frequency of occurrence of the concept in the corpus. The concepts are sorted by their saliences and grouped by a clustering algorithm such as hierarchical or k–means clustering. Each cluster is a product feature. A word cloud can be used to emphasize the importance of each feature. These features can be used to specify and design a new product. In one sense, they come directly from the customers via their written comments, but in another sense they are derived from the comments since few customers can clearly and succinctly indicate what they want. Customers can only complain about their problems; they cannot articulate their needs. This approach holds promise for uncovering those needs.

de Albornoz et al. [2011] outline several heuristics for associating each sentence with a product feature. This results in a mapping of each sentence to at least one product feature. Then all the sentences associated with a feature can be analyzed for the sentiment or opinion expressed for that feature.

7.3 Software

Most general statistical software can handle data visualization. R and Python have excellent data visualization capabilities but producing a graph, even a simple one, requires some program coding. Stata has a good graphics library but program coding is a bit awkward. The same holds for SAS. JMP is particularly good at data visualization because of its dynamic linking of a data table and a graph.

7.4 Summary

I presented a detailed case study of a drill-down of issues associated with a new product post-launch. The problems were identified through a dashboard but then investigated for root causes. The purpose of this detailed case study was to emphasize that Deep Data Analysis (DDA), the key message of this book, is not solely for new product development, but is also applicable for post-launch examination of that product. Just because a new product is launched does not mean that you should stop studying the data generated from it. Once launched, the product will succeed or fail, and as you know from Chapter 1, most fail. The root-cause analysis will help you identify why it failed so that the next new product would have a better chance for success.

7.5 Appendix

7.5.1 Demonstration of linearization using log transformation

Let $f(x)$ be some function we want to approximate at a point $x = a$. The *Taylor Series Expansion* (*TSE*) of $f(x)$ at $x = a$ is

$$f(x) = \sum_{i=0}^{\infty} f^i(a) \frac{(x-a)^i}{i!}$$

where $f^i(a)$ is the ith derivative of the function evaluated at a; $f^0(a)$ is the original function evaluated at a; and $i!$ is the factorial function with $0! = 1$. If you set $f(x) = \ln x$, then the *TSE* of the natural log is

$$\ln x = \ln a + \frac{x-a}{a} + R$$

where R is a remainder term that is usually ignored. Let $x = y_t$ and $a = y_{t-1}$. Then $\ln y_t = \ln y_{t-1} + (y_t - y_{t-1})/y_{t-1}$. The last term is the percent change in y. Denote this by g. Then

$$\ln y_t = \ln y_{t-1} + g. \tag{7.A.1}$$

Notice that the first term on the right-hand side in (7.A.1) is like the term on the left, just one step back. So you can write it as

$$\ln y_{t-1} = \ln y_{t-2} + g \tag{7.A.2}$$

and substitute (7.A.2) in (7.A.1) to get

$$\ln y_t = \ln y_{t-2} + 2 \times g. \tag{7.A.3}$$

Repeat this backward substitution until you get

$$\ln y_t = \ln y_0 + t \times g \tag{7.A.4}$$

where y_0 is the first or starting point for the y data series. Clearly, (7.A.4) is a linear equation with intercept $\ln y_0$ and slope g. So the natural log transformation linearized the original data.

7.5.2 Demonstration of variance stabilization using log transformation

Time series are often characterized by the property that their variance increases over time. Such a series is said to be *nonstationary*. See Wei [2006] for a discussion of nonstationarity. This property is not desirable from a statistical point of view because changing variances are difficult to work with; constant variances are more desirable. A time series that has a constant variance is called *stationary*. We require a function that when applied to a nonstationary time series converts it to a stationary one. That is, we require a function that converts the variance of a time series to a constant. This section closely follows the demonstration by Wei [2006] for finding the transformation function.

Assume a time series $Y_t, t = 1, 2, \ldots, T$. Then this series is nonstationary if we can write $V[Y_t] = c \times f(a_t)$ where c is a constant and $f(\cdot)$ is a function of the data. For example, we could assume that $V[Y_t] = c \times a_t^2$. We want a function $T(\cdot)$ that transforms Y_t so that $V[T(Y_t)] = c$. Following Wei [2006], we could use the Taylor Series Expansion (*TSE*) to determine the transformation function.

We want a transformation function $T(Y_t)$ evaluated at $Y_t = a_t$ such that

$$T(Y_t) \approx T(a_t) + T^1(a_t) \times (Y_t - a_t). \tag{7.A.5}$$

The variance of $T(Y_t)$ is

$$V[T(Y_t)] = [T^1(a_t)]^2 \times V(Y_t) \tag{7.A.6}$$

$$= c \times [T^1(a_t)]^2 \times f(a_t) \tag{7.A.7}$$

where $T^1(a_t)$ is the first derivative of T evaluated at a_t. We need

$$T^1(a_t) = 1 / \sqrt{f(a_t)}. \tag{7.A.8}$$

Integrating (7.A.8) and using $V[Y_t] = c \times a_t^2$, then $T(a_t) = \ln a_t$. So the natural log is the transformation that stabilizes the variance; i.e., makes it a constant. Wei [2006] shows that this approach can be extended to produce the *Box–Cox Power Transformations* which have the natural log as one option. This class of transformations is given by

$$T(Y_t) = \frac{Y_t^\lambda - 1}{\lambda}.$$

Transformations for different values of λ are shown in Table 7.10.

TABLE 7.10

λ	Transformation
-1.0	$1/Y_t$
-0.5	$1/\sqrt{Y_t}$
0.0	$\ln Y_t$
0.5	$\sqrt{Y_t}$
1.0	Y_t

Source: Wei [2006]

TABLE 7.11 Elasticity values and interpretations.

Elasticity Value	Interpretation
$\eta = \infty$	Perfectly Elastic
$1 < \eta < \infty$	Elastic
$\eta = 1$	Unit Elastic
$0 < \eta < 1$	Inelastic
$\eta = 0$	Perfectly Inelastic

7.5.3 Constant elasticity models

A useful concept is the elasticity. An *elasticity* is a unitless measure of the percent change in the dependent variable for a percent change in an independent variable:

$$\eta_X^Y = \frac{\text{Percent Change in Y}}{\text{Percent Change in X}}$$
$$= \frac{d\ln Y}{d\ln X}$$
$$= \frac{X}{Y} \times \frac{dY}{dX}.$$

Since an elasticity is a ratio of percent changes, it is natural to interpret values of η with respect to 1: the percent change in Y equals the percent change in X. Terminology is shown in Table 7.11.

A price elasticity of demand is

$$\eta_P^Q = \frac{d\ln Q}{d\ln P}$$
$$= \frac{P}{Q} \times \frac{dQ}{dP}.$$

For an inherently linear model, $Y_i = e^{\beta_0} \times X_i^{\beta_1}$, linearization using natural logs yields $\ln Y_i = \beta_0 + \beta_1 \ln X_i$. This is a *log-log model*. Note that

$$\frac{1}{Y_i}dY_i = \beta_1 \frac{1}{X_i}dX_i$$

or

$$\beta_1 = \frac{X_i}{Y_i} \frac{dY_i}{dX_i}$$

$$= \eta_X^Y.$$

The elasticity is the parameter and is a constant. The curve for Y is called an *isoelastic* curve. See Paczkowski [2018] for a discussion.

7.5.4 Total revenue elasticity

Total revenue is defined as $TR = P \times Q(P)$. Taking the first derivative with respect to price yields

$$\frac{dTR}{dP} = Q + \frac{dQ}{dP}.$$

To convert this to an elasticity, multiply the left-hand side by P and divide by TR which amounts to multiplying the left-hand side by $^1/_Q$ based on the definition of TR. The right-hand side also must be multiplied by $^1/_Q$ yielding $\eta_P^{TR} = 1 + {}^P/_Q \times {}^{dQ}/_{dP}$. The second term is the definition of a price elasticity, so $\eta_P^{TR} = 1 + \eta_P^Q$.

7.5.5 Effects tests F-ratios

The effects tests for the *OLS* models are based on the sum of squares for the respective effects. The sum of squares is from the Model component of the ANOVA table with that effect included and excluded. Basically, an ANOVA is created with the effect and then without. The sum of squares for the effect is the difference in the Model sum of squares from the two ANOVA tables. For example, the Region effect sum of squares is the difference between an ANOVA table's Model sum of squares with the Region variable and an ANOVA table's Model sum of squares without the Region variable. The corresponding F-ratio is the effect's mean square divided by the residual mean square from the ANOVA table.

Notes

1 B.Baesens. "Data Warehouses, Data Marts, Operational Data Stores, and Data Lakes: WhatâĂŹs in a Name?." Available at www.dbta.com/BigDataQuarterly/Articles/ Data-Warehouses-Data-Marts-Operational-Data-Stores-and-Data-Lakes-Whats-in-a-Name-127417.aspx. Last accessed June 9, 2019.

2 Also see https://en.wikipedia.org/wiki/Extract,_transform,_load for a high-level overview of this process. Last accessed on June 6, 2019.

3 There is another sense to dynamic – the real-time updating of the dashboard's contents. The continuous display of stock prices is an example. This is not my focus when I talk about a dynamic dashboard.

4 See https://quotes.deming.org/authors/W._Edwards_Deming/quote/3734. The quote is disputed as this link notes.

5 Based on http://en.wikipedia.org/wiki/Metadata. Last accessed June 7, 2019.

6 The color issue refers to difficulties color-challenged people face.

7 See https://en.wikipedia.org/wiki/Histogram. Accessed January 29, 2019.

8 I only consider two here, although actually there are more.

9 It could also *OLS* with appropriate transformation and use of polynomials, but I will focus on the logistic.

10 These steps hold regardless of the software used for model estimation. How they are implemented does vary, but only slightly.

11 From the sklearn User Guide. See https://scikit-learn.org/stable/user_guide.html. Last accessed June 10, 2019.

12 Recall that the odds ratio was discussed in Chapter 5.

13 The "box" is old survey terminology that is still in use. It refers to the boxes people checked on a paper questionnaire. Now, they check boxes on an online questionnaire. For a five-point Likert Scale, "top-two box" refers to the top two boxes checked.

14 Based on www.merriam-webster.com/dictionary/canine. Last accessed December 26, 2018.

15 See www.merriam-webster.com/dictionary/automaton. Last accessed December 26, 2018.

16 See http://wordnetweb.princeton.edu/perl/webwn?s=ENTITY for WordNet which defines an entity as "that which is perceived or known or inferred to have its own distinct existence (living or nonliving)."

17 de Albornoz et al. [2011]

8

RESOURCES

Making it work

I focused in this book on doing analytics for new product development from ideation to tracking. I discussed issues and some of the details for analysis. Nonetheless, this is not a managerial book. Management, however, played a role in some sections, but more for guidance and critical inputs on goals and objectives. It has a role above and beyond the analytical efforts. Executive managers provide the resources the organization needs and set the tone and agenda to successfully implement a data analytical approach to new product development. These resources are analytical talent and software and the agenda is the pursuit, the focus on, data-driven decisions. Executive managers also establish a collaborative framework so that analytical talent can share what they learn from the five stages of new product development and not hide what they know and have learned.

This chapter has three sections. The first covers the role and importance of collaboration, both internally and externally, for making more efficient use of data for the development of new products. Collaboration is important because it reduces costs and breaks down barriers that frequently block the development of ideas. In the second section, I discuss the analytical talent needed for all phases of a data-driven approach to new product development. The technical skill-sets required and the training needed to maintain those skills are covered. The third section covers software. Even though software was mentioned at the end of each chapter, this is such an important topic that it must be mentioned one last time.

8.1 The role and importance of organizational collaboration

The purpose of collaboration is to lower the overall cost of new product development allowing more products to be produced and brought to market faster and sooner than your competition. Given the analytical perspective of this book, it may seem that there is zero cost to doing analysis. In reality, of course, there is always an

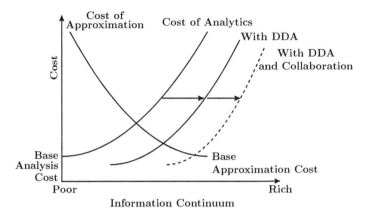

FIGURE 8.1 These are illustrative cost curves that show the effect of Deep Data Analysis (*DDA*) and then *DDA* with collaboration.

analytical cost. In particular, the more Rich Information managers need for making their decisions, the more analysis that is required. In economic terms, there is an upward sloping cost curve for analysis: the richer the information required the more analysis that has to be done and so the higher the cost of acquiring that information.

Management controls where they are on this cost curve by the requirements they establish. Whatever the requirements, however, the placement of the curve is determined by the level and extent of the collaboration of the staff involved in new product development. The less the collaboration, when departments and key personnel hoard data, information, and findings, the higher the cost of providing any level of information management needs. The more the level and extent of the collaboration, the lower the costs of doing analysis because information is shared. This is depicted in Figure 8.1.

The cost reduction I just described is based on collaboration internal to a business. External collaboration is just as important and is, in fact, the norm and necessity in key industries. Consider the automotive industry where there has been a convergence of consumer electronics and automotive technology, as automotive experts view a car not as a car but as a "mobile experience." This means that modern-day consumers, who are highly interconnected in all aspects of their lives, expect their transportation modes to be equally connected and provide them with the same experiences as they receive at home. Riding in a car (not necessarily driving one) should be an experience comparable to their other experiences as well as just providing mobility. As automotive experts realized and accepted this different view of the reason for buying a car, they changed its nature, composition, and function. More vehicles are now equipped with consumer electronics such as mobile phones for hands-free driving, video players for entertainment (of children), and enhanced stereo systems delivered not through the traditional radio but through satellite, Bluetooth, and wireless connections. See Forum [2016] for an analysis of the changing automotive landscape.

This change in perspective of a car to a mobility experience has altered the industry's supply chain. The traditional automotive establishment no longer develops all the complex electronics consumers demand for their "experience", so automotive manufacturers must look elsewhere for these developments. Development in-house is too costly; collaboration outside the industry is needed. Collaboration with outside organizations (universities, non-profit establishments, government agencies, and companies in other industries such as those in Silicon Valley) helps to develop not only the technology needed, but also develop new processes, problem solutions, analysis methods, and general intellectual property. See Pertuzé et al. [2010] for an analysis along these lines for industry-university collaboration.

A 2018 survey of the auto industry found that "nearly a quarter of the participants affirmed their belief that tech vendors with experience in consumer electronics and user experience will drive innovation [in the auto industry], compared to only 7 percent a year ago."[1] It is further noted that "Automakers are building research and development centers in Silicon Valley and partnering with technology giants from consumer markets. Many automotive OEMs are also considering the design and assembly resources of contract manufacturing partners ...that specialize in combining the rapid innovation and product introductions associated with consumer electronics with the rigorous engineering, testing manufacturing and reliability demands of the automotive industry."[2] This external collaboration is just as important and vital as internal collaboration.

Collaboration, however, does not always lead to successful new products. Pertuzé et al. [2010] note that 50% of the industry-university collaboration projects they examined lead to an outcome such as an idea or new process. But only 40% of these lead to something with impact. They argue that something new must have an impact; basically, it must lead to a new product. One reason for a low or even nonexistent impact is how a collaboration is managed. The effect of a collaboration is to establish a knowledge flow from one organization to another. A point-of-contact (POC), who could be an executive at the lead collaborator company (i.e., the company actually needing the results of the collaboration such as an automotive company that collaborates with a tech company), oversees the collaboration and thus the knowledge flows. This POC must ensure the dissemination to internal stakeholders of any and all knowledge gained. The POC also must oversee the sharing with the collaborating company. They may share strategic plans, internal knowledge about industry trends, and customer requirements perhaps based on market research. The knowledge flow is not one-way but two-way. This is illustrated in Figure 8.2. The internal and external collaboration are not two separate activities, but are one synergistic whole. If there is any impediment to this flow then collaboration will be less than perfect or will fail so the full cost reduction benefit of collaboration will not be realized.

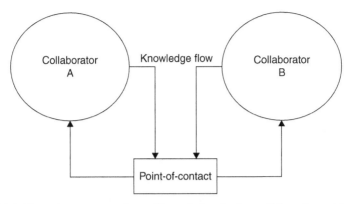

FIGURE 8.2 There is a two-way flow of knowledge during collaboration with an outside partner. The *POC* manages this flow and ensures that it is two-way and that any knowledge gained is disseminated internally to all the correct stakeholders.

8.2 Analytical talent

Analysts are needed for new product development, but not any analysts. Those with special skill-sets are needed. Not only are special skill-sets needed, but those skills must be maintained and updated as technology, software, and analytical tools are updated and new developments are introduced since, after all, developments in these areas are themselves new products. It is easy to fall behind in any one of these three areas, and falling behind could be a burden for the business. I will discuss these three skill requirements in the following subsections.

8.2.1 Technology skill sets

Big Data has become a big issue and a big opportunity for businesses in the first two decades of this millennium. As I noted in Chapter 1, it is usually defined in terms of the *Three Vs*: Volume, Variety, and Velocity. Regardless of which component you focus on, technology is behind that component in one form or another. Technology determines the data that are captured, how those data are stored, and how those data are analyzed.

As an example of how data are captured, consider sensors which are now ubiquitous. They are in medical facilities monitoring patients' bodily functions; at street intersections monitoring traffic flows; in vehicles monitoring vehicle functions, speed, distances, and driver alertness; in agriculture monitoring crops (for irrigation, for example) and livestock; in homes, office buildings, public places; and so on. They record a plethora of data almost in real-time which means that a tremendous amount of data is collected. This is the Volume part of Big Data. And those data must go somewhere. They go into data stores, data warehouses, data lakes, and data marts. Technology, in the form of sensors, generates and collects those data while other technology, in the form of more efficient computer storage, house and maintain those data. Sensors are making available, and will make available, volumes of data at real-time rates that are unprecedented. See Shi et al. [2018], Evans [2011], and Kim et al. [2019] for discussions of the development, challenges, and impacts of sensors.

In addition to data captured by sensors, different types of data are now collected in the form of text messages, audio, videos, and images, as I discussed in Chapters 2 and 6. Technology again plays a part in the generation and collection of these types of data as well as their storage. It causes the generation because of social media, for example, which is a newer form of communication technology that exploded on the market in the past two decades. This adds to the Variety component of Big Data.

Also, sensors and social media have made data available in real-time as I just noted. Analysts who access this data must know how to access it all, how to process and query it, how to wrangle it into a form they need, how to make sense of it, and how to report findings from it. This is true at the early ideation stage as well as at the tracking stage. Consider a new sensor device for monitoring home appliances, refrigerators in particular. It could, for example, monitor the compressor and alert the owner as well as a service provider when it begins to fault. Monitoring will be real-time since a refrigerator runs constantly. Analysts must know how to interpret signals sent from the sensor to distinguish between random noise from a compressor and a deviation from trend, thus indicating a pending fault. This would not be for one refrigerator, but for millions. Software, perhaps powered by an artificial intelligence system, would, of course, read and interpret the data and feed results to a human analyst. The human analyst still has to make a final determination of what action to take, if any. This is a special skill set because the human analyst has to interact with the software "analyst" to make a decision.

A data analyst cannot rely on just having statistical or econometric skills and knowledge. He or she must also be aware of and knowledgeable about rapid technology changes because they have direct implications for the data they are supposed to analyze. The basic tools for analyzing "big" data are the same as those required for analyzing "small" data. But the volume, variety, and velocity of the data means that some of these tools are less important and new ones are needed. For instance, data visualization became a hot buzz topic in the mid- to late 2010s. The idea of creating graphs to discover patterns in data has been around for a long time, so it is not new. See, for example, the classic book by Tukey [1977] who developed many of the now widely used methods of data visualization and, in fact, started a whole research line in this area. Yet visualization is getting a lot of attention because how visualization is approached has changed. New displays have been developed (e.g., hex bin plots, contour plots) that help the analysis of $Large-N$ data. At the same time, sampling methods, traditionally a mainstay of statistics, have been studied for their applicability to $Large-N$ situations. Furthermore, softwares (part of technological changes) have been developed to automate and enable the analysis of large quantities of data not to mention the different types of data. As another example, new statistical and econometric methods have been developed to deal with the

Large-N problem. See Varian [2014] for a discussion. Also see Kapetanios et al. [2018] for an extensive survey of econometric methods for Big Data.

Finally, as part of the Variety component of Big Data, an analyst must be conversant in text analysis as I developed it in Chapters 2 and 6. This is important both on the front-end of new product development (i.e., the ideation stage) but also on the back-end (the tracking stage) because customers write reviews on social media and review web sites, as well as the company's own web site. On the back-end, these reviews are important for understanding how your new product is being received in the market. Sales, of course, will certainly tell you how well it is received (high sales volume equates to being well received) but sales will not tell you why. Traditionally, market research methods (i.e., surveys and focus groups) were used to answer a "*Why?*" question. But because of the social media outlets and online reviews, text analysis can also be used, and probably at lower cost.

The implication for analytical talent is clear. Analysts must be conversant in a wide array of technologies:

- data collection methods;
- sampling from *Large-N* data sets;
- data visualization beyond simple pie and bar charts;
- programming tools to use with *Large-N* data (e.g., *SQL*);
- sophisticated software (e.g., SAS, R, Python);
- new statistical and econometric methods for *Large-N* data; and
- text analytic methods.

In addition, analysts must have domain-specific knowledge for determining the application and applicability of these technologies for their specific business. In summary, analysts must be conversant in Computer Science, statistics/econometrics, and domain-specific concepts, an area called *Data Science*.

8.2.2 Data scientists, statisticians, and machine learning experts

The analytical requirements outlined above cut across multiple disciplines. Figure 8.3 shows the intersection of three disciplines – computer science, statistics/econometrics, and application domain expertise – to produce one discipline: Data Science.

Computer Science contributes computer technology and programming languages for not only handling statistical and econometric problems, but also for handling data visualization and all that is associated with Big Data. For Big Data, the *Three V*s have to be managed in a way that allows end-users to efficiently access and process not just the right data for their problems, but also do so in a timely manner to solve or address a business problem.

Statistics and econometrics provide the estimation and analytical methods for extracting information from data. Some have been around for a long time. *OLS* regression is a good example. This technique has been known since 1805 and is now

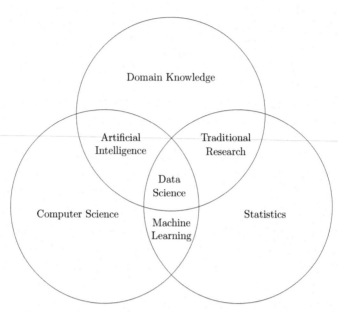

FIGURE 8.3 This Venn diagram shows the intersection of three main disciplines needed for new product development, not to mention for all business analytics whether for new products or not. This chart is based on a similar diagram in Duchesnay [2019].

well developed and understood.[3] Each discipline is separate yet tied together. They are separate in that they are concerned with different problem sets. Econometrics is concerned with economic (and business) problems while statistics is concerned with a wider array of problems which includes economics and business. Also, statistics covers a wider field of methods such as experimental design, ANOVA, data visualization, multivariate analysis, and sampling methodologies to mention a few. They are also intimately connected in that both are concerned with estimation methods. Together, they are a driving force in data analysis. The combination in conjunction with Computer Science is Machine Learning.

Domain Application is the specific set of problems that have to be addressed and the domain knowledge to frame solutions for those problems. In a business context, the Domain Application is business context (e.g., what the business does, its strategic goals, its organization, and so forth) as well as the industry the business operates in (e.g., the competitive structure and the regulatory environment). The overlap of Computer Science and Domain Applications is the province of Artificial Intelligence (*AI*). *AI* is the development and application of intelligent software to mimic thoughts and learning. As noted in Wikipedia:[4]

> *In computer science, artificial intelligence (AI), sometimes called machine intelligence, is intelligence demonstrated by machines, in contrast to the natural intelligence displayed*

by humans and other animals. Computer science defines AI research as the study of "intelligent agents": any device that perceives its environment and takes actions that maximize its chance of successfully achieving its goals.

This is a broad definition. I am taking a narrower perspective with a focus on business problems. In this context, *AI* will assess, i.e, "learn", from large and complex volumes of data looking for patterns and trends that are not only interesting but meaningful for the business. These patterns and trends could include operations as well as market conditions. For new product development, the volume of data generated by sensors could be processed through *AI* algorithms that learn how consumers use existing products and make recommendations for new ones. For example, Schnurrer et al. [2018] note how automobiles are equipped with an array of sensors that provide data on every aspect of a driver's driving behavior, not to mention the performance of the vehicle under different driving conditions. These data can be used to not only design new vehicles to better match consumers' driving preferences, but to also identify mechanical and electronic issues that might go undetected and that need to be resolved before a serious problem develops. The sensors in modern vehicles can transmit these data through the "cloud" to central data repositories (i.e., data stores) that then process the data into data warehouses accessible by engineering and design teams. In essence, the sensor data flow through a *Wireless Sensor Network* (*WSN*). See Kim et al. [2019] on *WSN*s. This has the effect of reducing product development costs and speeding the development of newer vehicles.

The implication is that future new product development teams must consist of people who are not only skilled in quantitative methods, the focus of this book, but must also possess technological knowledge and abilities to use the new *AI* systems and the plethora of data generated by the ever-expanding array of sensors in our modern economy. Because of the technology changes, however, newer approaches to data analytics are constantly being developed in academic and in industrial research laboratories. Data visualization, for example, once called Exploratory Data Analysis (*EDA*), has become an important component of statistical analysis when large quantities of data are available.

8.2.3 Constant training

Since technology is rapidly changing, those who are in the new product development area must constantly work to maintain their skill level and enhance it to keep pace with the technology changes. This includes methods for data access and data management, programming languages, data mining and text mining methodologies, and developing *AI* technologies to mention a few. In short, future new product development personnel have to be multiversed.

8.3 Software issues

Software is a major component of the analysis of data for new product development. Some issues with software are provided in the following subsections.

8.3.1 Downplaying spreadsheets

The days are long past when spreadsheets were the sole tool for data analysis, whether for new product development or not. In fact, they never had the capabilities required for extensive and comprehensive data analysis and statistical and econometric modeling that are now commonly used. Spreadsheets have well known and documented major issues. Seven reasons for not using spreadsheets for Business Intelligence and Business Analytics are:

1. They are not database managers.
2. They were not designed to handle large data sets (i.e., "Big Data").
3. They make it difficult to identify data.
4. The data are often spread across several worksheets in a workbook.
5. They are inadequate for complex data structures such as panel data.
6. They lack:
   - data wrangling operations: joining, splitting, and stacking;
   - programming capabilities, except Visual Basic for Applications (*VBA*) which is not a statistical programming language; and
   - sophisticated statistical operations beyond arithmetic operations and simple regression analysis.
7. Data visualization is limited: pie/bar charts and non-scientific visuals. Visualization is more infographic than scientific.

Other, more powerful software is required. I classify these software packages into Open Source and Commercial. The former are generally free while the latter are not. In addition, my brief comments on software are restricted to statistical and econometric packages and general programming languages.

8.3.2 Open source software

There are five open source software packages I will mention here because they are either the major ones available or have the potential to become major players. These are R, Python, Julia, Stan, and KNIME.

R

R is the *de facto* software for statistical analysis, although it does have issues that hinder its use for Big Data problems. The major problem is its memory handling: all data and objects created in R (e.g., functions) are stored in memory. R does not have any problems with small data sets that can easily be stored in memory. Its memory management becomes an issue with large data sets.

Another issue is its steep learning curve. It is not an easy language to learn. Finally, everything you want to do requires programming. If you are not a sophisticated analyst with programming capabilities, then R will prove a challenge. Aside from these issues, R is strong in the statistics domain and will remain in that position for some time to come.

An advantage of R is its package structure. Aside from the base R, which has many great statistical and graphing capabilities, R relies on user developed and contributed packages for all its major statistical and modeling functions. There is an extensive collection of packages that cover areas such as:

- Bayesian Inference
- Cluster Analysis and Finite Mixture Models
- Probability Distributions
- Econometrics
- Design of Experiments (DOE) and Analysis of Experimental Data
- Graphic Displays, Dynamic Graphics, Graphic Devices, and Visualization
- High-Performance and Parallel Computing
- Machine Learning and Statistical Learning
- Multivariate Statistics
- Natural Language Processing

to mention a few. For a complete list of topical areas, see https://cran.r-project.org/web/views/. For an extensive listing of packages, see https://cran.r-project.org/web/packages/available_packages_by_date.html. These packages give R an advantage but one which also comes at a cost. The advantage is that new packages with state-of-the-art methods and cutting-edge techniques can be easily and quickly made available. There is a wide and diverse community of developers who contribute these packages so a user can be almost guaranteed a needed capability will be found in R.

The cost associated with the package paradigm is twofold. First, not all developers are highly skilled programmers or program the function correctly. Although the source code is openly available for anyone to examine and audit, the sheer volume of packages and their complexities may make this impossible, or at least a daunting challenge. Second, there is no guarantee that the person or persons who developed a package will continue to maintain it. This can become problematic if a package is relied upon but the developer simply disappears and no one steps forward to become a new maintainer. Finally, some packages have functions with similar capabilities but with different syntax which makes their use confusing.

R can be downloaded at www.r-project.org/.

Python

Python is a challenger to R that in many respects has surpassed R. Python also has memory management issues, but its easier syntax and the Pythonic way of writing code make it much simpler to use and read. It also has a package structure that is simpler to access and use. The Pandas package is excellent for data manipulation using an intuitive syntax for access, management, and manipulation. The Statsmodels and Sk-Learn packages provide many excellent functions and capabilities for statistic and machine learning, respectively. For an introduction to Pandas, see McKinney [2018].

An interesting and useful side-by-side comparison of R and Python is available on the Dataquest website.[5] This comparison shows that in some instances, R is simpler to use while in others Python is simpler. The bottom line is that R and Python complement one another rather than being competitive. They each have strengths and weaknesses depending on applications. Dataquest further concludes that "Ultimately, you may end up wanting to learn Python and R so that you can make use of both languages' strengths, choosing one or the other on a per-project basis depending on your needs."

Python can be downloaded at www.python.org/downloads/.

Julia

Julia is a newer language developed at MIT. This is fast becoming a popular programming and statistical analysis language, but it still has development that must be done to make it a complete rival to R and Python. There are major plans for it in the data science area.

Julia can be downloaded at https://julialang.org/downloads/.

Stan

Stan is also a new language, but one that differs from R, Python, and Julia in that it focuses on Bayesian analysis. Bayesian analysis has become more accepted and useful in statistical analysis, especially since the development of the Markov Chain Monte Carlo (*MCMC*) methods.

Stan can be downloaded at https://mc-stan.org/.

KNIME Analytics Platform

KNIME is an open source software package specifically designed for data science applications. It has a graphical user paradigm that allows users to drag and drop icons on a canvas to paint a picture of the process they want to follow. This gives KNIME an intuitive appeal because the user can "see" how data flows from one application to another.

KNIME can be downloaded at www.knime.com/knime-software/knime-analytics-platform.

8.3.3 Commercial software

There are three commercial software packages I will mention, although two come from the same parent company, the SAS Institute: SAS and JMP. The third is Stata.

SAS

SAS is probably the granddaddy of all statistical software packages, whether commercial or open source. It was originally developed in the 1970s and has dominated the statistical software industry ever since, even though it has a hefty price tag. It is probably safe to say that any major statistical, data management, and data visualization capability that an analyst will need is in SAS. There is an extensive development structure behind the software at the SAS Institute that almost guarantees a high quality and powerful product. This is, however, a drawback because the Institute is slow in adding the latest statistical innovations.

I mentioned that all objects that R creates are maintained in memory. This makes using R with Big Data more than a challenge because there are memory limits. SAS, on the other hand, dynamically manages memory and is thus more efficient. Also, SAS has an extensive library of functions (called PROCs) with each library containing many sophisticated options. In fact, the depth of options far exceeds any other software package.

SAS is available at www.sas.com.

JMP

JMP is an interesting and powerful product also from the SAS Institute that has an intuitive graphical interface that makes working with data much simpler than in any other software package. It has many powerful and complete statistical options, although not as many as SAS and without all the depth SAS has on any one function. A major advantage of JMP is its close connection to SAS. If you have SAS installed on the same system as JMP, then JMP can be used as a front-end to SAS, easily passing data to SAS and retrieving data (and graphs) back as JMP objects and reports. In addition, JMP has interfaces to R and Python that greatly magnify its capabilities. Unfortunately, JMP also has a high price tag, although not as high as the one for SAS. See Paczkowski [2016] for a discussion of using JMP to analyze market data.

JMP is available at www.jmp.com.

Stata

Stata is a powerful statistical and econometric package although it is mostly targeted to econometrics. It has an intuitive graphical user interface (*GUI*) and powerful programming component. However, I have found the programming language difficult to use.

Stata is available at www.stata.com/.

8.3.4 SQL: A must-know language

All data analysts must have a working knowledge of the *Structured Query Language* (*SQL*) because accessing, manipulating, and querying large databases is a routine function all analysts have to perform. *SQL*, and its many dialects, is the major query language used by all database systems. It is the foundational language for accessing, and, by default, organizing vast quantities of data. It was introduced and standardized in the 1980s. It also enabled the development of data stores, data warehouses, data marts, and data lakes that are so common and prevalent in our current business environment.

8.3.5 Overall software recommendation

All data analysts need to know R, Python, and *SQL*. A working knowledge of SAS would also be beneficial but its availability may be hindered by its price tag.

8.3.6 Jupyter/Jupyter Lab

The open source software packages listed above can be used in one ecosystem: Jupyter. An ecosystem will handle multiple languages: Python, R, Julia, and SAS and many more.[6] In fact, about 120! Incidentally, a language is referred to as a *kernel* in Jupyter nomenclature. Jupyter allows you to document your workflow for reproducibility which is important in large and complex data science tasks. Documentation and reproducibility are two separate but connected tasks that are important in any research project. They should not be an afterthought. Trying to recall what you did is itself a daunting task usually subordinated to the other daunting tasks of research. Researchers typically document after the work is done but at this point the documentation is incomplete at best and error prone at worse. *Documentation* is the logging of steps in the research process and includes data sources, transformations, and steps to arrive at an answer to management or a client's question. *Reproducibility* is the ability to rerun an analysis. Quite often, analysts produce a report only to have management or the client call, even months later, requesting either a clarification of what was done, perhaps for a legal reason, or to request further analysis. This means you must recall exactly what you did, not to mention what data you used. This is where reproducibility comes in.

Jupyter uses a notebook paradigm which allows documentation and reproducibility through the use of a *cell-orientation* approach. There are two cells:

1. a code cell where code is entered; and
2. a "markdown" cell where text is entered.

Jupyter Lab is the next evolutionary step in the Jupyter notebook paradigm that allows you to have several notebooks open at once in tabs. You can drag and drop from one notebook to another, resize tabs, move tabs, and do much more.[7]

The best way to obtain Jupyter is by downloading and installing the Anaconda Navigator which comes with a large number of packages. Anaconda will load Python by default, but kernels for R, Julia, and SAS can be easily installed. Once installed, you can specify which language you want to use in a notebook.

Anaconda is available at www.anaconda.com/.

Notes

1 "Automotive Industry Trends Point to Shorter Product Development Cycles" available at www.jabil.com/insights/blog-main/automotive-industry-trends-point-to-shorter-product-development-cycles.html. Last access on April 8, 2019. The survey was conducted in December, 2018 by Jabil, a consulting company.
2 Ibid.
3 See the Wikipedia article on Least Squares at https://en.wikipedia.org/wiki/Least_squares#History. Last accessed April 4, 2019.
4 See the Artificial Intelligence article at https://en.wikipedia.org/wiki/Artificial_intelligence. Last accessed April 4, 2019.
5 www.dataquest.io/blog/python-vs-r/
6 "Jupyter" is a contraction of **Ju**lia, **Pyt**hon, and **R**.
7 As of the time of writing this book, Jupyter Lab is still in development.

BIBLIOGRAPHY

A. Agresti. *Categorical Data Analysis*. John Wiley & Sons, second edition, 2002.

P. Ahde. Jewelry as provocateurs of emotions. In *International Conference on Kansei Engineering and Emotion Research*, Mar. 2010.

E. Alpaydin. *Introduction to Machine Learning*. Adaptive Computation and Machine Learning series. The MIT Press, 2014.

D. Arthur, R. Motwani, A. Sharma, and Y. Xu. Pricing strategies for viral marketing on social networks. In S. Leonardi, editor, *Internet and Network Economics*, volume 5929 of *Lecture Notes in Computer Science*, pages 101 – 112. Springer, 2009.

W. B. Arthur. *The Nature of Technology: What it is and How it Evolves*. Free Press, 2009.

L. Baardman, I. Levin, G. Perakis, and D. Singhvi. Leveraging comparables for new product sales forecasting. Available through the SSRN, 2017.

A.-L. Barabasi and R. Albert. Emergence of scaling in random networks. *Science*, 286:509 – 512, Oct. 1999. www.sciencemag.org.

V. P. Barabba and G. Zaltman. *Hearing the Voice of the Market: Competitive Advantage through Creative Use of Market Information*. Harvard Business School Press, 1991.

K. E. Basford and G. J. McLachlan. The mixture method of clustering applied to three-way data. *Journal of Classification*, 2:109 – 125, 1985.

R. A. Beck. *Statistical Learning from a Regression Perspective*. Springer Series in Statistics. Springer, 2008.

M. A. Beltran, G. Narváez, and N. Aros. The semantic differential for the discipline of design: A tool for the product evaluation. In *Selected Proceedings from the 13th International Congress on Project Engineering*, volume Selected Proceedings from the 13th International Congress on Project Engineering, pages 422 – 433, July 2009.

G. Box, G. Jenkins, and G. Reinsel. *Time Series Analysis, Forecasting and Control*. Prentice-Hall, second edition, 1994.

J. Campos. *The Voice of the Customer for Product Development: Your Illustrated Guide to Obtaining, Prioritizing and Using Customer Requirements and Creating Winning Products*. Rapidinnovation, LLC, fourth edition, Aug. 2012.

D. B. Carr, R. J. Littlefield, W. L. Nicholson, and J. S. Littlefield. Scafferplot matrix techniques for large n. *Journal of the American Statistical Association*, 82(398):424–436, June 1987.

C. Chatfield. *Time-Series Forecasting*. Chapman and Hall/CRC, first edition, Oct. 2000.

K. Christensen, S. Norskov, L. Frederiksen, and J. Scholderer. In search of new product ideas: Idetifying ideas in online communities by machine learning and text mining. *Creativity and Innovation Management*, 26(1):17 – 30, 2017.

A. Christianson, M. B. Lenon, and S. M. Levin. Systems and methods for predicting the efficacy of a marketing message, 2008. URL https://patents.google.com/patent/US20080046317A1/en.

M. C. Chuang, C. C. Chang, and S. H. Hsu. Perceptual factors underlying user preferences toward product form of mobile phones. *International Journal of Industrial Ergonomics*, 27 (4):247 – 258, 2001.

P. Chwastyk and M. Kolosowskia. Estimating the cost of the new product in development process. *Procedia Engineering*, 69:351 – 360, 2014. Available online at www.sciencedirect.com.

W. S. Cleveland. *Visualizing Data*. Hobart Press, 1993.

W. S. Cleveland. *The Elements of Graphing Data*. Hobart Press, second edition, 1994.

W. G. Cochrane. *Sampling Techniques*. John Wiley & Sopns, Inc., second edition, 1963.

L. M. Collins and S. T. Lanza. *Latent Class Analysis and Latent Transition Analysis: With Applications in the Social, Behavioral, and Health Sciences*. John Wiley & Sons, 2010.

R. G. Cooper. *Winning At New Products: Accelerating The Process From Idea To Launch*. Basic Books, second edition, 1993.

R. G. Cooper. *Winning at New Products: Creating Value Through Innovation*. Basic Books, revised, updated edition, 2017.

J. D. Couger. *Creative Problem Solving and Opportunity Finding*. Boyd & Fraser Publishing Co., 1995.

I. Cox and M. Gaudard. *Discovering Partial Least Squares with JMP*. SAS Institute Inc., Oct. 2013.

T. Davenport and A. Spanyi. Improve new product development with predictive analytics. Blog: MIT Initiative on the Digital Economy, July 2016. Available at http://ide.mit.edu/news-blog/blog/improve-new-product-development-predictive-analytics.

J. C. de Albornoz, L. Plaza, and A. D. Pablo Gervás. A joint model of feature mining and sentiment analysis for product review rating. In P. Clough, C. Foley, C. Gurrin, G. J. F. Jones, W. Kraaij, H. Lee, and V. Mudoch, editors, *Advances in Information Retrieval - 2011*, volume 6611 of *Lecture Notes in Computer Science*, pages 55 – 66. Springer-Verlag, 2011. 33rd European Conference on IR Research, ECIR 2011, Dublin, Ireland, April 18-21, 2011. Proceedings.

S. de Jong. Simpls: An alternative approach to partial least squares regression. *Chemometrics and Intelligent Laboratory Systems*, 18(3):251 – 263, 1993.

J. P. Dillard. Language style and persuasion. In T. Holtgraves, editor, *The Oxford Handbook of Language and Social Psychology*. Oxford University Press, Jan. 2014.

J. P. Dillard, L. Shen, and R. G. Vail. Does perceived message effectiveness cause persuasion or vice versa? 17 consistent answers. *Human Communication Research*, 33:467 – 488, 2007a.

J. P. Dillard, K. M. Weber, and R. G. Vail. The relationship between the perceived and actual effectiveness of persuasive messages: A meta-analysis with implications for formative campaign research. *Journal of Communication*, 57(4):613 – 631, 2007b.

E. Duchesnay. Statistics and machine learning in python. Release 0.2 from ftp://ftp.cea.fr/pub/unati/people/educhesnay/pystatml/StatisticsMachineLearning PythonDraft.pdf. Last accessed April 4, 2019., Mar. 2019.

E. J. Dudewicz and S. N. Mishra. *Modern Mathematical Statistics*. John Wiley & Sons, 1988.

W. D. Dupont and J. W. Dale Plummer. Using density-distribution sunflower plots to explore bivariate relationships in dense data. *The Stata Journal*, 5(3):371 – 384, 2005.

W. W. Eckerson. *Performance Dashboards: Measuring, Monitoring, and Managing Your Business*. Wiley, second edition, 2010.

T. Edensor. Automobility and national identity: Representation, geography and driving practice. *Theory, Culture & Society*, 21(4/5):101 – 120, 2004.

F. Erlandsson, P. Brodka, A. Borg, and H. Johnson. Finding influential users in social media using association rule learning. *Entropy*, 18(5), May 2016.

D. Evans. The internet of things: How the next evolution of the internet is changing everything. White paper, Cisco Internet Business Solutions Group (IBSG), Apr. 2011.

R. D. Evans, J. X. Gao, S. Mahdikhah, M. Messaadia, and D. Baudry. A review of crowd-sourcing literature related to the manufacturing industry. *Journal of Advanced Management Science*, 4(3):224 – 231, May 2016.

B. S. Everitt, S. Landau, and M. Leese. *Cluster Analysis*. Arnold Publishers, fourth edition, 2001.

C. Fellbaum, editor. *WordNet: An Electronic Lexical Database*. MIT Press, 1998.

C. Ferguson. *Microeconomic Theory*. Richard D. Irwin, Inc., third edition, 1972.

S. Few. *Information Dashboard Design: The Effective Visual Communication of Data*. O'Reilly Media, 2006.

W. E. Forum. Digital transformation of industries: Automotive industry. White paper, World Economic Forum, Jan. 2016.

J. E. F. Fried. *Mastering Regular Expressions*. O'Reilly & Associates, second edition, 2002.

P. Geladi and B. R. Kowalski. Partial least-squares regression: A tutorial. *Analytica Chimica Acta*, pages 1 – 17, 1986.

W. Gilchrist. *Statistical Forecasting*. John Wiley & Sons, 1976.

A. S. Goldberger. *Econometric Theory*. John Wiley & Sons Inc., 1964.

J. P. Gould and E. P. Lazear. *Microeconomic Theory*. Irwin, sixth edition, 1989.

J. C. Gower and D. J. Hand. *Biplots*, volume 54 of *Monographs on Statistics and Applied Probability*. Chapman & Hall, 1996.

M. Greenacre and T. Korneliussen. Total inertia decomposition in tables with a factorial structure. *Statistica Applicata - Italian Journal of Applied Statistics*, 29(2 - 3):233 – 242, 2017.

M. J. Greenacre. *Theory and Applications of Correspondence Analysis*. Academic Press, 1984.

M. J. Greenacre. *Correspondence Analysis in Practice*. Chapman and Hall/CRC, second edition, 2007.

W. H. Greene. *Econometric Analysis*. Prentice Hall, fifth edition, 2003.

W. H. Greene and D. A. Hensher. A latent class model for discrete choice analysis: Contrasts with mixed logit. *Transportation Research Part B: Methodological*, 37(8):681–698, Sept. 2003.

D. Gujarati. *Basic Econometrics*. McGraw-Hill/Irwin, fourth edition, 2003.

L. Hardesty. Explained: Neural networks. Online at http://news.mit.edu/2017/explained-neural-networks-deep-learning-0414, Apr. 2017. MIT News Office.

R. Hardin. The free rider problem. https://plato.stanford.edu/archives/spr2013/entries/free-rider/, 2013. The Stanford Encyclopedia of Philosophy.

F. E. H. Jr. *Regression Modeling Strategies: With Applications to Linear Models, Logistic and Ordinal Regression, and Survival Analysis*. Springer Series in Statistics. Springer, second edition, Aug. 2015.

T. Hastie, R. Tibshirani, and J. Friedman. *The Elements of Statistical Learning: Data Mining, Inference, and Prediction*. Springer-Verlag, 2001.

S. G. Heeringa, B. T. West, and P. A. Berglund. *Applied Survey Data Analysis*. CRC Press, 2010.

R. C. Hill, W. E. Griffiths, and G. C. Lim. *Principles of Econometrics*. John Wiley & Sons, Inc, fourth edition, 2008.

E. Hoffman, N. M. Khanfar, C. Harrington, and L. E. Kizer. The lasting effects of social media trends on advertising. *Journal of Business & Economics Research*, 14(3), 2016.

K. Holtzblatt and H. R. Beyer. *The Encyclopedia of Human-Computer Interaction*, chapter Contextual Design. The Interaction Design Foundation, second edition, 2013.

R. J. Hyndman. The problem with sturges rule for constructing histograms. Unpublished Notes, July 1995.

R. J. Hyndman and G. Athanasopoulos. *Forecasting: Principles and Practice*. OTexts, second edition, May 2018.

R. J. Hyndman and A. V. Kostenko. Minimum sample size requirements for seasonal forecasting methods. *Foresight*, 2007.

B. Inmon. *Hearing the Voice of the Customer*. Technics Publications, 2018.

S. Isaksen. A review of brainstorming research: Six critical issues for inquiry. Creativity Research Unit. Creative Problem Solving Group - Buffalo. Buffalo, New York. Monograph No. 302., June 1998.

S. G. Isaksen and J. P. Gaulin. A reexamination of brainstorming research: Implications for research and practice. *The Gifted Child Quarterly*, 49(4):315–329, 2005.

G. James, D. Witten, T. Hastie, and R. Tibshirani. *An Introduction to Statistical Learning: With Applications in R*. Springer Science+Business Media, 2013.

J. Jobson. *Applied Multivariate Data Analysis*, volume II: Categorical and Multivariate Methods. Springer-Verlag, 1992.

S. Johnson. *Where Good Ideas Come From: The Natural History of Innovation*. Riverhead Books, reprint edition, 2011.

I. Jolliffe. *Principal Component Analysis*. Springer, second edition edition, Oct. 2002.

K. B. Kahn. *New Product Forecasting: An Applied Approach*. Taylor and Francis Ltd, 2006.

G. Kapetanios, M. Marcellino, and K. Petrova. Analysis of the most recent modelling techniques for big data with particular attention to bayesian ones. Statistical working paper, Eurostat, 2018.

J. Kazil and K. Jarmul. *Data Wrangling with Python: Tips and Tools to Make Your Life Easier*. O'Reilly Media Inc., 2016.

B.-S. Kim, K.-I. Kim, B. Shah, F. Chow, and K. H. Kim. Wireless sensor networks for big data systems. *Sensors*, 19(1565), 2019. Available at www.mdpi.com/journal/sensors.

H.-H. Lai, Y.-C. Lin, C.-H. Yeh, and C.-H. Wei. User-oriented design for the optimal combination on product design. *International Journal of Production Economics*, 100(2):253 – 267, 2006.

A. Landherr, B. Friedl, and J. Heidemann. A critical review of centrality measures in social networks. *Business & Information Systems Engineering*, June 2010.

J. R. Landis and G. G. Koch. The measurement of observer agreement for categorical data. *Biometrics,*, 33(1):159 – 174, Mar. 1977.

D. C. Lay. *Linear Algebra and Its Applications*. Pearson Education, fourth edition, 2012.

W. Lemahieu, B. Baesens, and S. vanden Broucke. *Principles of Data Management: The Practical Guide to Storing, Managing and Analyzing Big and Small Data.* Cambridge University Press;, first edition, 2018.

J. Leskovec, L. A. Adamic, and B. A. Huberman. The dynamics of viral marketing. *ACM Transactions on the Web*, 1(1), 2007.

J. Leskovec, A. Rajaraman, and J. D. Ullman. *Mining of Massive Datasets.* Cambridge University Press, second edition, Dec. 2014.

H. Levenbach and J. P. Cleary. *Forecasting: Practice and Process for Demand Management.* Duxbury, U.S.A., 2006.

P. S. Levy and S. Lemeshow. *Sampling of Populations: Methods and Applications.* John Wiley & Sons, Inc, fourth edition, 2008.

A. Liu and S. C.-Y. Lu. A crowdsourcing design framework for concept generation. *CIRP Annals - Manufacturing Technology*, 65(1):177 – 180, 2016.

A. M. Lokman, T. Yamanaka, P. Lévy, K. Chen, and S. Koyama, editors. *Proceedings of the 7th International Conference on Kansei Engineering and Emotion Research 2018*, volume 739 of *Advances in Intelligent Systems and Computing*, 2018. Springer.

B. G. Malkiel. *A Random Walk Down Wall Street.* W.W. Norton & Company, New York, revised edition edition, 1999.

C. D. Manning, P. Raghavan, and H. Schütze. *Introduction to Information Retrieval.* Cambridge University Press, 2008.

T. Matsubara, S. Ishihara, M. Nagamachi, and Y. Matsubara. Kansei analysis of the japanese residential garden and development of a low-cost virtual reality kansei engineering system for gardens. *Advances in Human-Computer Interaction*, 2011.

A. Mayer. Online social networks in economics. *Decision Support Systems*, 47:169 – 184, 2009.

D. McFadden. Conditional logit analysis of qualitative choice behavior. In P. Zarembka, editor, *Frontiers in Econometrics*, pages 105–142. Academic Press, 1974.

W. McKinney. *Python for Data Analysis: data Wrangling with Pandas, Numpy, and Ipython.* O'Reilly, second edition, 2018.

J.-F. Meullenet, R. Xiong, and C. J. Findlay. *Multivariate and Probabilistic Analyses of Sensory Science Problems.* IFT Press Series. Blackwell Publishing, 2007.

E. C. Mik. New product demand forecasting: A literature study. Research Paper Business Analytics, Vrije Universiteit Amsterdam, Jan. 2019.

G. A. Miller. Wordnet: A lexical database for english. *Communications of the ACM*, 38(11):39 – 41, 1995.

K. B. Monroe. *Pricing: Making Profitable Decisions.* McGraw-Hill, second edition, 1990.

D. C. Montgomery, C. L. Jennings, and M. Kulahci. *Introduction to Time Series Analysis qnd Forecasting.* John Wiley & Sons, 2008.

L. P. Morales, A. D. Esteban, and P. Gervas. Concept graph-based biomedical automatic summarization using ontologies. In *Proceedings of 3rd Textgraphs Workshop on Graph-Based Algorithms in Natural Language Processing*, Aug. 2008.

S. M. Mudambi and D. Schuff. What makes a helpful online review? a study of customer reviews on amazon.com. *MIS Quarterly*, 34(1):185 – 200, Mar. 2010.

T. T. Nagle and R. K. Holden. *The Strategy and Tactics of Pricing: A Guide to Profitable Decision Making.* Prentice Hall, third edition, 2002.

C. Narasimhan. A price discrimination theory of coupons. *Marketing Science*, 3(2):128 – 147, 1984.

C. R. Nelson. *Applied Time Series Analysis for Managerial Forecasting.* Holden-Day, Inc., 1973.

K. S. Ng. A simple explanation of partial least squares. Available at users.cecs.anu.edu.au/kee/pls.pdf, Apr. 2013.

J. Nunnally. *Psychometric Theory*. McGraw-Hill, 1978.

M. O'Mahony. *Sensory Evaluation of Food: Statistical Methods and Procedures*. Food Science and Technology: A Series of Monographs, Textbooks, and Reference Books. Marcdl Dekker, Inc., 1986.

A. F. Osborn. *Applied Imagination: Principles and Procedures of Creative Problem Solving*. Charles Scribner's Sons, 1953.

J. W. Osborne. Sample size and subject to item ratio in principal components analysis. *Practical Assessment, Research & Evaluation*, 9(11), 2004.

W. R. Paczkowski. *Market Data Analysis Using JMP*. SAS Press, 2016.

W. R. Paczkowski. *Pricing Analytics: Models and Advanced Quantitative Techniques for Product Pricing*. Routledge, 2018.

E. Parzen. *Stochastic Processes*. Holden-Day, Inc., 1962.

J. A. Pertuzé, E. S. Calder, E. M. Greitzer, and W. A. Lucas. Best practice for industry-university collaboration. *MIT Sloan Management Review*, 51(4):83 – 90, 2010. Summer.

A. Pigou. *The Economics of Welfare*. Macmillan and Co, fourth edition, 1932.

L. Plaza, A. Diaz, and P. Gervás. Automatic summarization of news using wordnet concept graphs. *IADIS International Journal on Computer Science and Information System*, V:45 – 57, 2010.

T. Qiao, W. Shan, and C. Zhou. How to identify the most powerful node in complex networks? a novel entropy centrality approach. *Entropy*, 19(11), Nov. 2017.

D. Raghavarao, J. B. Wiley, and P. Chitturi. *Choice-based Conjoint Analysis: Models and Designs*. Chapman & Hall/CRC, 2011.

S. Robertson. Understanding inverse document frequency: On theoretical argunents for idf. *Journal of Documentation*, 60(5), 2004.

R. E. Sanders. Style, meaning, and message effects. *Journal of Communication Monographs*, 51(2):154 –167, 1984.

D. Sarkar. *Text Analytics with Python: A Practical Real-World Approach to Gaining Actionable Insights from Your Data*. APress, 2016.

M. L. Sawatsky, M. Clyde, and F. Meek. Partial least squares regression in the social sciences. *The Quantitative Methods for Psychology*, 11(2):52 – 62, 2015.

H. N. J. Schifferstein and E. P. H. Zwartkruis-Pelgrim. Consumer-product attachment: Measurement and design implications. *International Journal of Design*, 2(3):1 – 13, 2008.

S. Schnurrer, M. Boilard, and S. Juckenack. How customer-generated data can help auto engineers cut product development costs. *Forbes*, Aug. 2018. https://www.forbes.com/sites/oliverwyman/2018/08/13/how-customer-generated-data-can-help-auto-engineers-cut-product-development-costs/#26764d42164a. Last accessed on April 8, 2019.

B. Schwartz. *The Paradox of Choice: Why More is Less*. HarperCollins, 2004.

S. S. Shaukat, T. A. Rao, and M. A. Khan. Impact of sample size on principal component analysis ordination of an environmental data set: Effects on eigenstructure. *Ekológia (Bratislava)*, 35(2):173 – 190, 2016.

M. Sheller. Automotive emotions: Feeling the car. *Theory, Culture & Society*, 21(4/5):221 – 242, 2004.

F. Shi, Q. Li, T. Zhu, and H. Ning. A survey of data semantization in internet of things. *Sensors*, 18(313), Jan. 2018. www.mdpi.com/journal/sensors.

B. R. Shiller. First degree price discrimination using big data. Working Paper, Department of Economics, Brandeis University, August 2013.

G. Strang. *Linear Algebra and Its Applications*. Thomson Brooks/Cole, fourth edition, 2006.

R. D. Tobias. An introduction to partial least squares regression. In *SUGI Proceedings*, 1995.

K. Train. *Discrete Choice Methods with Simulation*. Cambridge University Press, second edition, 2009.

P. Trott. *Innovation Management and New Product Development*. Pearson, sixth edition, 2017.

E. R. Tufte. *The Visual Display of Quantitative Information*. Graphics Press, 1983.

J. W. Tukey. *Exploratory Data Analysis*. Pearson, 1977.

G. L. Urban and J. R. Hauser. *Design and Marketing of New Products*. Prentice Hall, 1980.

R. Valliant and J. A. Dever. *Survey Weights: A Step-by-Step Guide to Calculation*. Stata Press, 2018.

H. R. Varian. Big data: New tricks for econometrics. *Journal of Economic Perspectives*, 28(2): 3 – 28, 2014.

J. K. Vermunt. A hierarchical mixture model fro clustering three-wy data sets. *Computational Statistics & Data Analysis*, 51:5368 – 5376, 2007.

L. Vicsek. Issues in the analysis of focus groups: Generalisability, quantifiability, treatment of context and quotations. *The Qualitative Report*, 15(1):122 – 141, 2010. Retrieved from http://nsuworks.nova.edu/tqr/vol15/iss1/7.

W. Vollenbroek, S. de Vries, E. Constantinides, and P. Kommers. Identification of influence in social media communities. *International Journal of Web Based Communities*, 10(3): 280 – 297, Jan. 2014.

A. Watt. *Beginning Regular Expressions*. Wiley Publishing Inc., 2005.

E. J. Wegman. Hyperdimensional data analysis using parallel coordinates. *Journal of the American Statistical Association*, 85(411):664 – 675, Sept. 1990.

W. W. Wei. *Time Series Analysis: Univariate and Multivariate Methods*. Pearson, second edition, 2006.

C.-H. Wen, W.-W. Huang, C. Fu, and P.-Y. Chou. A latent class generalised nested logit model and its application to modelling carrier choice with market segmentation. *Transportmetrica*, Jan. 2012.

P. V. Westendorp. Nss-price sensitivity meter (psm) - a new approach to study consumer perception of price. *Proceedings of the ESOMAR Congress*, 1976.

S. C. Wheelwright and S. Makridakis. *Forecasting Methods for Management*. John Wiley & Sons, third edition, 1980.

H. Wickham. *ggplot2: Elegant Graphics for Data Analysis*. Springer, first edition, 2009.

L. Wilkinson. *The Grammar of Graphics*. Springer, second edition, 2005.

H. Wold. Estimation of principal components and related models by iterative least squares. In P. R. Krishnaiah, editor, *Multivariate Analysis. Proceedings of an International Symposium held in Dayton, Ohio, June 14-19, 1965*, pages 391 – 420. Academic Press, 1966a.

H. Wold. Nonlinear estimation by iterative least square procedures. In F. N. David, editor, *Research Papers in Statistics. Festschrift for J. Neyman*, pages 411 – 444. John Wiley & Sons, 1966b.

D. Wong. Data is the next frontier, analytics the new tool five trends in big data and analytics, and their implications for innovation and organisations. Big Innovation Center. Executive Summary, Nov. 2012.

I. B. Yona. *Where Do Ideas Come From?: The Hidden Dimension of Creative Thinking*. Lindisfarne Books, 2011.

L. Zhang and B. Liu. Sentiment analysis and opinion mining. In C. Sammut and G. Webb., editors, *Encyclopedia of Machine Learning and Data Mining*. Springer, 2017.

D. Zhuang, B. Zhang, H. Zhang, J. Tantrum, T. Mah, H.-J. Zeng, Z. Chen, and J. Wang. Identifying influential persons in a social network, 2013.

INDEX

Printed in the United States
by Baker & Taylor Publisher Services